THE BOY WHO CRIED WOLF

THE BOY WHO CRIED WOLF

THE BOOK THAT BREAKS MASONIC SILENCE

RICHARD P. THORN, M.D.

M. EVANS AND COMPANY, INC.
NEW YORK

M. Evans and Company, Inc.
216 East 49th Street
New York, New York 10017

Excerpts from Douglas Hofstadter's "The Grim Riddle" appear on pages 92 and 93. "The Grim Riddle" is from *Metamagical Themas: Questing for the Essence of the Mind* by Douglas Hofstadter, copyright©1985 by Basic Books, Inc., and reprinted by permission of BasicBooks, a division of HarperCollins Publishers, Inc.

Library of Congress Cataloging-in-Publication Data

Thorn, Richard P.
    The boy who cried wolf : the book that breaks Masonic silence / Richard P. Thorn. — 1st ed.
      p. cm.
    Includes bibliographic references.
    ISBN 0-87131-760-5 (cloth) : $18.95
    1. Freemasonry—Religious aspects—Baptists. 2. Southern Baptist Convention—Controversial literature. 3. Religious fundamentalism.
I. Title.
HS495.T39   1994
366'.1—dc20

94-2376
CIP

Design by Charles A. de Kay
Typesetting by AeroType, Inc.
Manufactured in the United States of America
First Edition

9 8 7 6 5 4 3 2 1

Due credit has been given to the appropriate source for all concepts used in this book, wherever possible. It should be noted, however, that my reading is eclectic, so that many other writers have inevitably influenced my thinking. I apologize to anyone who finds that I have borrowed their ideas without rendering him or her proper acknowledgment.

—Dick Thorn

DEDICATION

To Pat and Bill Thorn. Mom and Dad are living examples of faith in action.

To Dr. Forrest Crocker. His living witness of love inspired me to find faith and peace in Jesus Christ.

To George E. M. Smith. "Bud" showed me what God's grace does for man.

To Dr. Richard Dobbins. Twenty-eight years ago, "Doc" was my pastor. In the years that followed, he has been my friend, counselor, and professor. He taught me how to understand God's word.

To my Lodge brothers, Byron "Shotty" Shotwell, Fred Boggs, George Stitt, John Hampton, Ralph "Clipper" Wells, John Gallon, and Bob Dye. It was through Shotty that I became a Mason. Fred, Clipper, and John Gallon came to my home to tell me something about Masonry, and to learn something about me. Fred was the Worshipful Master, Bob raised me on Junior Warden's Night, George was my coach, and John Hampton was my counselor. Through them all, I found fellowship and love for the fraternity.

To John J. Robinson. He encouraged me to write this book, and he told me how to do it.

To Tom Jackson, Grand Secretary, Grand Lodge of Pennsylvania. He reviewed the first manuscript, and without his support this book would not have been published.

To Betty Anne Crawford. She edited the manuscript and made many valuable suggestions that changed the book from a series of related essays to a cohesive whole. It was her idea to use the "wedding vows" as an example in Chapter IV, "Oaths and Obligations."

And finally, to my wife, Shirley, devoted companion, and friend. She got someone else to do all my "Honey, do" jobs so that I could devote my time to writing. Her love, help, patience, and confidence in me made it possible.

CONTENTS

FOREWORD

H OW GOOD IT IS TO find a man who tells the truth about the bigots who masquerade as spokesmen for God! Herein Richard Thorn unmasks some of those who pretend to be Christians, but who evidently lack the love and tolerance stressed by the Man from Galilee.

At length Dick graphically points out the hundreds of fabrications of the so-called Christian pastor called Ron Carlson, who claimed he had spent months researching the organization called "Freemasonry." This had to be an untruth. He spent most of his venom on the writings of one man—Albert Pike. Any honest researcher knows that no one man can, or does, speak for Freemasonry.

Carlson knew he was safe in quoting Pike. Few have read Pike's *Morals and Dogma*. It is difficult reading. It took me twenty years to complete its more than 850 pages of what I considered rambling text. Dick Thorn is to be congratulated for going through this page by page to point out the hundreds of errors of Carlson's interpretation of what he claims Pike wrote. The Southern Jurisdiction of the Scottish Rite wisely stopped reprinting it many years ago. And it's interesting to note that neither Carlson nor others of his ilk ever quote the Masonic works of contemporary authors.

Phrase by phrase Dick Thorn shows the reader how Carlson has distorted Pike's thesis. At considerable length Thorn shows us how Carlson twists innocent expressions into something he "proves" to be evil.

To a lesser extent Dick also proves that Pat (real name: Marion Gordon) Robertson, the multimillionaire evangelist-entertainer-businessman-television guru-politician (whose father was a Freemason), either doesn't know how to research, uses faulty researchers, or knowingly conveys outright falsehoods as truths.

Dick does an excellent job of telling us what theology (a mystery to most of us—including most evangelists) really is. He warns us, as does the Holy Bible,

9

to "beware false prophets, who come to you in sheep's clothing, but inwardly they are ravening wolves." Hundreds of charitable organizations have discovered this to be true after they had sent gifts to pleading media personalities posing as Men of God.

Fundamentalism is clarified at length by Dick. He concludes that "a fundamentalist is an American evangelical who is a militant crusader against modernism." He explains something that few of us know: there is a "fifth gospel," which is necessary to understand if we are to be able to interpret the well-known four Gospels.

Today's anti-Masons are little different from those of the past two centuries. Now they can and do use modern means of communication to convey their venom, while condemning modernizing religious thought. But they do not stop with condemning Freemasonry, they denounce everything that doesn't support their narrow religious views and teachings. This includes other Christian denomination, often including their own. As Dick points out: "Their lack of love for fellow believers in Christ leads to attacks on friend and foe alike."

These diabolic characters ignore the teachings of the Man they claim they worship. He admonished all to love their neighbors as they love themselves. He specified no color, sect, or religion. A couple of years ago a man named Ankerberg—one of these active anti-everything fundamentalists—attempted to have me appear on one of his Masonic-baiting television programs. He wouldn't take "no" for an answer. Finally I told his puppets I would take him up on his offer under certain conditions: That it would be a one-time live program—or that I have editorial control over the editing of the videotape—and that Ankerberg and his crew reread (or read for the first time) the Sermon on the Mount. I never heard from him again.

Dick suggests Freemasonry ought to stop turning the other cheek when unfairly criticized and answer its critics honestly and forthrightly. This is what a few of us have been strongly advocating for years. For a decade, beginning in 1826, a handful of vocal anti-Masons came close to destroying the organization. It wasn't until a small group of Masonic leaders fought these bigots that the "antis" pulled up stakes and went back to their holes. A lesson that should be remembered.

Freemasonry unites men of every country, sect, and opinion. It discriminates against no one of good will. It supports the freedom of all, regardless of their race or religion. It endeavors to help all peoples to live together in peace and harmony. It helps those who honestly cannot help themselves. Its charity knows no bounds.

These, and more, are the lessons Dick Thorn passes on to his readers. Those who put them into practice will be rewarded beyond the dreams of the most optimistic.

Allen E. Roberts,
Fellow, Past President, and Executive Secretary of the Philalethes Society,
Past Grand Master of the Allied Masonic Degrees of the United States,
and author of *House Undivided; Brother Truman; The Mystic Tie;*
and twenty-six other books

INTRODUCTION

MANY BOOKS AND ARTICLES HAVE been written in response to the allegations of anti-Masons, and this book was also originally intended to answer the questions they raise. But three months into the process of writing it, I read *The Cloud of Prejudice*, Art deHoyos's response to the tape-recorded anti-Masonic sermon by Ron Carlson, president of Christian Ministries, International; and the February 1993 issue of the *Scottish Rite Journal*, which addressed anti-Masonic charges made by James Holly at the Southern Baptist Convention in Indianapolis, in June 1992. At first there seemed no point in continuing to write this book, and then it occurred to me that the real issues are the theological assumptions of the fundamentalists who make these allegations. In other words, I feel it is necessary to go beyond their allegations and address the theological mind-set that makes them.

UNDERSTANDING THE MAN WHO LIES ABOUT MASONRY
There is a biblical precedent found in 2 Corinthians, chapters 10–13, where the apostle Paul found it necessary to defend his ministry in the same way, when he addressed the issues raised by the false apostles who were his critics at Corinth. We do not know the exact nature of their charges, nor do we know what they were teaching, because we can only read Paul's reply. But this much is clear: Paul's opponents attacked his ministry and attempted to undo his work, claiming that they had Christ's authority and that Paul did not. Paul replied that if they were confident that they belonged to Christ, they could not deny him the right to say that he, too, belonged to Christ. Paul said that the authority that the Lord had given him was for "building you up rather than tearing you down."[1] Paul refused to compare himself with those who measured themselves by comparison with one another. He preferred to boast of things according to the measure of the rule that God had given him, and would not go beyond that measure. The assumed authority of the false

apostles was destructive. It was dividing the body of Christ, rather than building it up. Paul respected his limits, but their boundless conceit showed that his opponents were false apostles and servants of Satan, masquerading as apostles of Christ.[2] Paul's point seems to be that any religion that causes a man to look down upon his fellow men, and to think that he is better than they are, is a false religion.

There is a certain type of person, among fundamentalists, whose usual method of preaching is to attack the faith and practice of another person or group. One can only infer what such men believe from the context of their judgmental attacks, because they seldom make any positive statement of their own doctrine and faith. Their assumed authority to judge others is destructive. They divide the body of Christ, and according to Paul's criteria, their actions are those of false apostles.

Unless someone else is doing all their thinking, no two people can always agree on every issue. This was one of the fundamental reasons for the Protestant Reformation. (All forms of Protestantism have a tradition of arguing about theology, Biblical interpretation, ethics and error. This book is a part of that tradition). The same principle is also the source of the Masonic belief in the right of the individual to interpret the Bible for himself. Masons do not teach a plan of salvation because that is the function of religion and Freemasonry is not a religion. Just as Paul's ministry had certain limits, Freemasonry limits itself to teaching men to show their faith by what they do. Paul's credentials were proven by positive results in the lives of his converts. In the same way, Masons seek to make good men better, by putting their faith in action.

The allegations against Paul concerned his character. Paul was fighting for a principle. Freemasonry has also been wrongfully accused, and so we, too, are fighting for that same principle. Most of our opposition comes from those who believe that Freemasonry is a danger to *their religious* views. It is valid to oppose Freemasonry from a true spirit of concern, but most of their concern is over issues that do not even exist. Masons are charged to avoid argument with those who, *through ignorance,* may ridicule our Order. But Ron Carlson's ridicule is not through ignorance; his ridicule is through false witness. I wish to respond to his allegations from the perspective of a fundamentalist, who has been a lay student of theology for more than thirty years.

Carlson says, among other things, that:

1. Masonry is a religion.
2. Masonry is in error because it is pantheistic.
3. Masonry is in error because it gives works more importance than faith.
4. Masonry is a secret society.
5. Masonry has its roots in the mystery religions.
6. Masonry is anti-Christian.
7. Masonry is Satanic.

The purpose of this book is to show that most of his charges are false, and that in those instances where there may be an honest difference of opinion, to show that there is a sound scriptural basis for a different view. Other fundamentalists will disagree with my views at several points. We will agree that 2 Timothy 2:15 tells us to "Study to show thyself approved unto God," but we will often disagree on "rightly dividing the word of truth." Even Paul and Peter disagreed about "walking uprightly according to the truth of the Gospel."[3] Because we bring our personal experience, as well as our belief, into Bible study, it is always appropriate to differ with my views, but it is *never appropriate* to lie about them. When you hear a man of God bear false witness, and when it becomes obvious that he *knows* it is false witness, you must ask yourself this vital question: "What is his *real issue?*" What possible motive can he have for breaking the ninth commandment, while pretending that "this is *God's* message?"

The Mason's charge to avoid argument is based on common sense and courtesy. Even the most impeccable logic will not dissuade an emotional man or woman, nor will it convince the obstinate person. It is not through argument, but through reconciliation, that they are won. It is an act of love and courtesy to respect their dignity, their integrity, and their right to their opinion. It has been said that the best way to destroy an enemy is to make him your friend. It is *not* the best way. It is the *only* way.

Masonic tradition opposes *any discussion* of religious issues *in the Lodge* because history teaches us that any attempt to *impose* a religious viewpoint is a fertile source of dissension. But I must *write* from the viewpoint of the fundamentalist Christian, first, because it *is* my viewpoint, and second, because that is the viewpoint of our accusers. Thus I would find it far more difficult to reach the same conclusions from neutral ground.

The aims of Freemasonry are to make good men better by promoting Brotherhood, Relief and Truth. Brotherhood refers to equality, justice, companionship, love, and respect for others. Relief is love in action, lending spiritual, emotional, and material support to those in need. Truth has to do with a belief in God and life after death, ethics, morality, avoiding hypocrisy and deceit, following the Golden Rule, and seeking knowledge.

Masonry's emphasis on secrecy is limited to keeping to ourselves our modes of identification, and those things told to us in confidence, and specifically excludes any felony.

1 || A SOUL SET FREE

B OTH SIDES OF MY FAMILY are fundamentalist Christians. Our family activities centered around Sunday school and morning worship, evening youth fellowship and evangelistic services, Wednesday prayer meeting, Thursday choir practice, and Friday men's fellowship. Then suddenly, in 1943, church-related activities no longer seemed important to me. The city of Akron had emerged from the depression into a wartime economy. War-related industry provided jobs for thousands who came to Akron to find work. East High School was on a split schedule to accommodate the influx of new students. My classes were scheduled from 7:30 A.M. until noon, to allow me to work at the Firestone Tire and Rubber Company from 2:00 to 10:00 P.M. I bought new clothes, a watch, and a car, and found new friends at work. Then I began to rebel against my parents' rules concerning my choice of friends and a midnight curfew hour.

At school I was studying Old Testament Literature as an elective. The teacher was an atheist who used the classroom to "debunk the myths of the Bible." He told us that Abraham's willingness to offer Isaac on the altar *proved* that the ancient Hebrews practiced human sacrifice; that Moses couldn't have written the first five books of the Bible because writing hadn't been invented yet; and that the Bible itself says there is no God. Becoming an atheist made it easy for me to justify a new life-style, as I told my parents to look at the difference between what Christians said, and what they did. To me, God was only an adult version of Santa Claus.

In 1945 I enlisted in the army, and served as a paratrooper and a medic with the 82nd Airborne Division. After discharge from the service, I married a Christian girl, returned to church, and studied pre-med at the University of Akron. In zoology class the professor compared and contrasted the story of creation in Genesis with Darwin's theory of evolution. When I asked my pastor how to *reconcile* the two, he lent me a book that argued against Darwinism as it was taught in the 1890s. Instead of focusing on current issues, the book had set up a *straw man* and attacked *it*. No man, and I counseled with many, showed me that there can be no conflict between the Bible and true science, because *God is the Author of both!* Instead, each tried to prove that his particular view was right, and that the other view was a lie. Because all of the clergymen I talked to had obvious gaps in their knowledge of the scientific method, I came to believe that God was only an Ideal, created by man, and often used to exploit others; I became a militant atheist.

After graduating from the Ohio State University College of Medicine, I returned to Akron to serve my internship. While working with Dr. Forrest Crocker, a resident at Children's Hospital, I saw true Christian love and personal peace in action, as he ministered to his patients. As a result of his living witness, I accepted Jesus Christ as my personal savior, August 16, 1958. For the first time in my life, I experienced a very real personal peace and a love for other people. The continuing daily experience of peace and love changed my life so deeply, that I felt called to share that experience with others. I served as a medical missionary with the fundamentalist Christian and Missionary Alliance Church in Congo (now called Zaïre), West Africa, doing surgery and obstetrics, teaching in the nursing school, and preaching the Gospel.

In preparation for the mission field my pastor tutored me in theology, using William Evans's *The Great Doctrines of the Bible* as a textbook, so that I could preach the Gospel, as well as serving the mission as a medical doctor. The study of theology became a lifelong hobby; a burning passion to find answers that respected the validity of both science and the Bible. I know obedience to God produces profound changes in the lives of men and women; and I also know that science improves the quality, the comfort, and the length of their lives.

As I study the Bible, I still use Evans's book as my guide to doctrine and theology, and Mickelsen's *Interpreting the Bible* to learn how the Bible should be understood today; taking into account the differences in time, place, language, logic, and culture; as well as the differences between God's covenant with Abraham, and how we should relate to God through Jesus Christ in *this* Dispensation.

After returning home in 1965 because of my wife's health, I continued in Christian service as a Sunday school teacher; as a regular participant and board member of a fundamentalist television Bible-study program; and as a speaker and member of the board of the Cleveland Chapter of The Full Gospel Businessmen's Fellowship International. Through the years I have taught Sunday school classes ranging from teenagers to senior citizens, served as a deacon and member of the board of my church, and preached the sermon in the absence of the pastor.

Atheism was a time of darkness in my life, because my mind was closed to the truth of God's grace. Then, beginning in 1971, I passed through a second era of darkened understanding because guilt about divorce drove me to avoid church and fellowship with other Christians. Marital problems had seemed so severe that I could see no options but divorce or suicide, but divorce did not solve my problems. It only provided the opportunity for a series of disastrous relationships. Then, in early March 1981, I walked into Huebner Chevrolet, intending to buy a car. Before I could say a word, the salesman, Bud Smith, was saying, "Hey, Dick, come here, I want to talk to you. You know, Bill and Beth Urey, my preacher and his wife, have a love for God I've never seen before." As he continued talking, my mind went back to those years when a man's love, freely and openly shared, had drawn me into an awareness of the love and grace of God. As I recounted this, Bud sat back, scratched his white head, and with a puzzled expression on his face, he asked, "What happened to you, Dick?"

As I told him how I had fallen away from fellowship with the Lord, he scratched his head again as he asked, "Don't you know God's grace is sufficient for that?" The burden of years of guilt was suddenly gone as the true significance of his words sank in. I left Huebner's without remembering why I had come. I stepped into a world literally made new again by a restored sense of the depth of God's love and forgiveness. I was seeing the world with different eyes, and I found a new joy in Christian fellowship and church activities. Years later, while preparing a sermon, I tried to recapture the emotion of that experience by writing "A Soul Set Free," a parody of William Ernest Henley's "Invictus:"

Released from sin that shackled me,
The curse of man, from pole to pole.
Because, in Christ, I am set free,
There are no fetters on my soul,

I am not free of circumstance,
I often wince and cry aloud.
Buffeted still by winds of chance,
Yet His grace keeps my head unbowed.

While in this place of sin and tears,
Resting in the choice I have made,
I find no menace of the years,
For His love keeps me, unafraid.

I need not fear, though strait the gate,
His, the punishments on the scroll.
T'was Christ, the Master of the gate,
Who set free my guilt-burdened soul.

In September 1982, I took a leave of absence from the practice of medicine, to attend the Ashland (Brethren) Theological Seminary, majoring in Pastoral Counseling at the Emerge Ministries campus.

I believe in the inerrancy of the Bible, which means that I agree with Evans that the Bible is "just as much the Word of God as though God spoke every word of it with His own lips."[1] But I do not believe in the inerrancy of the *interpretation* of the Bible by those who teach it. The problem is not just a difference in our view of inerrancy, but in how men read and understand the Bible. Some try to understand the Bible as though it were written in twentieth-century America. The teachings of Jesus and the major doctrines of the Bible are clear enough to permit this. But keep in mind that Biblical scholars often differ in their understanding of certain scriptural passages. (The Protestant tradition of arguing about theology and Biblical interpretation is why we have different denominations in the church today.) Scholars are not always certain of the original meaning, and what those who heard it, or first read it, understood it to mean, as well as how its message might be phrased, if it were first preached or written today.

Almost any word we use has three or more different meanings. When we translate something from another language, we must decide which meaning is appropriate and use its equivalent in English. A simple example illustrates the problem: The preposition *before* can mean: in front of, earlier, next to, of higher rank, and so forth. When the Bible says David danced before the ark, the reader will understand that this means David danced in front of the ark, not that David danced first and then the ark did! But the original meaning is not always that clear. This leads to an honest difference of opinion among Bible-believing scholars when translating or interpreting the Bible. But sometimes the problem lies in someone using a passage of Scripture to prove a point, instead of allowing the Bible to speak for itself. My atheistic teacher told me, "The Bible says, 'There is no God.' " But when I read the verse,[2] I see that it really says, "The fool hath said in his heart, 'there is no God.' " The atheist omitted some words to make the Bible *appear to say* what *he wanted me to believe,* not to understand what the Psalmist really meant.

It saddens me to hear a minister or Bible teacher ignore *the context* of Bible verses to "prove" what he *says* the Bible teaches. He might disregard the context, for the same reason my atheistic teacher did: to make the Bible *appear to say* what he wants me to believe. He may ignore the context because he is not aware, or does not believe, that sound methods of interpretation are needed; and finally, he may be someone who thinks interpretation is just one more way that human secularism "despiritualizes" the Bible.

But it grieves me even more to see someone twist the words of a human author, and make him *appear to say something* he never intended to say, because this is not ignorance. *He knows it isn't true* because *he made it up;* he is like the fox in Aesop's fable who could not reach a beautiful bunch of ripe grapes hanging high over his head; so he walked off scornfully, saying, "Why should I wear myself out trying to get a bunch of sour grapes?" He pretends to despise, and belittles that which is beyond his reach or understanding. Keep in mind the sacred nature of the minister's call to proclaim God's Truth, and you will understand why **telling a lie in the pulpit is taking God's name in vain.** "Because they . . . have spoken lying words in my name, which I have not commanded them; *even I know, and am a witness, saith the Lord.*"[3]

Consider then, how I reacted when I first heard, and then saw, evidence to the contrary. One night, during evangelistic services at our church, the visiting evangelist said that seven thousand elderly people had lost their lives in a recent flu epidemic. Later, over coffee and dessert, I said that I didn't know the loss of life was so high. He replied, "Oh the real number was seven hundred; that was just a little evangelistic exaggeration!" I was shocked to hear a man of God tell a lie from the pulpit.

In Seminary, I was asked to write a paper on Jay Adam's *The Use of the Scriptures in Counseling*. Adams said (page 38) that Thomas Harris, M.D., author of *I'm OK – You're OK*, urges us to become OK without the aid of the Christ of the Scriptures. "After all, he tells us, 'Truth is not bound in a black book.' " Harris actually said, "The truth is not something which has been brought to finality at an ecclesiastical summit meeting or bound in a black book. The truth is a growing body of data of what we observe to be true."[4] This chapter of Harris's book was devoted to moral values and the concept of Christ's grace. Adams, who teaches pastors how to counsel, had distorted Harris's meaning, context, and purpose, by omitting some of Harris's words.

In February 1986, Shotty, an 81-year-old retired barber and a member of our church, asked me why I had never become a Mason. I said, "Because no one ever asked me to join." He explained that the only way to become a Mason was to ask a Mason for a petition. I was raised a Master Mason June 16, 1986, received the Knight Templar degree December 7, 1987, became a Shriner June 11, 1988, and received the 32nd degree in the Scottish Rite October 29, 1988. I was elected Worshipful Master of Carroll Lodge #124, Carrollton, Ohio, November 5, 1990.

I have applied the same diligence in the study of Freemasonry that I was taught to use in Bible study. I enrolled in the Grand Lodge of Ohio's "The Exceptional Lodge Leader" study course and in its Masonic Training Course, Series IV. I joined the Ohio Lodge of Research and the Philalethes Society. I read the *Northern Light*, the *Knight Templar*, *The Philalethes*, and numerous other masonic publications. I have read Pike's *Morals and Dogma*, ten of Allen Roberts's books, two by Joseph Fort Newton, and many other books by masonic authors. I have the *Little Masonic Library, Coil's Masonic Encyclopedia, History of Freemasonry in Ohio*, and several other Masonic reference works. I have also read all of the anti-Masonic literature I can get my hands on, and viewed and listened to many of their video and audio tapes. **Without exception, all of them distort the teachings of Freemasonry.** Some of them are based on misinformation, or an honest difference in interpretation, but others unmistakably demonstrate a deliberate and misleading rewording of the works of Masonic authors to make them appear to say things that they never intended to say.

My father was asked to resign from Masonry in order to be considered eligible for the office of elder in his church. He did so because holding that office was more important to him than Masonic membership. Dad is a devout man who sees nothing wrong in Freemasonry. He says his church objects to the secrecy in Masonry: "What are they trying to hide?" Nothing! "The secrets of Freemasonry" is a term used in the same context as "The mystery of the Gospel." No man can understand a relationship he denies. He must be open to the leading of the Holy Spirit to fully understand what Jesus taught and he must be a Mason to understand the secrets of Freemasonry. Anyone wishing to know more about Freemasonry can find it in the public library, or by buying a copy of *Born in Blood* by John Robinson, or a copy of Allen Roberts's *The Craft and Its Symbols*.

Freemasonry is often attacked because it "leaves out Jesus Christ." Those who say this believe that Masonry is a religion that teaches men how to get to heaven through their good works. This shows why the principles of interpretation are so important. Masonry says that it is not a religion. An honest interpretation of the teachings of Freemasonry will show that instead of teaching men what to believe, men are simply asked to put the religion they already have, when they become a Mason, into everyday practice. People look at the difference between what Christians say, and what they do. The ideal Mason will practice what he believes, so that there will be no difference between what he says and what he does. Again, this is why careful interpretation of Scripture is so important. Only Jesus could perfectly fulfill the Law. As a Christian, His righteousness is imputed to me, but the Law remains my guide as I seek to follow Him. Masonry seeks only to reinforce my decision to use that guide. It makes no claims for itself.

Shortly after I received the 32nd degree in the Scottish Rite, a former pastor handed me a copy of Ron Carlson's tape, and advised me to listen to it closely. As I listened, I became horrified, and wondered what I had gotten myself involved in. But as I continued to listen, I realized that I had not heard any of the things that Carlson says are taught in the higher degrees. All of my friends in Scottish Rite agreed. At the time, I had never seen a copy of Albert Pike's *Morals and Dogma*. It took me almost a year to find one that I could borrow, because the book is out of print and many small Lodge libraries do not own a copy. (The one I found was printed in 1914.) As I compared Carlson's tape with Pike's book, I saw that Carlson was distorting Pike's meaning, context, and purpose, in exactly the same way Adams had distorted Harris's book.

By tradition, Freemasonry never defends itself. That is one reason misinformation about its teachings has persisted. But the principles of Christian ethics impose a higher obligation on defending a principle than on maintaining courtesy. This book was written to correct false views of Freemasonry. It is true, as I understand the truth, and the reader is free to reject or dissent from my view, as he chooses.

In Luke's Gospel we read that an expert in the law asked Jesus what he must do to inherit eternal life. Jesus asked him, "What is written in the Law? How do you read it?" He answered: " 'Love the Lord your God with all your heart and with all your soul and with all your strength and with all your mind'; and, 'Love your neighbor as yourself.' " "You have answered correctly," Jesus replied. "Do this and you will live." But he wanted to justify himself, so he asked Jesus, "And who is my neighbor?" In reply Jesus said: "A man was going down from Jerusalem to Jericho, when he fell into the hands of robbers. They stripped him of his clothes, beat him and went away, leaving him half dead. A priest happened to be going down the same road, and when he saw the man, he passed by on the other side. So, too, a Levite, when he came to the place and saw him, passed by on the other side. But a Samaritan, as he traveled, came where the man was; and when he saw him, he took pity on him. He went to him and bandaged his wounds, pouring on oil and wine. Then he put the man on his own donkey, took him to an inn and took care of him. The next day he took out two silver coins and gave them to the innkeeper. 'Look after him,' he said, 'and when I return, I will reimburse you for any extra expense you may have.' "Which of these three do you think was a neighbor to the man who fell into the hands of robbers?" The expert in the law replied, "The one who had mercy on him." Jesus told him, "Go and do likewise."[5]

Jesus chose the Good Samaritan as an example of loving your neighbor because the Jews and the Samaritans were enemies.[6] Jesus said, "You have heard that it was said, 'Love your neighbor and hate your enemy.' But I tell you: Love your enemies and pray for those who persecute you, that you may be sons of your Father in heaven. He causes his sun to rise on the evil and the good, and sends rain on the righteous and the unrighteous. If you love those who love you, what reward will you get? Are not even the tax collectors doing that? And if you greet only your brothers, what are you doing more than others? Do not even pagans do that? Be perfect, therefore, as your heavenly Father is perfect."[7] Perfect can mean flawless, but in this context, perfect means that God treats men just the same whether they are evil, and therefore enemies, or righteous; and we are commanded to do the same thing.

The church tends to emphasize orthodoxy in belief and behavior as a test of righteousness. Jesus said that those who emphasize insignificant details "Strain out a gnat but swallow a camel"[8] In Matthew 25, Jesus seems to emphasize following Him and obeying His commandments as the test of righteousness.

Jesus said that in the final judgment, all nations will be gathered before Him, and He will separate the people as a shepherd separates the sheep from the goats. He will then invite the righteous to accept their reward. "For I was hungry and you gave me something to eat, I was thirsty and you gave me something to drink, I was a stranger and you invited me in, I needed clothes and you clothed me, I was sick and you looked after me, I was in prison and you came to visit me." Then the righteous will ask when they saw Him in need and did those things. He will reply, "Whatever you did for one of the least of these brothers of mine, you did for me."

Then He will say to the unrighteous, "Depart from me, you who are cursed, into the eternal fire prepared for the devil and his angels. For I was hungry and you gave me nothing to eat, I was thirsty and you gave me nothing to drink, I was a stranger and you did not invite me in, I needed clothes and you did not clothe me, I was sick and in prison and you did not look after me. They, too, will ask when they saw Him in need and did not help Him. Then He will reply, "Whatever you did not do for one of the least of these, you did not do for me."[9]

This is faith or love in action. There was no question about what they believed. It was a question about what they did. "For in Christ Jesus neither circumcision nor uncircumcision has any value. The only thing that counts is faith expressing itself through love."[10] Fundamentalists are quick to point out that Ephesians 2:8–9 teaches us that salvation is through faith, not by works, so that no one can boast; but often fail to add that verse 10 tells us that we were created "to do good works, which God prepared in advance for us to do" (NIV). In the words of James the Apostle: "What good is it, my brothers, if a man claims to have faith but has no deeds? Can such faith save him? Suppose a brother or sister is without clothes and daily food. If one of you says to him, 'Go, I wish you well; keep warm and well fed,' but does nothing about his physical needs, what good is it? In the same way, faith by itself, if it is not accompanied by action, is dead. . . . Show me your faith without deeds, and I will show you my faith by what I do."[11]

Jesus showed God's love and compassion by healing the sick and feeding the poor, but instead of praising God for His miracles, some of the religious leaders accused Him of breaking the Sabbath and sought to kill Him. They were more interested in protecting their view of the Law, than in the good that had been done in the power of God.[12] When Jesus healed a blind and mute man, these same religious teachers said His powers were Satanic.[13] He taught us to love our enemies, but when He ate with tax collectors and sinners they criticized Him.[14]

One branch of the church tends to emphasize salvation at the expense of the social gospel, while another branch tends to emphasize the social gospel at the expense of teaching salvation. There is a third position: Sin is more than an act of transgression. The true origin of sin is rebellion and estrangement. When man is wrong in his relationship with God, he will be wrong in relation to his neighbor. The law has more to do with relationships than it has to do with moral absolutes. A simple example is the so-called "little white lie." If a man views Truth as an absolute, there is no such thing as a "little" lie. If he views the law as supporting relationships, white lies are not only permissible, but required—he will not tell his wife that he doesn't like her dress at the cost of damaging their relationship. The essence of Christianity is not legalism, but reconciliation with God and our fellow man, through a personal relationship with Jesus Christ.

Many people consider those of a different religion to be their enemies. Jesus said to love our enemies. Freemasonry teaches us to accept other people, and to respect their religious beliefs. It does not teach that all religions are equal, only that we should respect them. My religious concepts were formed long before I became a Mason, but I consider Freemasonry to be a work of the Lord Jesus Christ, raised up to emphasize that part of His teaching so often neglected by the church: to love your enemy. Just look at the strife between Catholics and Protestants in Ireland, and the struggle between Jews and Arabs in the Middle

East. Consider the religious warfare in India, the former Yugoslavia, and Iran. History tells us that *heresy* was considered the greatest crime in medieval Europe—not murder, not lawless violence, not rape—but heresy. Heresy was the only reason for the hideous tortures of the Inquisition.

What delights me most about Freemasonry is to see its teachings used to encourage Jews and Christians of all denominations to bond together around the beliefs that they hold in common, and to live and practice what they believe, instead of arguing about differences in their belief. I have found the same love and fellowship with some of my brothers in the Lodge, that I have shared with some of my brothers and sisters in church. The great secret of Freemasonry is its teachings concerning Brotherly Love, Relief, and Truth. Those teachings are best expressed in the words of Romans 12:9-13:1 [NIV].

> Love must be sincere. Hate what is evil; cling to what is good. Be devoted to one another in brotherly love. Honor one another above yourselves. Never be lacking in zeal, but keep your spiritual fervor, serving the Lord. Be joyful in hope, patient in affliction, faithful in prayer. Share with God's people who are in need. Practice hospitality. Bless those who persecute you: bless, and do not curse. Rejoice with those who rejoice; mourn with those who mourn. Live in harmony with one another. Do not be proud, but be willing to associate with people of low position. Do not be conceited. Do not repay anyone evil for evil. Be careful to do what is right in the eyes of everybody. If it is possible, as far as it depends on you, live at peace with everyone. Do not take revenge, my friends, but leave room for God's wrath, for it is written: "It is mine to avenge; I will repay," says the Lord. On the contrary: "If your enemy is hungry, feed him; if he is thirsty, give him something to drink. In doing this, you will heap coals on his head." Do not be overcome by evil, but overcome evil with good. Every one must submit himself to the governing authorities, for there is no authority except that which God has established.

Some of the principle teachings of Freemasonry, which are expressed in Romans 12:9-13:1, include:

1. Be devoted to one another in brotherly love.
2. Honor one another above yourselves.
3. Keep your spiritual fervor, serving the Lord.
4. Be joyful in hope, faithful in prayer.
5. Share with God's people who are in need.
6. Practice hospitality.
7. Bless and do not curse.
8. Rejoice with those who rejoice; mourn with those who mourn.
9. Live in harmony with one another.
10. Do not be proud, but be willing to associate with people of low position. Do not be conceited.
11. Do not repay anyone evil for evil.
12. Be careful to do what is right in the eyes of everybody.
13. If it is possible, as far as it depends on you, live at peace with everyone.
14. Do not take revenge.
15. If your enemy is hungry, feed him; if he is thirsty, give him something to drink.
16. Do not be overcome by evil, but overcome evil with good.
17. Everyone must submit himself to the governing authorities.

11 || Understanding the Fundamentalist

I N ORDER TO UNDERSTAND CARLSON, and his allegations against Freemasonry, we must understand the tradition from which he comes. Evangelicals and fundamentalists are theological conservatives. Their religious beliefs are basically the same as those of the Protestant Reformers, who set the authority of the Bible above that of men, and accepted as orthodox, the great creeds of the early church fathers. Fundamentalist and evangelical concerns are rooted in hostility toward American Protestant liberal or modern theology, and Darwin's theory of evolution. Liberals consider some of the traditional orthodox doctrines unimportant. Their theology is best described as the social gospel.

The fundamentalist movement began as a scholarly debate that degenerated into bitter theological politics, and separation from those it saw as apostates. A fundamentalist is an American evangelical who is a militant crusader against modernism. A new evangelical group has emerged in reaction to what they view as the excesses of fundamentalism. Carl F. H. Henry is its best-known spokesman.

The best history of this uniquely American conflict forms the first section of *Carl F. H. Henry,* one of a series of books entitled "Makers of the Modern Theological Mind." Bob E. Patterson, professor of religion at Baylor University in Waco, Texas, is the editor of the series, as well as the author of this book. In writing this chapter, I have drawn freely from his book as my primary source of information.

According to a 1976 Gallup poll, membership in four mainline churches: Methodists, Presbyterians, Episcopal, and Church of Christ, declined by 2.7 million. Conservative evangelicals had an increased membership, with the Southern Baptist Convention alone gaining almost 2 million. Patterson believes that one reason for the evangelicals' growth is that they are changing their traditional style and approach, while retaining the basic Christian doctrines. The Southern Baptists are now the nation's largest Protestant body. (The *1993 World Almanac* says they had over 15 million members in 1991).

Carl Henry is a Baptist. Henry says the Baptist tenets that impressed him while he was a student at Wheaton College are: 1) The final authority of Scripture above all creeds and speculation; 2) the priesthood of all believers; 3) believer's baptism by immersion; 4) the autonomy of the local church; and 5) the separation of church and state. Although these tenets are not exclusively Baptistic, Henry says that their combination and their emphasis is unique to Baptists.

Henry says: "Reliance upon Scripture to reveal the saviorhood and lordship of Jesus Christ, and His plan and purpose for mankind, is more than the first tenet of Baptist belief; it is the foundation stone for the other principles." He does not feel that the Baptist position conflicts with ecumenical interest. While he prefers to communicate the life of Christ in His church, in the Baptist tradition, he does not deny that there is some measure of genuine Christian status in other traditions, "even as we are quick to admit that something less than full Christian status often intrudes into our own!"

Henry believes that resolute devotion to the demands of the scriptural revelation will best secure and advance specific Baptist beliefs and ecumenical Christian priorities. Henry does not approve of some of the trends in his denomination. He says that any Baptist activity that does not relate to the Bible becomes a mere abstraction.

By 1943 Henry was married and had earned B.A. and M.A. degrees at Wheaton College; and B.D. and Th.D. at Northern Baptist Theological Seminary. In 1949 he finished his Ph.D. at Boston University. In 1947 he was selected to help Fuller Theological Seminary get started. He remained there until 1956, when Billy Graham and his father-in-law, L. Nelson Bell, asked Henry to be the first editor of *Christianity Today*. Through his editorials, essays, and interviews, Henry has helped to define and defend conservative Protestantism.

Christian Orthodoxy

Henry is trying to restore the traditional orthodoxy of the nineteenth-century American Protestant movement. To understand the reason for this effort, we need to know what was lost.

Evangelical theology finds its origin in the Reformation. The Reformers set the Bible above Catholic tradition, refused to accept the Apocrypha as Scripture, and denied the authority of Church councils. The Reformers believed that sinners were saved by God's grace through faith alone, that the church had no authority to control grace, and accepted as orthodox, the great creeds of the early church fathers. From the Reformation came a large body of orthodox literature, that has helped shape the thinking of both early American and contemporary evangelicals.

The eighteenth-century Evangelical revival included Pietism in Germany, Methodism in England, and the Great Awakening in America. The Pietist revival began with Philipp Spener, who condemned the sins of the day, and presented six requirements for reformation: Better knowledge of the Bible, restoration of mutual Christian concern, emphasis on good works, avoiding controversy, better spiritual training for ministers, and more fervent preaching. His teaching influenced A. H. Francke, whose work grew out of his concern for destitute and deprived people. Foreign missions were emphasized and a whole series of institutions were founded, including a school for the poor, an orphanage, a hospital, a widow's home, a teacher's training institute, a Bible school, a book depot, and a Bible house.[1]

This movement influenced the American Puritans, The Great Awakening (Jonathan Edwards), George Whitefield, John and Charles Wesley, and the nineteenth-century holiness movement (Charles Finney). In England an evangelical group in the Anglican church cooperated with the nonconformist churches in social welfare and missionary endeavors. Similar alliances of Protestant churches that were formed in the United States helped shape American culture.

The foundation of the traditions and values of our American culture was largely the Evangelical Protestant ethic, and its impact on our priorities, education, and social legislation was enormous. Between 1830 and 1860 evangelical Protestantism dominated American religion. Although the War between the States caused regional and racial realignment of churches, their theology remained orthodox. But between 1870 and 1920, the emergence of the rationalism and skepticism of the "Enlightenment" movement in philosophy, and fundamental changes in the ideas of science, removed the evangelical tradition from the established theological community. Skeptics had combined the new techniques of biblical criticism and Darwin's theory of evolution to attack biblical ideas.

Protestant liberalism began with the need for a response to the skeptics. Theologians who were impressed with the new ideas, and not overly concerned with the importance of orthodox doctrine, tried to protect the Christian faith by redefining it, so that it would be more acceptable to the mind of modern man. The pioneer American liberal, according to Patterson, was Horace Bushnell. Barker says, "Bushnell criticized the chilling Calvinistic orthodoxy of his time and stressed faith, while taking emotion and intuition into consideration. During the mid-nineteenth century in America, theology was primarily an exercise in logic, and Christianity an appeal to the intellect. Bushnell tried to offset these tendencies but encountered stern opposition from . . . most other theologians. . . . He presented fresh ideas on the Atonement, the Trinity, conversion, and man."[2]

Patterson says that liberals "emphasized personality as the key to reality, experience and reason as the final authorities in religion, and the moral teachings of Jesus as the key to understanding Christianity. . . . The social gospel movement became the most characteristic expression of liberal theology in America. The differences between liberals and conservatives were institutionalized in 1908 when the Federal Council of Churches was founded to combine the social programs of liberal congregations. The conservatives counterorganized and began to harden into the fundamentalist movement."

Most evangelicals remained in the major denominations and tried to counter modernistic ideas and the liberals' contempt for orthodox doctrine from within. But some of them left the main denominations and formed a new alliance under Dwight L. Moody, and later under Billy Sunday. Other groups that retained the revivalist tradition were the Holiness and Pentecostal movements. They emphasized the supernatural transformation of the believer in the power of the Holy Spirit, and a complete separation from the world. These groups also emphasized the second return of Christ and biblical inerrancy. Some of them rejected the social gospel and higher education. These conservative evangelicals formed the basis of the fundamentalist movement. Hostility toward liberal theology sprang from nineteenth-century opposition to Darwinism and popular revivalism. The movement finally coalesced with the publication, between 1910 and 1915, of a series of pamphlets called *The Fundamentals*.

Five of their theological ideas were known as the "fundamentals of the faith:" 1) the verbal inspiration of the Bible; 2) the virgin birth of Christ; 3) His substitutionary atonement; 4) His bodily resurrection; and 5) His imminent and visible second coming. Patterson says the pamphlets were written by Princeton Seminary Professors Charles Hodge and B. B. Warfield, and other writers. (Cairns adds the names of James Orr, R. A. Torrey, and C. I. Scofield.) These and other conservative theologians of genuine academic ability, do not fit today's stereotypical image of the fundamentalist. Patterson says that many of the later fundamentalists were so strict that some of the original writers would not have been welcome in their circles. Both Cairns and *The New International Dictionary of the Christian Church* credit Curtis Laws, editor of *The Baptist Watchman-Examiner*, with coining the title "fundamentalists" for conservatives who believed that the modernists were surrendering the fundamentals of the Gospel. It was later used in a pejorative sense to describe militant theological conservatives in their crusade against modernism. Patterson defines a fundamentalist as an evangelical who has added the element of opposition to his creed.

Scholarly debate was displaced by the bitterness of theological politics, and the fundamentalists' separation from theological error and evil in society. Their fight against liberalism turned to the courtroom in the 1925 trial of John T. Scopes for teaching evolution in Tennessee public schools. William Jennings Bryan, the three-time Democratic presidential nominee and Freemason,[3] was the acknowleged spokesman for the fundamentalists, and assisted the prosecution. Clarence Darrow, the most famous criminal lawyer of his generation, was chief defense counsel. Bryan was devastated by Darrow's animated, sarcastic cross-examination about his beliefs relative to the fundamentalist view of science and biblical authority.[4] He left the impression that fundamentalism was an outdated, intellectually repressive religion. For many people, especially those in higher education, conservative orthodoxy was heresy, and fundamentalism only an offensive theological weed. Fundamentalism, in turn, saw only apostasy in the historic denominations, and chose to defend itself by withdrawing. The doctrine of separation had become part of their creed.

The theology of fundamentalism particularly stressed the supernatural origin of Scripture and the divine nature of Christ in His person and work. The phrase "inerrancy of the Bible in all its details" became a catchword, and is now one of their most characteristic expressions. They vehemently opposed the optimistic doctrines of the liberals, and many of them began to teach dispensational-premillennialism, which Patterson describes as a very anti-progressive scheme of history that postpones most of the benefits of Christianity until Christ returns to earth. This doctrine became the basis for separation from both the apostate church and the world, and was often considered a test of orthodoxy. Other important positions were godly living (the deeper life movement), prohibition of alcohol, rejection of the natural sciences, revivalism, and political conservatism.

Around 1940 Carl Henry emerged as a leader of a group of evangelicals who deliberately began to distinguish themselves from the older fundamentalists. Harold J. Ockenga was perhaps their most significant leader. In 1942 he became the first president of the National Association of Evangelicals, and in 1947, the first president of Fuller Seminary. Since the 1920s, fundamentalists had refused to cooperate with apostates, fearful of compromise of any sort. By contrast, the newer evangelicals sought to cooperate through an intelligent discussion of differences. Where the fundamentalists demanded conformity and feared academic liberty, the new evangelicals rejected anti-intellectualism and emphasized scholarship. Their schools continued to oppose liberal theology, but dropped militancy, and permitted debate on the question of the inerrancy of Scripture. The evangelicals used the tools of research developed during the Enlightenment while Fundamentalism feared biblical criticism. Some fundamentalists think the Bible is a book of facts that are *all* historically and scientifically true; they think *any interpretation* is heresy. Many of those who do understand and use the principles of hermeneutics think that literary criticism is an attempt to discredit what the Bible teaches; Evangelicals believe that skeptical criticism is not due to *form criticism* itself, but to the theological assumptions of the *form critic;* in other words, don't blame the tool for the fault in the craftsman.[5]

Henry and the new evangelicals rejected the fundamentalists' cultural isolation, and contended that Christianity has important social factors. They continued to be predominantly conservative and patriotic, but they were seriously concerned about the need for more radical social application (they often dropped dispensationalism, though not usually premillennialism). The new Evangelicalism wanted to resume its role of helping shape the American culture. While evangelism was still their central focus, the new evangelicals were characterized by ecclesiastical cooperation, growth in scholarship, and a more sophisticated political understanding to express renewed social concern. The fundamentalists became a strict subculture within orthodoxy, while the new evangelicals became *the* evangelicals to the American public at large.

Rejection of Fundamentalism

Years later, Carl Henry wrote, "What distressed the growing evangelical mainstream about the Fundamentalist far right were its personal legalisms, suspicion of higher education, disdain for biblical criticism per se, polemical orientation of theological discussion, judgmental attitudes toward those in ecumenically related denominations, and an uncritical political conservatism."

Better than anyone else, Henry has singled out the weaknesses of fundamentalism and firmly repudiated them. In 1947, he published *The Uneasy Conscience of Modern Fundamentalism* to point to their harsh temperament and spirit of lovelessness and strife, that had seen heresy in liberal untruth but not in their own lack of love. In this book Henry criticized the fundamentalist theological tradition as he pointed the evangelicals in some new directions. The fundamentalists' primary interest was in the preservation of the orthodox doctrine of salvation and the inerrancy of Scripture. They also rejected a "social gospel" without individual regeneration, a philosophy of history without a final judgment, and an ecumenical movement that minimized the absoluteness of Christianity.

Henry disagreed more with the fundamentalist temperament than he did their theology, and yet the two views of orthodox Christianity are so different, that the distinction between them actually is theological. To ignore correct theological elements, and to elevate secondary doctrines to cardinal ones, is theological error.

What were the elements in fundamentalism that Henry examined and rejected? First, he rejected the attitude of fundamentalism—its lack of love for fellow believers in Christ. Many fundamentalists were guilty of a divisive spirit of discord, which led to isolation and ineffective evangelism. This lack of love led to militant, intemperate attacks on both friend and foe, a dogmatism of personal ethics and experience, and schismatic strategies as the normal strategy.

By contrast, Henry proposed unity and fellowship among evangelicals, liberality over minor issues, a strategy of influencing the major denominations from within instead of from without, the rejection of a "thou shalt not" Christianity, an informed attitude toward newer forms of liberal theology, and love for all believers in Christ. He urged cooperation among all evangelicals for the purposes of evangelism and of educating believers in orthodox theology. Evangelicals have responded to this appeal and are showing a willingness to converse with liberals for common purposes of scholarly pursuit, to welcome the charismatics, and to be tolerant of differences in eschatology.

Second, Henry rejected the anti-educational position of the fundamentalists. The militant fundamentalists were anti-intellectual, had a general disregard for scholarship, failed to produce academically competent books and journals, over-simplified theology (their gospel was little more than the biblical plan of salvation), lacked intellectual honesty in dealing with evolution, and opposed the natural sciences. To correct this situation among the new evangelicals, Henry emphasized an educated ministry, scholarly research and writing, careful clarification of theological issues, an intellectual defense of the evangelical position, and a Christian approach to education.

The new evangelicals are concerned with quality education at all levels. They have an open attitude toward scientific studies and an increased emphasis on scholarship. Their emphasis on intellectual respectability has moved them toward an honest dialogue on specific scientific-biblical problems. It has given them a greater openness to biblical higher criticism with a new desire to define the nature of biblical inerrancy, and it has caused them to study the nature of history to see how it relates to the Christian faith.

The third characteristic of fundamentalism that Henry examined and rejected was its failure to apply Christianity to the whole of life. Fundamentalism did not insist on a thorough statement of, and concern for, personal and social ethics. Henry chided the fundamentalist tradition for being extremely dogmatic on minor points of eschatology while failing to produce any adequate system of social-personal ethics based on Christian-biblical resources. If liberals depreciated the prophetic element in the Bible and misconstrued its historical message, the fundamentalists depreciated the legitimate demand of the gospel upon every area of culture.

A properly balanced Evangelicalism can learn from both liberals and fundamentalists. The liberals are right in their conviction that Christianity implies solutions for all the problems of human existence. The fundamentalists were right in assuming that history has a final chapter but wrong in assuming that *"this is it."* Until the Lord returns, the gospel provides for solutions to all of mankind's problems, and the news of His second coming is equally important.

Henry has been especially active in the area of social and ethical concerns, making it one of his doctrinal priorities. He has insisted that orthodox theology is not complete without a thorough system of *personal and social* ethics.

More than forty years after Henry's 1947 attack on fundamentalism's indifference to ethics, extreme separatist fundamentalism still has no social conscience. Their dogmatic theology prevents them from returning to biblical theology, and from developing a program for reconciliation among Christians.

III ‖ NATURE WORSHIP

C ARLSON'S LECTURE MAKES A VARIETY of false charges, which are best discussed one at a time. To avoid tedious repetition, only his most flagrant fabrications were selected to expose Carlson's duplicity in the method he used to perpetrate his hoax. Anyone wishing to find answers to his other allegations may compare the appendices to this book,* or consult Art Dehoyos's *The Cloud of Prejudice* and the February 1993 issue of *The Scottish Rite Journal*. This chapter addresses his claim that Freemasonry is a religion. Carlson says that Masonry is Pantheism and nature worship because "Masons teach that the universe is God, and tolerates the worship of all gods. Masonry borrows ideas from all religions and mixes them together to form a universal religion."

FREEMASONRY IS NOT A RELIGION

Carlson's audiocassettes introduce him as follows:[1]

> Ron Carlson, lecturer in Conservative Religion, has studied at seven universities, including working on and specializing in non-Christian Cults in Eastern Philosophy. He has traveled extensively in over thirty countries and many major universities.

Notice that Carlson was introduced as a "lecturer in Conservative Religion," not as an ordained Minister. His introduction implies that he is an expert "in

*Note: Appendix A is a true and complete transcript of an audiocassette of Carlson's anti-Masonic lecture. Index numbers locate corresponding positions on Carlson's tape. An ellipsis ". . ." shows where portions of Pike's text were omitted by Carlson. Parentheses enclose Carlson's words where they were substituted for Pike's. [Brackets] enclose my added explanations or mark a page number to reveal his source – where Carlson added selected phrases to those found on the page he cited. In my response, **bold print** identifies all text that Carlson omitted. *Italics* within Pike's text are those that Pike used. All pages cited from Albert Pike's *Morals and Dogma*, either by Carlson or myself, are reproduced as Appendix B for comparison.

non-Christian Cults in Eastern Philosophy," but it does not tell us where Carlson received his university training. It only says that he "has studied at seven universities," and that "he has traveled extensively in over thirty countries and many major universities." Does his introduction mean that his name is listed as a student on the records of seven different universities? Or that he read some books in seven different university libraries?

Carlson begins his anti-Masonic lecture by saying,[2]

> It is good to have you here tonight, as we deal with a very timely and important subject to deal with. Tonight we want to speak on the subject of Freemasonry and the Masonic Lodge, the Shriners. I have prayed much about tonight's message. . . . It is our purpose tonight not to attack or tear down any individual. I have no quarrel with Masons as people. I have a great love for them. My quarrel tonight though, is with an organization, which claims to be the supreme universal religion, and denies Jesus Christ, our Lord. . . .
>
> This message is a combination of eighteen months of research. I have not gone to anti-Masonic writers, but rather to the authoritative works of Masonry. What I am going to say tonight is from their own source books, from the authorities of Masonry , including Albert Pike, his *Morals and Dogma* of which all Masons have a copy of . . . I have spent hours interviewing across this country, talking with some of the leading authorities in Masonic Law . . . [3]

Carlson says his charges are based on his study of the "authoritative works" of Masonry, but when I first heard this tape, I had never heard of Albert Pike's *Morals and Dogma*. It took me almost a year to find a copy that I could borrow. Keep in mind that Carlson says he spent eighteen months preparing this message from the works of Masonry. The transcript of his lecture shows, beyond any shadow of doubt, that *he could not have written his lecture* without reading and re-reading Pike's *Morals and Dogma*. It therefore follows that *it took him eighteen months to make up all the lies he tells about Freemasonry!*

Carlson says:

> To begin with, one of the things that you will hear from Masons, is they will tell you that Masonry is not a religion. They say, "Oh I'm not in it

for religion, I'm in it for the social advantage, the business advantage." The Mason simply does not understand what he is involved in. Tonight I would like to quote from their authoritative works, mainly from the book which all Masons have, that of Albert Pike's book *Morals and Dogma*. Tonight when I quote a reference, a page number, it will be from *Morals and Dogma* unless I otherwise specify. To begin with, in Albert Pike's *Morals and Dogma*, I'll quote the page numbers, so you can go home and look them up, if anyone questions what I am saying. Beginning on page 213, Pike says, "every Masonic Lodge is a temple of religion, and its teachings are instructions in religion."[4]

Pike actually meant that Masonry teaches us that the true religious philosophy of an imperfect being is not a creed; it is an unlimited search. A man's religious or moral character is not formed in a moment. It is the habit of our minds, the result of many thoughts and feelings and efforts. His thought here is the same as Paul's in Galatians 6:7, "God cannot be mocked. A man reaps what he sows."[5]

In the sentence that follows the one that Carlson quoted, Pike said, "**For here are inculcated disinterestedness [freedom from selfish motive or interest], affection, toleration, devotedness, patriotism, truth, a generous sympathy with those who suffer and mourn, pity for the fallen, mercy for the erring, relief for those in want, Faith, Hope, and Charity.**" Carlson altered Pike's meaning by quoting only part of what Pike said. The two sentences, taken together, clearly mean that Freemasonry impresses on men's minds the lesson taught in James 1:27: "Pure religion and undefiled before God and the Father is this, to visit the fatherless and widows in their affliction, and to keep himself unspotted before the world," and in James 2:17: "Even so faith, if it hath not works, is dead, being alone." The marginal note in Dake's *Annotated Reference Bible* provides insight into the meaning of these verses: "Faith without works is dead; works without faith is dead. Neither is complete in itself, like fire burning without fuel, and fuel burning without fire."

Freemasonry is *not* a religion, but it teaches Masons that their daily life should reflect the principles of their own religion, whatever *their religion* might be. Even here, Pike does not claim any authority to speak for Masonry. He clearly states, in the preface to *Morals and Dogma*, that the teachings of these Readings are not sacramental; that the Ancient and Accepted Scottish Rite uses the word "Dogma" in its true sense, of *doctrine,* or *teaching;* and is not *dogmatic;* and "Every one is entirely free to reject and dissent from whatsoever herein may seem to him to be untrue or unsound. It is only required of him that he shall weigh what is taught, and give it fair hearing and unprejudiced judgment."[6]

Carlson continues:

> Page 210, quote, "Masonry is . . . from the earliest times the custodian and depository of the great . . . religious truths, unknown to the world at large, and handed down from age to age by an unbroken current of tradition, embodied in symbols, emblems, and allegories."

Earlier in this chapter, on page 206, Pike says that except for a few persons, the people of Judah and Israel were prone to worship other gods, and did not believe in the existence of only one God until a late period in their history. Only a few understood the true nature and attributes of God. The rest either could not understand, or refused to believe it. Those who did understand and believe, used symbols, emblems, and allegories to teach their knowledge to the next generation. Pike regarded Masonry as the spiritual heir to their method of teaching religious truths.

FREEMASONRY IS NOT A UNIVERSAL RELIGION
BASED ON GOOD WORKS

Carlson distorts Pike's meaning in the following paragraph by omitting several key words and phrases. Although Carlson says it is found on page 219, he actually introduces the paragraph with a phrase quoted from page 218:

> Page 219, quote, "Much of the Masonic secret manifests itself . . . to him who even partially comprehends all of the Degrees in proportion as he receives them; and particularly to those who advance to the highest degrees of the Ancient and Accepted Scottish Rite. That Rite raises a corner of the veil, even in the Degree of Entered Apprentice; for it is there declared that Masonry is a *worship.* [Masonry] . . . is

the universal . . . religion . . . in the heart of universal human-ity. . . . The ministers of this religion are all Masons. . . . Its sacrifices to God are good works, . . . and perpetual efforts to attain to all the moral perfection of which man is capable." Unquote.

In order to appreciate what Pike actually said, the phrases that Carlson omitted are shown in bold print. The omitted portions include two scripture verses, whose origin can be found in the notes:

It is the universal, **eternal, immutable** religion, **such as God planted it in the heart of universal humanity. No creed has ever been long-lived that was not built on this foundation. It is the base, and they are the superstructure. "Pure religion and undefiled before God and the Father is this, to visit the fatherless and widows in their affliction, and to keep himself unspotted before the world."[7] "Is not** _this_ **the fast that I have chosen? to loose the bands of wickedness, to undo the heavy burdens, and to let the oppressed go free, and that ye break every yoke?"[8]** The ministers of this religion are all Masons **who comprehend it and are devoted to it;** its sacrifices to God are good works, **the sacrifices of the base and disorderly passions, the offering up of self-interest on the altar of humanity,** and perpetual efforts to attain to all the moral perfection of which man is capable.

Carlson sums up his charge that Masonry is a religion by saying:

Albert Pike, their leading authority, says first of all, that the Masonic Lodge is a temple of religion, that Masonry is a worship; it is a universal religion, that all Masons are ministers of this religion; its sacrifices to God are good works and perpetual moral efforts of man. We now understand what we're dealing with. We're dealing with a religion which claims to be the universal worship of man. What is this universal religion that Masons are the ministers of? I quote Albert Pike's _Morals and Dogma_, page 311: "In all religions, there is a basis of Truth; in all there is pure Morality . . . all teachers and reformers of

mankind we admire and revere. Masonry . . . has her mission to perform . . . she invites all men of all religions to enlist under her
banners."⁹

CALUMNY

The following paragraph commands particular attention because it exposes
Carlson's false charges as deliberate and malicious misrepresentations calculated to damage Freemasonry. *Pike did not write this paragraph;* it does not
even exist in Pike's book. *Carlson wrote it:* He stole six lines of text from
page 708 and cut out a few key words; he lifted eight more lines from page 715
and chopped out some more key words; then he took two lines from page 714,
and pasted them all together. He added a few words here, changed some
there, and Carlson, not Pike, became the author of this entire paragraph.
Once again, in order to appreciate what Pike actually said, the phrases that
Carlson omitted are shown in bold print. Words that Carlson added are
enclosed in parentheses:

> They go on, page 708: "Thus we . . . are in communion with the great
> philosophies . . . and . . . the religions which cover the earth, and all
> repose on the sacred foundation of natural religion . . . that religion
> which reveals to us the natural light given to all men, without the aid
> of (any) particular revelation . . . [From page 715:] (Beautiful), above
> the great white chaos of human errors, shines the calm, clear light of
> natural human religion; . . . the Universe, (is) the Great Bible of God.
> Material nature is (the) Old Testament, . . . Human Nature is the New
> Testament. . . . [From page 714:] The material was and has been the
> element of communion between man and God. Nature is full of
> religious lessons to . . . (the Mason)."

Carlson used Pike's words to make up his own paragraph, and claimed he
was quoting what Pike said on page 708:

> Thus we **reach the threshold of religion; and** are in communion with
> the great philosophies **which all proclaim a God** and **at the same time
> with** the religions which cover the earth, and all repose on the sacred

foundation of natural religion; of that religion which reveals to us the natural light given to all men, without the aid of a particular revelation. So long as philosophy does not arrive at religion, it is below all worships, even the most imperfect; for they at least give man a Father, a Witness, a Consoler, a Judge. By religion, philosophy connects itself with humanity, which, from one end of the world to the other, aspires to God, believes in God, hopes in God. Philosophy contains in itself the common basis of all religious beliefs.

FREEMASONRY IS NOT A PANTHEISTIC RELIGION

And then, continuing as though it were the next paragraph, Carlson skips ahead, to add from page 715:

Beautifully, above the great white chaos of human errors, shines the calm, clear light of natural human religion, revealing to us God as the Infinite Parent of all, perfectly powerful, wise, just, and perfectly holy, too. Beautiful around stretches off every way the Universe, the Great Bible of God. Material nature is its Old Testament, millions of years old, thick with eternal truths under our feet, glittering with everlasting glories over our heads; and Human Nature is the New Testament from the Infinite God, every day revealing a new page as Time turns over the leaves. Immortality stands waiting to give a recompense for every virtue not rewarded, for every tear not wiped away, for every sorrow undeserved, for every prayer, for every pure intention and emotion of the heart. And over the whole, over nature, Material and Human, over this Mortal Life and over the eternal Past and Future, the infinite Loving-kindness of God the Father comes enfolding all and blessing everything that ever was, that is, that ever shall be.

Everything is a thought of the Infinite God. Nature is His prose, and man His Poetry. There is no Chance, no Fate; but God's Great Providence, enfolding the whole Universe in its bosom, and feeding it with everlasting life. In times past there has been evil which we cannot understand; now there is evil which we cannot solve, nor make square with God's perfect goodness by any theory our feeble intellect enables us to frame. There are sufferings, follies, and sins for all mankind, for every nation, for every man and every woman. They were all foreseen by the infinite wisdom of God, all provided for by His infinite power and justice, and all are consistent with His infinite love.

Still pretending that he is quoting from page 708, Carlson turns back to page 714, to add: "The material was and has been the element of communion between man and God. Nature is full of religious lessons to a **thoughtful man.**"

Once again, Carlson sums up his false charges:

Here we find what the true basis of Masonic religion is, as we're gonna see in a moment, that of natural religion, nature worship. The universe is God, the natural world is the Old Testament, human nature is the New Testament. You do not need any revelation, you do not need the revelation of Jesus Christ because your own intellect and nature will lead you to the path. What we find summed up then is that this universal religion, which all Masons claim to be Ministers of, is a universalism of morality; it's a syncretism of all religion, taking a little from everything, mixing it in a blender, and coming up with Freemasonry. It worships all gods and deities.

PIKE'S TEXT REFUTES NATURE WORSHIP

Pike traces the origin of pagan idolatry in this very long and involved chapter, which is often quoted, *out of context*, by anti-Masons, as *"proof* that Masonry is a false religion." Pike was a brilliant man who passionately believed that God revealed His relationship to man in the Bible. He never intended to create a cultic philosophy of Nature worship, as Carlson and others accuse him of doing. He believed that the beauty and complexity of Nature reveals his Creator, and proves that God exists.

Beginning on page 708, and continuing through page 715, is the section Carlson skipped to make up his hoax. Pike says that "philosophy contains in itself the common basis of all religious beliefs; . . . From the necessity of His Nature, the Infinite Being must create, preserve, bless, and reveal Himself to man, in forms man can understand." Page 709: "Among the primary ideas of consciousness, we find the idea of God. Carefully examined by the scrutinizing intellect, it is the idea of God as an infinite, perfectly powerful, wise, just, loving, holy; absolute being with no limitation. [God] made us, made all, sustains us, sustains all; made our body, . . . made our spirit, our mind, conscience, affections, soul, will, appointed for each its natural mode of action. Thus self-consciousness leads us to consciousness of God, . . . That is the highest evidence of . . . His [existence]."

If there is a God at all, He must be omnipresent in space. He must be beyond the last stars, as He is here. He is in the little cell of life the microscope discovers. He must also be omnipresent in time. God was in every second of time before the stars began to burn. He is in the smallest imaginable portion of time, and in every second of its vast and unimaginable volume; His Here includes All of Space, His Now is the same age as All of Time.

Page 710: "All this is philosophy, the unavoidable conclusion of the human mind. It is not the *opinion* of the philosophers, but their *science;* not what they *guess,* but what they *know.* In virtue of this in-dwelling of God in matter, we may say that the world is a revelation of Him; He *is* in His work, and all material things are in communion with Him. All grow and move and live in Him. Let Him withdraw from anything, and it ceases to be. He dwells in all things, yet is prior to, above, and beyond all material existence. The title of Saint has commonly been claimed for those whose boast it is to despise philosophy; yet faith will stumble and sentiment mislead, unless knowledge be present, in amount and quality sufficient to purify the one, and to give beneficial direction to the other."

Page 711: "The study of nature is a mystery, adapted to display the wisdom and power of the Great Creator. Thus science teaches us that we are but an infinitesimal portion of a great whole, that stretches out on every side of us, and above and below us, infinite in its complications, and which infinite wisdom alone can comprehend. Infinite wisdom has arranged the infinite succession of beings, involving the necessity of birth, decay, and death, and made the loftiest virtues possible by providing those conflicts, reverses, trials, and hardships, without which even their names could never have been invented."

Page 712: "Doubt, the essential preliminary of all improvement and discovery, must accompany all the stages of man's onward progress. The faculty of doubting and questioning, without which those of comparison and judgment would be useless, is itself a divine prerogative of the reason. Knowledge is always imperfect in which discovery multiplies doubt, and doubt leads on to new discovery. The boast of science is its admitted imperfection and unlimited capacity for progress. The true religious philosophy of an imperfect being is not a creed; it is an unlimited search. Finality is just another name for bewilderment or defeat."

Page 713: "God and truth are inseparable; a knowledge of God is the possession of the saving oracles of truth. In the same proportion that the individual subjects his thought and purpose to the rule of right prescribed by Supreme Intelligence, his happiness is promoted and the purpose of his existence is fulfilled. A new way of life arises in him; he is no longer isolated. His erring will is directed, informed, and molded by the influence of a higher will."

Now Pike turns to metaphor, to poetically describe how the splendor of Nature confirms His Word, and reveals the truth and the power of God to those who have not received the Scripture: "Even to the Barbarian, Nature reveals a mighty power and a wondrous wisdom, and continually points to God. It is no Wonder that men worshiped the several things of the world. The world of matter is a revelation of fear to the savage . . . , and he sees the divine in the extraordinary. The grand objects of Nature perpetually constrain men to think of their Author. The Alps are the great altar of Europe; the nocturnal sky has been to mankind the dome of a temple, starred all over with admonitions to reverence, trust, and love."

Page 714: "The Scriptures for the human race are writ in earth and Heaven. Nature is full of religious lessons to the thoughtful man. He cannot fail to be filled with reverence, with trust, with boundless love of the Infinite God, who devised these laws of matter and of mind. The great Bible of God is ever open before mankind. The great sermon of Jesus was preached on a mountain, which preached to Him as He did to the people."

If tomorrow I am to perish utterly, then I shall only take counsel for today. Page 715: "Passion may enact my statutes today; and ambition repeal them tomorrow. I will know no other legislators. Morality will vanish, and expediency will take its place. Heroism will be gone; no longer the cool, calm courage that, for truth's sake, and for love's sake, looks death firmly in the face.

Affection, friendship, and philanthropy will be only the wild fancies of the mentally ill.

"Beautifully, above the great white chaos of human errors, shines the calm, clear light of natural human religion, revealing to us God as the Infinite Parent of all, perfectly powerful, wise, just, and perfectly holy, too. Beautiful around stretches off every way the Universe, the Great Bible of God. Material nature is its Old Testament, millions of years old, thick with eternal truths under our feet, glittering with everlasting glories over our heads; and Human Nature is the New Testament from the Infinite God, every day revealing a new page as Time turns over the leaves. Immortality stands waiting to give a recompense for every virtue not rewarded, for every tear not wiped away, for every sorrow undeserved, for every prayer, for every pure intention and emotion of the heart. And over the whole, over nature, Material and Human, over this Mortal Life and over the eternal Past and Future, the infinite Loving-kindness of God the Father comes enfolding all and blessing everything that ever was, that is, that ever shall be."

Everything is a thought of the Infinite God. Nature is His prose, and man His Poetry. There is no Chance, no Fate; but God's Great Providence, enfolding the whole Universe in its bosom, and feeding it with everlasting life. Page 716: "In times past there has been evil which we cannot understand; now there is evil which we cannot solve, nor make square with God's perfect goodness by any theory our feeble intellect enables us to frame. There are sufferings, follies, and sins for all mankind, for every nation, for every man and every woman. They were all foreseen by the infinite wisdom of God, all provided for by His infinite power and justice, and all are consistent with His infinite love."

CARLSON'S MISINTERPRETATION OF MASONIC SYMBOLS
On side B of Carlson's tape, he elaborates his charge that Freemasonry is a Pantheistic religion:

What you soon discover, as you get into Freemasonry, is that the god of Freemasonry, in nature worship, of the Universal Pantheistic All, underneath it all is the philosophy of the generating principle of life.[10]
I quote Albert Pike, Morals and Dogma, page 13: "The Sun is the

ancient symbol of the life-giving . . . generative power of the Deity. . . . The Moon was the symbol of the passive capacity of nature to
produce, the female, of which the life-giving power and energy was the
male. . . . The Master of Light and Life, the Sun and the Moon, are
symbolized in every Lodge . . . "

Carlson has once again selected only part of Pike's words, to give a 'false
picture of Pike's meaning: On page 13, Pike really said: "The Sun is the ancient
symbol of the life-giving **and** generative power of the Deity. **To the ancients,
light was the cause of life; and God was the source from which all light
flowed; the** *essence* **of Light, . . . The sun was His manifestation and
visible image; and the Sabaeans worshiping the Light—God, seemed to
worship the Sun, in whom they saw the manifestation of the Deity.**

"The Moon was the symbol of the passive capacity of nature to produce, the
female, of which the life-giving power and energy was the male. **It was the
symbol of Isis, Astarte, and Artemis, or Diana. The** *'Master of Life'* **was the
Supreme Deity, above both, and manifested through both; Zeus, the son of
Saturn, become King of the Gods; Horus, the son of Osiris and Isis, become
the Master of Life; Dionusos or Bacchus, like Mithras, become the author
of Light and Life and Truth.**

"The Master of Light and Life, the Sun and the Moon, are symbolized in
every Lodge **by the Master and Wardens: and this makes it the duty of the
Master to dispense light to the Brethren, by himself, and through the
Wardens, who are his ministers.**

" 'Thy sun,' says Isaiah to Jerusalem, 'shall no more go down, neither
shall thy moon withdraw itself; for the Lord shall be thine everlasting light,
and the days of thy mourning shall be ended. Thy people also shall be all
righteous; they shall inherit the land forever.'[11] Such is the type of a free
people.''

ORIGIN OF THE MYSTERIES

When Pike quoted Isaiah, he showed that he had a far different reason for
describing the religion of the ancients, than Carlson would have you to believe,
a purpose that becomes increasingly clear as you follow his thought.

Pike traces the origin of pagan idolatry, and with it, the origin of the Mysteries, in several of his chapters, and those passages are often quoted, *out of context,* by anti-Masons, as "proof" that Masonry is a false religion. On pages 583–584, Pike says that "in some of the preceding Degrees, you have heard of the ancient worship of the Sun, the Moon, and of other Elements and Powers of Universal Nature."

"Perhaps you have supposed that we, like many who have written on these subjects, have intended to represent this worship to you as the most ancient and original worship of the first men that lived. To undeceive you, if such was your conclusion, we have caused the Personifications of the Great Luminary of Heaven, under the names by which He was known to the most ancient nations, to proclaim the old primitive truths that were known to the Fathers of our race, before men came to worship the visible manifestations of the Supreme Power. . . . We ask now your attention to a still further development of these truths, after we shall have added something to what we have already said in regard to the Chief Luminary of Heaven, in explanation of the names and characteristics of the several imaginary Deities that represented Him among the ancient races of men."

PIKE SAYS THAT NATURE IS A REVELATION OF GOD'S NATURE
Pike continues with a discussion of the Deities and beliefs of several Eastern religions: On pages 598–600, Pike says traces or remnants of God's original revelation to mankind appear in the sacred traditions of all primitive nations.

Instead of preserving the original dowry of truth imparted to man by God, pride led each of the early nations to make these fragments, as far as possible, their private property. They reproduced them under peculiar forms, wrapped them up in symbols, concealed them in allegories, and invented fables to account for their own special possession of them. This primeval word of revelation was falsified, obscured, confused, and disfigured almost beyond recognition, but by close and severe examination we discover the truth which the apparent fable contains. What was originally revered as the symbol of a higher principle, became gradually confounded or identified with the object itself, and was worshiped; until this error led to a more degraded form of idolatry. False faiths easily sprung up when the Divine Truth was not preserved in its pristine purity.

Pike goes on to describe the forms of false religion adopted by the Eastern nations, and says, on page 601, "Increasing familiarity with early oriental records seems more and more to confirm the probability that they all originally emanated from one source." Pike then presents the details of Nature-worship in the Eastern religions, and shows the remnants of Truth, held in common by each of them, on page 609: "Behold the great fundamental primitive truths! Matter, not eternal nor self existent, but created – created by a thought of God. After matter, and worlds, then man, by a like thought: and finally, after endowing him with the senses and a thinking mind, a portion, a spark, of God Himself penetrates the man, and becomes a living spirit within him. [Pages 610–11:] The fundamental doctrine of the ancient religion of India and Persia was at first nothing more than a simple veneration of nature. . . . This pure and simple veneration of nature is perhaps the most ancient, and was by far the most generally prevalent in the primitive and patriarchal world. It was not originally a deification of nature, or a denial of the sovereignty of God. Those pure elements and primitive essences of created nature offered to the first men, still in a close communication with the Deity, not a likeness of resemblance, nor a mere fanciful image or a poetical figure, but a natural and true symbol of Divine power."

In summary, Pike says, "Nature is full of religious lessons to the thoughtful man. He cannot fail to be filled with reverence, with trust, with boundless love of the Infinite God, who devised these laws of matter and of mind." We find the same thought in Psalm 19:1–3: "The heavens declare the glory of God; and the firmament sheweth his handywork. Day unto day uttereth speech, and night unto night sheweth knowledge. There is no speech nor language, where their voice is not heard."

Pike's purpose in tracing the development of pagan idolatry, was to warn us that, in every culture, what men once saw as God revealed in nature, degenerated into worship of nature itself. Pike's view is the same as Paul's in Romans 1:18–23, 25: "The wrath of God is revealed from heaven against all ungodliness and unrighteousness of men, who hold the truth in unrighteousness; Because that which may be known of God is manifest in them; for God hath shewed it unto them. For the invisible things of him from the creation of the world are clearly seen, being understood by the things that are made, even his eternal power and Godhead; so that they are without excuse: Because that, when they knew God, they glorified him not as God, neither were thankful; but became vain in their imaginations, and their foolish heart was darkened. Professing themselves to be wise, they became fools, and changed the glory of the uncorruptible God into an image made like to corruptible man, and to birds, and four-footed beasts, and creeping things. . . . Who changed the truth of God into a lie, and worshiped and served the creature more than the Creator, who is blessed for ever. Amen."

IV || Oaths and Obligations

A FTER DESCRIBING HIS IMPRESSION OF the nature of the penalties involved, when taking Masonic oaths or obligations, Carlson states his view that Jesus forbade the taking of oaths.[1]

When I first petitioned for the degrees of Freemasonry, it was in response to a friend's interest in me as a person. I had no idea of the nature of the Order, much less that any controversy existed. But I must admit that some questions did come to my mind as I progressed through the initiation. Perhaps sharing my experience may have more value than argument.

At first I hesitated when I was asked if I was willing to take an oath or obligation. Then the memory of the Oath of Service when I enlisted in the army, and of the Hippocratic Oath when my medical class graduated flashed into my mind. The obligation itself amused me and I had to smother a laugh. The idea that grown men would actually take such an oath seriously seemed ludicrous. But then I recalled that just before entering the Lodge, I had been told that the only penalties Freemasonry ever imposes are reprimand, suspension, or expulsion, and that all references to any other penalties are only symbolic in nature.

Carlson asks:

> What does the Bible say about things like this, even taking of an oath? If you have your Bibles, I'd like you to turn with me to Matthew 5:34–37. Jesus says, "But I say to you, (Make no oath) at all, either by heaven, for it is the throne of God, or by the earth, for it is the footstool of His feet, or by Jerusalem, for it is the city of the Great King; nor shall you (make an oath) by your head, for you cannot make one hair white

or black; so let your statements be yes or no, and anything beyond this is of evil." Turn with me to James 5:12: "But above all, my brethren, do not swear, either by heaven or by earth, or of any other oath; but let your yes be yes, your no be no, so that you may not fall under the judgment." 1 Corinthians 3:16–17: "Do you not know that you are the temple of God, and that the Spirit of God dwells in you? If any man destroys the temple of God, God will destroy him, for the temple of God is holy and that is what you are."

My friends, to take an oath as a Mason, to swear an oath that you will rip your body to shreds if you should reveal any of the secrets, have your throat cut across, your tongue ripped out; God says, as a Christian, you should have no part of it. After the oaths are taken, the Mason is then told what he is to believe. It's interesting to me that Masons are sworn to secrecy on the oath of death, before they are told anything about what is going on inside the Masonic Lodge.

Jesus did not say, "(Make no oath) at all;" "Nor shall you (make an oath) by your head." He said, **"Do not swear at all;"** "Nor shall you **swear** by your head."[2]

BIBLICAL REFERENCES TO OATH-TAKING
The Illustrated Bible Dictionary says the Hebrew word for *oath* is related to a verb whose basic meaning is 'to pronounce a conditional curse.' It owed its power to the sovereign response of God Himself.[3] The seriousness of oaths is emphasized in the laws of Moses,[4] but false swearing by a witness could be atoned for by a sin offering.[5] According to *The Interpreter's Dictionary of the Bible,* the more serious the issue at stake, the more terrible would be the curses that are designed to enforce the oath.

Carlson's view that Jesus forbade us to take *any oath,* without exception, is a belief shared by many. But we know that is *not* the lesson Jesus intended to teach us, because of what we read in Matthew 26:62–64: "And the high priest arose and said to Him, 'Do You answer nothing? What *is it that* these men testify against You?' But Jesus kept silent. And the high priest answered and said to Him, 'I adjure You by the living God, that You tell us if You are the Christ, the Son of God.' Jesus said to him, *'It is as* you said. Nevertheless, I say to you, hereafter you will see the Son of Man sitting at the right hand of the Power, and coming on the clouds of heaven.' " Notice that Jesus was silent before His accusers until *after He was put under oath.*

Eight different sources—Barclay, Dake, Meyer, *The Illustrated Bible Dictionary, The Interpreter's Dictionary of the Bible, The New Bible Commentary, Tyndale New Testament Commentaries,* and *The Zondervan Pictorial Encyclopedia of the Bible*—all agree that Jesus's answer was given under oath.

Meyer says that *"to swear not at all"* interdicts all *kinds of swearing* in general. Christianity as it should be according to the will of Christ should know no oath at all. To the consciousness of the Christian, God should always be so vividly present that, to him, and others in the Christian community, his yea and nay are, in point of reliability, equivalent to an oath. His yea and nay are oath enough. The kinds of swearing censured by Jesus were very common amongst the Jews. Not merely the Jews, but also the heathen, swore by their head. The meaning of the whole passage is: Ye shall not swear by all these objects; for all such oaths are nothing less than the oath directly by God Himself, on account of the relation in which those objects stand to God.[6] Meyer says that the high priest answered Jesus's refusal to speak in self-defense by repeating a formal oath, in which Jesus is called upon to swear whether He was the Messiah or not. To give an affirmative answer to this formula was to take the full oath usually administered in any court of law. Jesus not only affirmed it, He said that He was the Messiah who was seen by Daniel in his vision.[7]

Barclay says that Jesus did not protest at being put on oath at His trial before the High Priest: the High Priest said to Him: "I adjure you by the living God—I put you on oath by God Himself—tell us if you are the Christ, the Son of God."[8] In Barclay's view, Jesus found two things about taking oaths that were not satisfactory. The first was unnecessary or frivolous swearing: "By thy life," or "By my head." Its modern equivalent would be: "I swear by my mother's grave," or the child's "Cross my heart and hope to die." The second was evasive swearing. Any oath that contained the name of God was held to be absolutely binding; but if an oath evaded the use of God's name, God was not considered to be a partner in the transaction. In effect Jesus is saying that God is involved in all transactions, whether God is actually named or not. An honest man will never need to take an oath; the truth of what he says and the reality of his promises need no such guarantee. But oaths are still necessary because all men are not honest, and this is not an ideal world.[9] Most ministers who believe that Jesus forbade us to take an oath under any circumstance willingly perform conventional marriage ceremonies that require the bride and groom *to take their vows* "in the sight of God and these witnesses."

The *Illustrated Bible Dictionary* says that Christ taught that oaths were binding.[10] The Christian's daily conversation is to be as sacred as his oaths, and he is not to have two standards of truth in regard to oaths. In the kingdom of God oaths finally become unnecessary.[11] Christ Himself accepted the imprecatory oath,[12] and there were occasions when Paul swore by an oath: *"But I call God to witness against me* – it was to spare you that I refrained from coming to Corinth;"[13] "In what I am writing to you, *before God,* I do not lie!"[14]

OATHS TAKEN BY GOD

In the Old Testament oaths formed a regular part of treaties and covenants.[15] Ezekiel 17:19 is especially interesting because it not only shows that God honors an oath, but also that He makes them: "Therefore thus saith the Lord God; *As I live,* surely *mine oath* that he hath despised, and *my covenant* that he hath broken, *even it will I recompense upon his own head."* In Hebrews 6:13–17, we read that God bound Himself by an oath: "When God made his promise to Abraham, since there was no one greater for him to swear by, he swore by himself, saying, 'I will surely bless you and give you many descendants.' And so after waiting patiently, Abraham received what was promised. Men swear by someone greater than themselves, and the oath confirms what is said and puts an end to all argument. Because God wanted to make the unchanging nature of his purpose very clear to the heirs of what was promised, he confirmed it with an oath."[16] The Lord bound Himself to perform His promises to His covenant people.[17] The coming of Christ was the fulfillment of God's ancient oaths.[18]

The Zondervan article says that an oath is a solemn appeal to God in attestation of the truth of a statement or the binding character of a promise. The credibility of a claim is enhanced by the use of an oath.[19]

THE OATH AND ORDEALS

The oath in Numbers 5:11–31 refers to a trial by ordeal, designed to absolve an innocent woman, when her husband accused her of being unfaithful. It was believed that God would protect the innocent from death and permit the guilty to succumb in the ordeal. The priest had the woman drink a mixture of holy water and some dust from the Tabernacle floor, into which was washed the written curses laid upon her. If she was not affected by the "bitter water that brings a curse," it was assumed that God had cleared her of guilt.

Noah's flood, Moses escaping through the Red Sea, and Joshua crossing the Jordan may all be understood as examples of an ordeal by water, through which the chosen people safely passed by an act of God, referred to as "baptism" in 1 Corinthians 10:2 and 1 Peter 3:21. The Old Testament utilized the concept of ordeal in connection with God's covenant-oath of redemption, where circumcision was a symbol of the ordeal.[20]

When the Sanhedrin demanded the truth of Jesus's claim to be the Messiah, Jesus accepted the solemn charge of a judicial oath and its implication of ordeal by death. The Resurrection is God's witness to the validity of the oath taken by Christ.[21]

PURPOSE OF OATH-TAKING

In the Old Testament, taking an oath put a person's statement under the judgment of God, and served to reinforce a will that tended to lie, because of the universal belief that all actions and intentions of men were observed by God. A higher measure of integrity and dependability was the undoubted result of the common use of oaths in human relationships.

The practical value of an oath was only a part of its importance in a religious culture. For the people of the Old Testament, an oath underlined the sincere concern and effectual strength of the life and words of men when brought into the presence of God. The Hebrew took joy in making an oath before God,[22] and found peace and comfort in his holy vows taken in the name of God.[23] In this way he expressed his faith and loyalty. Had not God Himself accompanied His words with an oath[24] guaranteeing the truth of what He had spoken and that His promises were irrevocable?[25] The use of God's name in an oath was treasured as an act in which God participated and gave assurance of His presence. It remained a purely religious form with profound meaning and became an essential element in God's covenant-oath of redemption.

The verbal form of the oath varied considerably. Some were not far from the "on-my-word-of-honor" formula that God used when He said, "By myself I have sworn, . . ."[26] or "As I live, surely my oath. . . ."[27] God also swore by His "great name"[28] and by "His holiness."[29] Paul used the same type of restrained oath in 2 Corinthians 1:23; Galatians 1:20; and Philippians 1:8.

The form of an oath that included a curse was intended to call man's attention to God, rather than calling God's attention to the transaction. The oath explicitly specified the punishment in case of perjury, the classic example being the oath in the covenant God made with Abraham, where animals were severed in two and the parties to the transaction passed between the pieces.[30] Jeremiah says: "The men who have violated my covenant and have not fulfilled the terms of the covenant they made before me, I will treat like the calf they cut in two and then walked between its pieces. The leaders of Judah and Jerusalem, the court officials, the priests and all the people of the land who walked between the pieces of the calf, I will hand over to their enemies who seek their lives. Their dead bodies will become food for the birds of the air and the beasts of the earth."[31]

Circumcision is a sign of the curse to be applied if the covenant-oath is broken, and a pledge of sincerity of the covenant-oath of allegiance.[32] Such thoughts could not have taken root in the Hebrew mind without the concept of an oath that involved punishment to make it binding.

God made use of the sign of circumcision to disclose His intentions of redeeming the race by the sacrifice of His Son: "For in Christ all the fullness of the Deity lives in bodily form, and you have been given fullness in Christ, who is the head over every power and authority. In him you were also circumcised, in the putting off of the sinful nature, not with a circumcision done by the hands of men but with the circumcision done by Christ, having been buried with him in baptism and raised with him through your faith in the power of God, who raised him from the dead. When you were dead in your sins and in the uncircumcision of your sinful nature, God made you alive with Christ. He forgave us all our sins, having canceled the written code, with its regulations, that was against us and that stood opposed to us; he took it away, nailing it to the cross."[33]

In other words, circumcision is a sign of the curse Jesus suffered in order to reconcile fallen man with his Creator: "Christ redeemed us from the curse of the law by becoming a curse for us, for it is written: "Cursed is everyone who is hung on a tree."[34] "If a man guilty of a capital offense is put to death and his body is hung on a tree, you must not leave his body on the tree overnight. Be sure to bury him that same day, because anyone who is hung on a tree is under God's curse."[35]

MASONIC OATHS AND THE CHRISTIAN FAITH

So what does all this theology have to do with Freemasonry? Simply this: God Himself instituted the concept of an oath that provided for a specific punishment, in the form of a conditional curse, in order to guarantee a man's performance of his promise, or the truth of his statement. Just as it is also true of Masonic oaths, the agent who was to carry out the penalty was not stated in the curse itself. But the fact that it was sworn before God implies that the person taking the oath was asking God Himself to be the agent of death. Since the Bible says that Jesus fulfilled the requirements of the Law and became cursed in our behalf,[36] it is evident that the imprecatory oath was the instrument used by God to show us our need for reconciliation with the Creator. Masonic oaths follow the precept and example of the Volume of Sacred Law. Since the oath was an instrument of Grace, it takes a perversion of the truth of Scripture to declare the oath to be an instrument of evil when it is used in Freemasonry.

V | THE MYSTERIES

C ARLSON ADDS TO HIS CHARGE that Masonry is a religion by saying that Masonry is identical with the ancient Mysteries, and then goes on to describe the doctrines of the mystery religions, as though these were the teachings of Freemasonry. However, the ancient Mysteries, as the term was used by Pike, and the mystery religions are two entirely different things, and are not to be confused.

According to the *Dictionary of the Christian Church*, the mystery religions were adaptations of national religions of the Middle East. They became cults as they spread throughout the Greco-Roman world by means of migration, trade, and military service abroad. The mystery religions were "clubs" of individual initiates, whose name derived from the secret symbols and rites revealed to initiates only. Most were originally fertility religions with a death-resurrection mythology representing the annual cycle of nature.[1]

The term "ancient Mysteries" as used by Pike specifically referred to their teaching method which used symbols, emblems, and allegories to teach religious knowledge that was hidden from all but a select few initiates. Pike regarded Masonry as the spiritual heir to their method of teaching religious truths.

Carlson says:

> Albert Pike, *Morals and Dogma*, page 352: "Among most of the Ancient Nations there was, in addition to their public worship, a private one styled the Mysteries; to which (only those who were admitted by initiation and ceremonies could be welcomed)." Page 353: "Where the Mysteries originated is not known. It is supposed that they came from India, by . . . way of Chaldea, into Egypt, and then were carried into Greece. Wherever they arose, they were practiced (by) all the ancient nations;"[2]

Pike actually said, on page 352, "Among most of the Ancient Nations there was, in addition to their public worship, a private one styled the Mysteries; to which those only were admitted who had been prepared by certain ceremonies called initiations." And on page 353, "Where the Mysteries originated is not known. It is supposed that they came from India, by the way of Chaldea, into Egypt, and thence, were carried into Greece. Wherever they arose, they were practiced among all the ancient nations; . . ."

Near the end of page 352, Pike quotes the first known Christian scholar: "Clemens [Clement] of Alexandria says that what was taught in the great Mysteries concerned the Universe, and was the completion and perfection of all instruction; wherein things were seen as they were, and nature and her works were made known." William P. Barker, in *Who's Who in Church History,* says, "Clement and the Alexandrians . . . looked upon philosophy as the handmaid to Christianity, and in no way inconsistent with it. Combining the best of ancient philosophy with the Gospel . . . Clement built . . . the idea that, although faith is enough for salvation, the man who adds knowledge to his faith has an even greater good."[3]

THE MYSTERIES AS A TEACHING METHOD
Carlson continues:

Page 22, "Masonry, successor of the Mysteries, still follows the ancient manner of teaching. . . . [from page 23:] Masonry is identical with the ancient Mysteries." The powers revealed in the Mysteries were all, in reality, nature gods. The Mysteries taught that doctrine of the Divine Oneness. Here we get into the fact that Freemasonry claims to be identical to the ancient Mysteries, that the Mysteries revered Nature and the Nature God, and held to the pantheistic Divine One as their god.

In this section, Pike was *not* referring to the *Mystery Religions.* He intended for us to understand the true purpose of *the Mysteries, as a teaching method:* how their symbols were used to teach the Initiate his obligation to maintain the established religion, as it was before it degenerated into a worship of imaginary Deities, and idols. The two sentences, supposedly found on page 22, are actually found on pages 22 and 23; they are qualified by text that precedes the first sentence, and follows the second; text that Carlson *had to read* before he could find and misuse them.

Page 22:

> In the ancient Orient, all religion was more or less a mystery and there was no divorce from it of philosophy. The popular theology, taking the multitude of allegories and symbols for realities, degenerated into a worship of the celestial luminaries, of imaginary Deities, . . . of idols, . . . Of course the popular religion could not satisfy the deeper longings and thoughts, the loftier aspirations of the Spirit, or the logic of reason. The first [religion], therefore, was taught to the initiated in the Mysteries. There, also, it was taught by symbols. The vagueness of symbolism, capable of many interpretations, reached what the palpable [clear, plain] and conventional creed could not. Its indefiniteness acknowledged the abstruseness [difficulty] of the subject: it treated that mysterious subject mystically: it endeavored to illustrate what it could not explain; to excite an appropriate feeling, if it could not develop an adequate idea; . . . Thus the knowledge now imparted by books and letters, was of old conveyed by symbols; and the priests invented or perpetuated a display of rites and exhibitions, which were not only more attractive to the eye than words, but often more suggestive and more pregnant with meaning to the mind. Masonry, successor of the Mysteries, still follows the ancient manner of teaching. **Her ceremonies are like the ancient shows,** [and then, on page 23:] **Though** Masonry is identical with the ancient Mysteries, **it is only so in this qualified sense: that it presents . . . a** system that has experienced progressive alterations, . . . the Mysteries were modified by the . . . religious systems of the countries into which they were transplanted. To maintain the established government, laws, and religion, was the obligation of the Initiate everywhere; and everywhere they were the heritage of the priests, who were nowhere willing to make the common people coproprietors with themselves of philosophical truth. . . .

Pike goes on to say, "Christianity taught the doctrine of FRATER-NITY; but repudiated that of political EQUALITY, by continually inculcating obedience to Caesar, and those lawfully in authority. Masonry was the first apostle of EQUALITY. In the Monastery there is *fraternity* and *equality*, but no *liberty*. Masonry added that also, and claimed for man the three-fold heritage, LIBERTY, EQUALITY, and FRATERNITY.

"It was but a development of the original purpose of the Mysteries, which was to teach men to know and practice their duties to themselves and their fellows, the great practical end of all philosophy and all knowledge."[4]

THE ORIGIN OF THE MYSTERIES

Carlson says that Freemasonry claims to be identical to the ancient Mysteries, that the Mysteries revered Nature and the Nature God, and held to the pantheistic Divine One as their god.

But Pike said that Masonry is identical with the ancient Mysteries only in the sense that it presents a system that has experienced progressive alterations. Pike describes the origin, not the present meaning of the symbols. Those who devised them had a reason for their symbolism, which was changed by local priests as the Mysteries traveled. As we follow their history, the symbols had many and various meanings, but the Mysteries were modified by each local religious system to maintain their own established government, laws, and religion; only one specifically assigned meaning was used and taught to the local initiate. Pike seeks to inform us that, in every nation, the same *method* was used to teach the local religion, and that in every case, the local populace took the symbols literally, and for them, the religion degenerated into idolatry, as the symbols took on base meanings that were not originally given to the initiates.

Again, Pike's purpose was to show the steadying influence of the Mysteries, whose initiates retained the original meaning that was intended, while those who were not initiated gradually assigned new meanings. [The warning is clear—it happened in every nation—and it is happening today, in the United States of America!] Pike said that Masonry was only a development of the original purpose of the Mysteries, which was to teach men to know and practice their duties to God, to their fellow men, and to themselves.

Pike continued his discussion of the Mysteries on pages 64 and 65: "The Mysteries were a Sacred Drama, exhibiting some legend significant of nature's changes, of the visible Universe in which the Divinity is revealed . . . Nature is the great Teacher of man; for it is the Revelation of God. It neither dogmatizes nor attempts to tyrannize by compelling to a particular creed or special interpretation. It presents its symbols to us, and adds nothing by way of explanation. It is the text without the commentary; and, as we well know, it is chiefly the commentary and gloss that lead to error and heresy and persecution. The earliest instructors of mankind not only adopted the lessons of Nature, but as far as possible adhered to her method of imparting them. In the Mysteries few explanations were given to the spectators, who were left, as in the school of nature, to make inferences for themselves. No other method could have suited every degree of cultivation and capacity. To employ nature's universal symbolism instead of the technicalities of language, rewards the humblest inquirer, and discloses its secrets to every one in proportion to his power to comprehend them. If their philosophical meaning was above the comprehension of some, their moral and political meanings are within the reach of all."

WHEN MYSTERIES BECOME IDOLATRY

These mystic shows and performances were not the reading of a lecture, but the opening of a problem. Requiring research, they were calculated to arouse the dormant intellect. They implied no hostility to philosophy, because philosophy is the great expounder of symbolism; although its ancient interpretations were often ill-founded and incorrect. The alteration from symbol to dogma is fatal to beauty of expression, and leads to intolerance and assumed infallibility.[5]

The Mysteries dramatized the original teachings of the local religion. The priests used the symbolic form to teach the Initiates, because the symbols never varied unless they were intentionally changed. Thus religious beliefs, portrayed by the Mysteries to the Initiates, remained intact. The priests used verbal explanations for the common people because they were more precise than visual illustration alone; but verbal explanations varied with each generation of teachers until the original symbols were transformed into idols.

On pages 598–600, Pike says that traces or remnants of God's original revelation to mankind, appear in the sacred traditions of all primitive nations. Instead of preserving the original dowry of truth imparted to man by God, pride led each of the early nations to make these fragments, as far as possible, their private property. They reproduced them under peculiar forms, wrapped them up in symbols, concealed them in allegories, and invented fables to account for their own special possession of them. This primeval word of revelation was falsified, obscured, confused, and disfigured almost beyond recognition, but by close and severe examination we discover the truth, which the apparent fable contains. What was originally revered as the symbol of a higher principle, became gradually confounded or identified with the object itself, and was worshiped; until this error led to a more degraded form of idolatry. False faiths easily sprung up when the Divine Truth was not preserved in its pristine purity.

PROPER MEANING OF THE MYSTERIES
In *A Pilgrim's Path,* John Robinson says, "It is, apparently, very confusing for non-Masons to learn that Freemasonry doesn't tell men what they are supposed to believe."[6] "It is important to understand that Freemasonry does not *teach* a man to believe in God, or in religious freedom, or in moral conduct, or in acts of charity. He must bring those beliefs with him into the brotherhood, where he will find them encouraged and reinforced. George Washington, Benjamin Franklin, and Paul Revere were not taught to love liberty in their Masonic Lodges. They joined because the beliefs they already cherished were shared by other Masons and encouraged by the brotherhood. They became Masons in order to be with like-minded men."[7]

One form of interpretation is to allow symbols to speak for themselves without verbal elaboration. Masonry, seen in this light, is the heir to the teaching method of the Mysteries, because Masonry does not teach men what to believe and this is the proper meaning of the Mysteries.

Pike continues:[8] "In the Mysteries, wherever they were practiced, was taught the truth of the primitive revelation, the existence of One Great Being, Infinite and pervading the Universe, Who was there worshiped without superstition; and His marvellous nature, essence, and attributes taught to the Initiates; while the vulgar attributed His works to Secondary Gods, personified, and isolated from Him in fabulous independence.

"These truths were covered from the common people as with a veil; and the Mysteries were carried into every country, that, without disturbing the popular beliefs, truth, the arts, and the sciences might be known to those who were capable of understanding them, and maintaining the true doctrine incorrupt; which the people, prone to superstition and idolatry, have in no age been able to do; nor, as many strange aberrations and superstitions of the present day prove, any more now than heretofore."

Page 625: "Masonry, when properly expounded, is at once the interpretation of the great book of nature, the recital of physical and astronomical phenomena, the purest philosophy, and the place of deposit, where, as in a Treasury, are kept in safety all the great truths of the primitive revelation, that form the basis of all religions. In the modern Degrees three things are to be recognized: The image of primeval times, the tableau of the efficient causes of the Universe, and the book in which are written the morality of all peoples, and the code by which they must govern themselves if they would be prosperous."

Pages 62–64: "*All* religious expression is symbolism; since we can *describe* only what we *see* . . . All language is symbolic . . . 'To retract,' is to *draw back,* and when applied to a *statement,* is symbolic, as much so as a picture of an arm drawn back would be. . . . To present a visible symbol to the eye of another, is not necessarily to inform him of the meaning which that symbol has to you. Hence the philosopher soon superadded to the symbols, explanations addressed to the ear, susceptible of more precision, but less effective and impressive than the painted or sculptured forms that he endeavored to explain. When Philosophy resorted to definitions and formulas, its language was more complicated symbolism, attempting to grapple with and picture ideas impossible to be expressed. For as with the visible symbol, so with the word; to utter it to you does not inform you of the *exact* meaning which it has to *me;* and thus religion and philosophy became to a great extent disputes as to the meaning of words. The most abstract expression for Deity, which language can supply, is a *sign* or *symbol* for an object beyond our comprehension. . . . Thus language too is symbolism, and words are as much misunderstood and misused as more material symbols are.

"Symbolism tended continually to become more complicated; and all the powers of Heaven were reproduced on earth, until a web of fiction and allegory was woven, partly by art and partly by the ignorance of error, which the wit of man, with his limited means of explanation, will never unravel. Even the Hebrew Theism became involved in symbolism and image worship. . . . The priests were monotheists; the people idolaters.

"There are dangers inseparable from symbolism. Names that stand for things are confounded with them; the means are mistaken for the end; the instrument of interpretation for the object; and thus symbols come to be seen as truths and persons. Though perhaps a necessary path, they were a dangerous one by which to approach the Deity; in which many, mistaking the sign for the thing signified, fell into a ridiculous superstition; while others, in avoiding one extreme, plunged into irreligion and impiety."

CHRISTIAN INTERPRETATION OF THE BLUE DEGREES

In this section, Pike speaks as a Christian. It should be noted that these same symbols will have different interpretations for Masons of other faiths.

On pages 638–642 Pike repeats the Christian interpretations of the Blue Degrees. The full account of the interpretations will be found in Appendix B. The following is only a brief summary:

In the First Degree there are three symbols to be applied:

1st. After the fall man was prone to evil, and staggered blindly into the thick darkness of unbelief, bound fast by the cable-tow of the natural and sinful will. This condition of blindness, destitution, misery, and bondage, from which to save the world the Redeemer came, is symbolized by the condition of the candidate, when he is brought up for the first time to the door of the Lodge.

2d. Not withstanding the death of the Redeemer, man can only be saved by faith, repentance, and reformation. His confidence in his guide, his trust in God, and the point of the sword are symbolical of the faith, repentance, and reformation necessary to bring him to the light of a life in Christ the Crucified.

3d. Having repented and reformed, and bound himself to the service of God by a firm promise and obligation, the light of Christian hope shines down into the darkness of the humble penitent. This is symbolized by the candidate's being brought to light, after he is obligated, by the Worshipful Master, who in that is a symbol of the Redeemer, and so brings him to light, with the help of the brethren, as He taught the Word with the aid of the Apostles.

In the Second Degree there are two symbols:

4th. The new Christian assumes new duties toward God and his fellows. Toward God, of love, gratitude, and veneration, and an anxious desire to serve and glorify Him; toward his fellows, of kindness, sympathy, and justice. And this assumption of duty, this entering upon good works, is symbolized by the Fellow-Craft's obligation.

5th. The Christian, reconciled to God, sees the world in a new light. This great Universe is no longer a machine set in motion, and left to run forever, by a law of mechanics created at the beginning; it has now become the product of God's thought, a thing of life, over which God watches continually, and produces every moment of its present action, the law of harmony being the essence of the Deity, reenacted every instant. This is symbolized by the instruction given in the Fellow-Craft's Degree, in the sciences, and particularly geometry, connected as the latter is with God Himself in the mind of a Mason, because the same letter, suspended in the East, represents both.

There are also two symbols in the Third Degree, making a total of seven:

6th. The candidate is told of a difficult and dangerous path yet to be traveled, and is advised that it depends upon that journey whether he will become a Master. This is symbolical of that which our Savior said to Nicodemus, that his morals might be beyond reproach, but he could not enter the kingdom of Heaven unless he were born again, symbolically dying, and again entering the world regenerate, like a spotless infant.

7th. The murder of Hiram, his burial, and his being raised again by the Master, are symbols of the death, burial, and resurrection of the Redeemer; and of the death and burial in sins of the natural man, and his being raised again to a new life, or born again, by the direct action of the Redeemer, after Morality and Philosophy had failed to raise him. Christ embraces the whole human race as closely and affectionately as brethren embrace each other in fellowship.

Masons are taught to plant firmly and deep in their hearts the foundation stones of principle, truth, justice, temperance, fortitude, prudence, and charity, on which to erect that Christian character that all the storms of misfortune and all the powers and temptations of Hell shall not prevail against.

"The Master's word, supposed to be lost, symbolizes the Christian faith and religion, supposed to have been crushed and destroyed when the Savior was crucified, after Iscariot had betrayed Him, and Peter deserted Him, and when the other disciples doubted whether He would arise from the dead; but [the Christian faith and religion] rose from His tomb and flowed rapidly over the civilized world; and so that which was supposed to be lost was found. It symbolizes also the Savior Himself; the Word that was in the beginning—that was with God, and that was God; the Word of life, that was made flesh and dwelt among us, and was supposed to be lost, while He lay in the tomb, for three days, and His disciples 'as yet knew not the scripture that He must rise again from the dead,' and doubted when they heard of it, and were amazed and frightened and still doubted when He appeared among them." "Such are the explanations of our Christian brethren; entitled, like those of all other Masons, to respectful consideration."

VI | THE BOY WHO CRIED WOLF

I F CARLSON'S DISCUSSION OF THE Mysteries had been limited to the allegations that have been countered in the previous chapter, a good case could possibly be made that he simply misunderstood Pike's view. But he goes on to accuse the leaders of the Masonic Order of using the Mysteries to deliberately mislead the average Mason, leaving no room for doubt that his attack is deliberate calumny. Carlson says:

> Now as we get into what the Mysteries are, these secrets which Masons are sworn to secrecy on, they say that you cannot know the Mysteries unless you're a Mason. The problem is, most Masons don't know them, themselves. These Mysteries, which are the basis of true Masonry, are hidden even from the Masons. Now this is one of the things which, as I talked with Masons, they do not understand themselves; that the leaders of Freemasonry, and the authorities, are consciously lying and seeking to mislead the average Mason, so that he does not understand what he is involved in.[1] Let me read for you their authority, Albert Pike, *Morals and Dogma*, page 104, I quote: "Masonry, like all the Religions, all the Mysteries, . . . *conceals* its secrets from all except the Adepts and Sages, . . . and uses false (interpretations) and misinterpretations of its symbols. . . ."[2]

WHY MASONS TEACH THROUGH SYMBOLS

Pike referred to the *reason* for the Masonic teaching methods on pages 104–105, which can be easily seen by simply allowing him to finish his sentence: "Masonry, like all the Religions, all the Mysteries, . . . *conceals* its secrets from all except the Adepts and Sages, **or the Elect,** and uses false explanations and misinterpretations of its symbols to mislead those who deserve only to be misled; to conceal the Truth, which it calls Light, from them, and to draw them away from it. Truth is not for those who are unworthy or unable to receive it, or would pervert it."

WHY JESUS TAUGHT IN PARABLES

Jesus taught in parables for the same reason: to impart hidden knowledge to a select few; not for capricious reasons, but because the larger group was not yet prepared to hear and understand. Neither for that matter were His disciples, but their minds were open, and they were willing to follow Him as their teacher. It was not until after His resurrection that His disciples understood the "mysteries" in terms of the revelation of formerly hidden knowledge, rather than in terms of knowledge hidden from all but a select few. But it seems to me that, in His early ministry, there is a strong parallel to Pike's description of the Mysteries as a teaching method, because Jesus indicated that His disciples *were* a select few: "And the disciples came, and said unto Him, Why speakest thou unto them in parables? He answered and said unto them, Because it is given unto you to know the mysteries of the kingdom of heaven, but unto them it is not given."[3] "Therefore speak I to them in parables: because they seeing see not; and hearing they hear not, neither do they understand. And in them is fulfilled the prophecy of Esaias [Isaiah], which saith, 'By hearing ye shall hear, and shall not understand; and seeing ye shall see, and shall not perceive: For this people's heart is waxed gross, and their ears are dull of hearing, and their eyes they have closed; lest at anytime they should see with their eyes, and hear with their ears, and should understand with their heart, and should be converted, and I shall heal them.'[4] But blessed are your eyes, for they see: and your ears, for they hear."[5] "All these things spake Jesus unto the multitude in parables; and without a parable spake He not unto them; That it might be fulfilled, which was spoken by the prophet, saying, 'I will open my mouth in parables; I will utter things which have been kept secret from the foundation of the world.' "[6] "With many similar parables Jesus spoke the word to them, as much as they could understand. He did not say anything to them without using a parable. But when he was alone with his own disciples, he explained everything."[7]

INITIATION
Carlson misquotes:[8]

"The rites of initiation became progressively more complicated. Signs and tokens were invented by which the Children of Light could with facility make themselves known to each other. Different Degrees were invented, as the number of Initiates enlarged, in order that there might be (an) . . . inner (apartment) of the Temple, a favored few, to whom alone the more valuable secrets were entrusted, . . . All persons were initiated into the lesser Mysteries, but few attained the greater, in which the true spirit of them, and most of their secret doctrines were hidden. The veil of secrecy was impenetrable, sealed by oaths and penalties the most (treacherous) and appalling."

Pike actually says:

The rites of initiation became progressively more complicated. Signs and tokens were invented by which the Children of Light could with facility make themselves known to each other. Different Degrees were invented, as the number of Initiates enlarged, in order that there might be **in the** inner **apartments** of the Temple, a favored few, to whom alone the more valuable secrets were entrusted, **and who could wield effectually the influence and power of the Order. Originally the Mysteries were meant to be the beginning of a new life of reason and virtue. The initiated or esoteric companions were taught the doctrine of the One Supreme God, the theory of death and eternity, the hidden mysteries of Nature, the prospect of the ultimate restoration of the soul to that state of perfection from which it had fallen, and the states of reward and punishment after death. The uninitiated were deemed Profane, unworthy of public employment or private confidence, sometimes proscribed as Atheists, and certain of everlasting punishment beyond the grave.** All persons were initiated into the lesser Mysteries, but few attained the greater, in which the true spirit of them, and most of their secret doctrines were hidden. The veil of secrecy was impenetrable, sealed by oaths and penalties the most **tremendous** and appalling.

Carlson says that the true meaning of the first three degrees of Masonry is known only to the leaders of Masonry, who intentionally mislead the Initiate by false interpretations, so that he does not understand what he is involved in.

Page 819, Albert Pike: "The Blue Degrees (which are the first three degrees of Masonry, that all go through), The Blue Degrees are but the outer court of the Temple. Part of (its) symbols are displayed there to the Initiate, but he is intentionally misled by false interpretations. It is not intended that he shall understand them; . . . Their true explication is reserved for the Adepts, the Princes of Masonry. The whole body of the Royal and Sacerdotal Art was hidden so carefully, centuries since, in the High Degrees. . . . It is well enough," listen to this, "it is well enough for the mass of those (so) called Masons, to imagine that all is contained in the Blue Degrees;"

For those who take the trouble to read the entire chapter, it becomes obvious that Pike is quoting from the Allocution of Pio Nono, a formal speech containing a story fabricated by the successors of Pope Clement V, in an effort to justify the betrayal of the Knights Templar, and its last Grand Commander, Jacques de Molay, by Clement and Philip le Bel, the French King called Philip the Fair in England.

Compare the differences in spelling of the names in this account, with the forms of their names in Masonic use. Also note that, in this account, Jacques de Molay, an illiterate man, supposedly organized and instituted Scottish Rite Masonry, while awaiting his execution, more than four hundred years before its actual origin.[9] (See Art deHoyos's *The Cloud of Prejudice,* page 23, for a more detailed account.) It is also worthwhile to note what John Robinson says: "The charges to which the Templars were asked to confess were profuse and included several that frequently showed up in allegations of heresy and witchcraft and would for centuries to come. The Templars were asked to admit . . . that they worshiped idols; . . . Two Templars confessed to worshiping a bearded idol, apparently a head, which they called Baphomet."[10] Compare this with Pike's commentary in *Morals and Dogma:* "It is absurd to suppose that men of intellect adored a monstrous idol called Baphomet."[11]

THE KNIGHTS TEMPLAR AS PRECURSORS TO FREEMASONRY

In this chapter, Pike attributes the origin of Papal hostility to Freemasonry to the Vatican's belief that our Masonic Order is the successor to the Knights Templar. He quotes an "enemy of the Templars," who tells us the "secret," and assures us that it will be easy, as we read, to separate the false from the true, the audacious conjectures from the simple facts:[12]

> The avowed object of the Templars was to protect the Christians who came to visit the Holy places: their real object was to rebuild the Temple of Solomon on the model prophesied by Ezekiel. The Templars took as their models, in the Bible, the Warrior-Masons of Zorobabel, who worked holding the sword in one hand and the trowel in the other. They concealed themselves under the name of Brethren Masons. [This name, *Frère Maçons* in the French, was corrupted into English to *Free*-Masons.][13]
>
> Hugues de Payens, founder of the Order, was a secret member, and the Chief of a Gnostic Sect of Johannite Christians, who claimed to be the only true Initiates into the real mysteries of the religion of the Saviour. Thus the Order of the Knights of the Temple was at its very beginning devoted to the cause of opposition to the tiara of Rome and the crowns of Kings. The tenets of the Order were enveloped in profound mystery, and it externally professed the most perfect orthodoxy.
>
> The Chiefs alone knew the aim of the Order. To acquire influence and wealth and to establish the Gnostic dogma were the object and means proposed to the Initiated Brethren. The Templars, like all other Secret Orders, had two doctrines, one concealed and reserved for the Masters, which was Johannism; the other public, which was *Roman Catholic*.[14] Hence Free-Masonry adopted Saint John the Evangelist as one of its patrons, associating with him Saint John the Baptist, and thus covertly proclaiming itself the child of the Kabalah and Essenism together.[15]

TAXIL'S HOAX

In keeping with the context of this account, let us address a further allegation of Carlson:[16]

Albert Pike, before he died, finally addressed, on July 14th, 1889, gave his final instructions to the twenty-three supreme councils of the world. Let me quote Albert Pike, the leading authority as to what is going on. I quote, "That which we must say to the crowd is, We worship a God and it is the God that one adores without superstition. To you sovereign grand inspectors general, we say this, that you may repeat it to the brethren of the 32nd, to the 31st, and to the 30th degrees: The Masonic religion should be, by all of its initiates of the high degrees, maintained in the purity of the Luciferian Doctrine. Yes, Lucifer is god, the god we worship, and the pure philosophic religion is the belief in Lucifer." Unquote.

Carlson is quoting from the elaborate hoax perpetrated by Leo Taxil, who is described in Mackey's *Encyclopedia*,[17] as the author of a pornographic book, *The Private Love Affairs of Pius IX*. Pope Pius IX, who died shortly before Taxil's book was published, had announced the dogma of the Immaculate Conception of the Virgin Mary in 1854, and the dogma of Papal Infallibility in 1871.[18] The allegations made by the Roman Church in this chapter were exaggerated and enlarged upon by the fertile imagination of Leo Taxil, and were the likely basis and source of his ideas. Taxil's hoax is described in detail by Mackey,[19] and his books and speeches on the evils of Masonry are described as a hoax in *The New Catholic Encyclopedia*,[20] as cited in deHoyos's *The Cloud of Prejudice*.[21] DeHoyos says the quote by Carlson is from a discredited anti-Masonic book, *Occult Theocrasy*, by Edith Starr Miller, who was apparently unaware that Taxil confessed, in 1897, that it was all a hoax at the expense of the Catholic Church.[22]

Carlson said he was quoting Pike, but Taxil's confession that it was a hoax is well documented, so how can Carlson possibly be quoting Pike? Earlier in his lecture Carlson said, "Tonight when I quote a reference, a page number, it will be from *Morals and Dogma*, unless I otherwise specify."[23] One more lie!

Returning to Carlson's allegation that Masonry deceives, misleads, and lies to the Initiates in the Blue Degrees:

Page 545: "All the (Mysteries) should be kept concealed, . . . (The Mason) sins against God, who divulges to the unworthy the Mysteries confided to him. The danger is not merely in violating truth, but in telling truth, . . ." How different this is from the Gospel of Jesus Christ. The danger is not simply telling the truth, but revealing the truth. He who sins against God is he who reveals the truth. My friends, as Christians, we're told to go into all the world and proclaim the good news! Jesus said, "I am the truth and the truth will set you free," not enslaving you to pagan oaths and initiations to be kept secret. You are consciously misled.

This paragraph is one of the most glaring examples of how Carlson re-created Pike's text *to represent his own ideas in Pike's words,* while *reversing Pike's meaning.*

If you turn to page 545 in Appendix B, you can read for yourself that Pike really said, "**St. Ambrose, Archbishop of Milan, who was born in 340, and died in 393, says in his work** De Mysteriis: 'All the **Mystery** should be kept concealed, **guarded by faithful silence, lest it should be inconsiderately divulged to the ears of the Profane.** . . . It is not given to all to contemplate the depths of our Mysteries . . . that **they may not be seen by those who ought not to behold them; nor received by those who cannot preserve them.' And in another work:** 'He sins against God, who divulges to the unworthy the Mysteries confided to him. The danger is not merely in violating truth, but in telling truth, . . . **if he allows himself to give hints of them to those from whom they ought to be concealed.** . . . **Beware of casting pearls before swine!'** "

Now let's take Carlson's words, and use *his* method to show how *Carlson's own words condemn him:* (Words that are changed are in bold print in both versions).

1. Carlson's original words: "The danger is not merely in **violating** truth, but in **telling** truth. How different this is from the Gospel of Jesus Christ. The danger is not simply telling the truth, but **revealing** the truth. He who sins against God is he who **reveals** the truth. My friends, as Christians, we're told to go into all the world and proclaim the good news! Jesus said, "I am the truth and

the truth will set you free," not enslaving you to pagan oaths and initiations to be kept secret. You are consciously misled."

2. After using Carlson's method: "The danger is not merely in telling truth, but in violating truth. How different this is from the Gospel of Jesus Christ. The danger is not simply telling the truth, but violating the truth. He who sins against God is he who violates the truth. My friends, as Christians, we're told to go into all the world and proclaim the good news! Jesus said, "I am the truth and the truth will set you free," not misleading you about Masonic oaths and initiating slander. You are consciously misled by Carlson, not by Masonry!"

Abraham Lincoln said, "Truth is generally the best vindication against slander."[24] Lincoln also said, "If you once forfeit the confidence of your fellow citizens, you can never regain their respect and esteem. It is true that you may fool all the people some of the time; you can even fool some of the people all the time; but you can't fool all of the people all the time."[25]

Carlson's slander and false witness has fooled some of the people for some time. He has forfeited the confidence of those who look to him as *Pastor* Carlson. The title of Pastor symbolizes the *Good Shepherd,* Jesus; but when those who look to him as *Pastor* find out they have been fooled, Carlson can never regain their respect and esteem. They will show him the same contempt that was shown to the *shepherd boy* who cried, "Wolf!" Liars are not believed even when they speak the truth.

As Jesus spoke in parables, and said, "To whom it is given, let him hear," so Masonry teaches in allegories: "To whom it is given, he becomes a better man." Masonry cannot make a knave into a good man, so our membership is selective. To whom it is not given, men who cannot accept the brotherhood of man, Masonry is seen as a danger to their religious viewpoint. It is a valid duty, from their viewpoint, to object, and *to make their case* against Freemasonry; but when they take one more step, and *make a false case* against Freemasonry, by distorting its teaching, they violate the very principles of Christian ethics, which are the teachings of Jesus Christ Himself.

VII || Blessed Are the Peacemakers

S INCE CARLSON CLAIMS PROFESSIONAL EXPERTISE that qualifies him to judge the ethics of Freemasonry, and since Carlson's own ethics are in question, it follows that we should know something about the professional ethics that govern the activities of a Christian pastor. The task of a Christian pastor is to "feed my sheep;"[1] to instruct by precept, example, or experience. In other words, part of his task is to be a role model. He should teach Christian ethics by example.

CHRISTIAN ETHICS

Formulating the principles of Christian ethics is not an easy task. Following the suggestion of my sister, Hope Thorn Hörst I used the first section of Dietrich Bonhoeffer's *Ethics* as a model, and abridged and amended it, to write the following summary.

All ethical systems define good and bad and discuss moral duty and obligation, but Christian ethics looks beyond classical ethical systems, to the origin of the whole problem of ethics.

In Christian ethical reflection, the fact that it is even *possible* for a human being to *know* good and evil, shows that man has fallen away from God. Knowing good and evil, he knows *only himself,* in *separation from God.* But it is only in union with God, that it is possible for man to truly know the mind of God, of other men, of other created beings, and himself. Originally created in the image of God, and now separated from God, man no longer knows God at all; he sees himself as creator and judge, the only possible origin of good and evil.

When he ate the forbidden fruit, man learned what only God *ought to know,* at the price of separation from God, and in opposition to God's plan. Man tore himself away from eternal life, from the unifying, reconciling life in God, and became subject to sin and death. Man's life is now in disunion with God, with men, with other created beings, with things, and with himself.

Shame

Man is ashamed of his nakedness because he has lost something essential to his original character. Man covers himself to hide himself from God and other men. Every mind wears a mask to hide its disunion, but behind that mask there is a longing for reconciliation. This longing breaks through its cover when two human beings become one flesh, or when a human being seeks union with God; but then, more than ever, shame demands the very deepest secrecy.

The reason man finds it hard to say, "I love you," is the fear that expressing affection in words may allow the other person to get a glimpse of his nakedness. Not even the closest fellowship is permitted to unmask his shame. The most profound and intimate joy or grief cannot be expressed in words. Shame also keeps a man from making any kind of display of his relationship with God.

The Masonic tenet of Brotherly Love specifically relates to this dilemma. Masons are not afraid to share personal problems, because of their obligation as a Master Mason to keep the secrets of a brother. Masons are taught to begin every activity with prayer, to pray for guidance, and to pray for one another. A Mason's prayers are a display of his relationship with God.

Finally, man protects himself against any ultimate disclosure; he keeps his own secret, even from himself, when he refuses to be aware of certain feelings, memories, desires, and motives. Masons are taught to warn a falling brother that he is in error.

Shame is not overcome by concealment and exposure; they only confirm it. Shame can only be overcome when the original unity is restored, when man is once again clothed by God in the "house which is from heaven."[2] Masonry's assistance here is in the form of guidance, consolation, and silence before others.

Conscience

Shame reminds man of his disunion with God and with other men, but conscience is the sign of man's disunion with himself. It is the mark of the man who is already disunited from God. Conscience is *the voice of apostate life,* which desires to at least remain united with oneself. This is evident because the voice of conscience is always negative: "Thou shalt not . . ." "You ought not to have . . ." For conscience, life is governed by what is permitted and what is forbidden. Conscience has no positive commandment. For conscience, "permitted" is identical with "good." In forbidden actions, conscience sees a peril to union with oneself. The range of experience and knowledge does not extend to the fact that the voice of conscience arises from the disunion with God. This means that conscience is not concerned with man's relationship to God and other men, but only with how man relates to himself. It derives the relationship to God and men from the relation of man to himself. Conscience pretends to be the voice of God and the standard for other men. Armed with his knowledge of good and evil, man has become judge over God and man, just as he is judge over himself.

Instead of his original understanding of all things in God, knowledge now means the recognition of all things in himself, and of himself in all things. If man is in disunion with God, all things are in disunion: what is and what should be, idea and reality, duty and desire, necessity and freedom; even truth, justice, beauty, and love come into opposition with one another. The course of human history constantly adds to the list: legalism and holiness, art and pornography, choice and right to life. The point of any ethical decision is *always conflict*. In conflict the decision is always based on the knowledge of good and evil.

This is one reason for the Mason's charge not to argue with those who ridicule our Order. People who are convinced that Masonry is evil become angry and upset when they are faced with truth. Argument will not change their attitude. It only reinforces their opinion.

New Testament Ethics
In the New Testament, the focus of discussion is no longer the world of disunion, conflict, and ethical problems. In place of man's separation from God, from men, from things, and from himself; the new birth, *reconciliation,* is the basis of discussion and the point of ethical decisions.

Masonic Ethics
In Freemasonry, the focus is on the tenets of Brotherly Love, Relief, and Truth. Love for God and one's fellowman is the basis of discussion and the point of ethical decisions.

The Pharisee

It is when Jesus confronts the Pharisee that the old and the new are most clearly contrasted. The Pharisee is not just a phenomenon of a particular time in history. He is the man, even in our day, to whom the knowledge of good and evil is the only important thing in his life. He subordinates his entire life to his knowledge of good and evil, and is as severe a judge of himself as he is of his neighbor, and he humbly thanks God for this knowledge. For the Pharisee every moment of his life becomes a situation of conflict, in which he has to choose between good and evil. His entire thought is devoted to anticipation of possible conflicts, and to making a decision in each of those conflicts.

These men can only confront a man in one way: Examine his decisions in the conflicts of life. Even when they come face to face with Jesus, they try to force Him into conflicts and into decisions, to see how He will conduct Himself. This constitutes the basis of their temptation of Jesus. The crucial point is that Jesus does not allow Himself to be drawn into a single one of these conflicts and decisions. Each of His answers leave the conflict beneath Him. The Pharisees' question and temptation come from disunion, and from the knowledge of good and evil. Jesus's answers come from His unity with God and from reconciliation. The Pharisees and Jesus are speaking on totally different levels. That is why Jesus's answers do not appear to be answers at all, but rather attacks of His own against the Pharisee, which in fact they are.

The Pharisees' question is a repetition of the first temptation of Jesus.[3] Satan tried to lure Him into a disunion with the word of God. Jesus overcame him by virtue of His unity with the word of God. This temptation of Jesus, in turn, echoes the question the serpent asked Eve: "Yea, hath God said?" This question implies disunion, against which man is powerless, because it constitutes his essential character; it is the question that can only be overcome (but not answered) from beyond the disunion. And finally, all these temptations are repeated in the questions we ask Jesus when we appeal to Him for a decision in cases of conflict. In the New Testament there is no single question put by men to Jesus, which Jesus answers with an acceptance of the human "either/or" that every such question implies. Every one of Jesus's answers, to the questions of His enemies and His friends alike, leaves this either/or behind it in a way that shames the questioner. Jesus does not allow Himself to be invoked as an arbiter in vital questions. He refuses to be held by human alternatives: "Man, who appointed me a judge or an arbiter between you?"[4]

This is an exact parallel of how God answers Job in chapters 38–41. The silent or spoken responses of Job's friends apparently parallel the response of the Pharisees, because the Lord said to Eliphaz the Temanite, "I am angry with you and your two friends, because you have not spoken of me *what is right*, as my servant Job has."[5]

Jesus often seems to be missing the point. He does not answer the question, He addresses Himself directly to the questioner. Jesus speaks with a complete freedom that ignores the logical alternatives. He casts aside all the distinctions that the Pharisee so laboriously maintained. Jesus evades all the questions that are clearly intended to determine His position. To the Pharisee, He is a man who knows and respects only His own law, a blasphemer of God. The freedom of Jesus is in the simplicity of His action, which is confronted by only one thing, the will of God. There is only one will of God: Reconciliation. In it the origin is recovered and in it there is established freedom and simplicity of all action.

This is the second reason for the Masonic tradition of not defending itself. To do so is to descend to the level of our enemies. "Do not judge, or you too will be judged. For in the same way you judge others, you will be judged, and with the measure you use, it will be measured to you."[6]

Judging

"Do not judge, or you too will be judged" is a *warning* that every judgment a man makes on the basis of good and evil, will fall back on himself. The Pharisee's action seeks public judgment. He desires to be seen, to be judged, and to be acknowledged as good. The Pharisee's action is based on knowing good and evil, and impedes real action, which is reconciliation. In this sense, his action is false action or hypocrisy. Seeking public judgment is his way of doing good. It is intended to overcome disunion, but only leads to further disunion.

The disunion of the man who sits in judgment over another man reveals itself in forms that can be understood in terms of psychology. It is precisely *when a man sees his own weakness in the other man,* that he is impelled to condemn him with particular severity. In other words, the spirit of judgment brings forth poisonous fruit, because of his own internal struggle with the same problem. Judgment is evil because it is itself apostasy; and that is precisely the reason why it brings forth evil fruit. Extremely noble motives may be the thought of the man who judges, but this fact has no bearing on the character of judgment itself. "Judging" is not just vice or wickedness in the disunited man; it is his *essence*, which is easy to recognize in his speech, his action, and his sentiment. The Pharisee has no insight, or understanding of his essence, because of his apostasy from his origin. When Jesus says, "do not judge," it is the call to reconciliation.

There is a true "judging" and "knowing" that come from reconciliation with God in Christ. True "judging" and "knowing" create reconciliation, not further disunion. Jesus Christ's judgment consisted precisely in His having come, not to condemn but to save. "And this is the judgment, that light is come into the world."[7] Men who are reconciled with God and man in Christ will judge all things and know all things as though they do not know good and evil. Their judgment is brotherly help, lifting up the fallen, showing the way to the straying, exhortation, and consolation.[8]

Masonry, through its tenets of Relief and Truth, teaches us to contribute to the relief of the distressed, especially widows and orphans; and that hypocrisy and deceit should be unknown among us.

Man cannot live simultaneously in reconciliation and in disunion. There are no intermediate stages. That is why Jesus summons us to forsake disunion, and the apostasy of knowing good and evil; to return to unity with the origin, to new life in Christ. It is the call to reconciliation.

Freemasonry's equivalent of reconciliation is that bond of brotherly love and affection that unites us as friends and brothers, and teaches us to avoid the basis of hypocrisy: comparison and contention with one another.

Proving

The will of God is not always obvious; it is not whatever the mind may think, and it is not a system of rules. The will of God is new and different in each new and different situation. A man must always search for the will of God *in reconciliation*. It is disclosed only to him who proves the will of God in doing it, in living it.

Freemasonry is a philosophy or system of morals and ethics based on the commonly held beliefs of all monotheistic religions. It therefore cannot, and does not, tell any man how to find the will of God, because it is not a religion.

But it can, and does, encourage and reinforce a man's search for truth, as he understands truth.

Doing

The sermon on the mount was given *for the purpose of being done:* "Therefore whosoever *heareth* these sayings of mine, *and doeth* them, I will liken him unto a wise man, which built his house upon a rock."[9] It is only in *doing* that man submits to the will of God. In doing *God's* will man renounces every right and every justification of *his own.* The Scriptures insist on *doing* His will because God refuses self-justification.

Barclay says it is "perfectly possible for a man to pass an examination in Christian Ethics with the highest distinction, and yet not to be a Christian. Knowledge must become action; theory must become practice; theology must become life. There is little point in going to a doctor, unless we are prepared to do the things we hear him say to us." There is one word that sums up hearing and doing, and that word is obedience.[10] "But be ye doers of the word, and not hearers only, deceiving your ownselves."[11]

The fundamental tenets of Freemasonry are Brotherly Love, Relief, and Truth. The primary emphasis, in all three tenets, is on "doing." Masonry is not a religion; instead of teaching men what to believe, men are taught to put the religious beliefs they held before they were initiated into our Order, into everyday practice. The ideal Mason will practice what he believes, so that there will be no difference between what he says and what he does. In other words, Masonry seeks only to reinforce my own faith, so that it becomes faith in action.

False Prophets

"Beware of false prophets, who come to you in sheep's clothing, but inwardly they are ravening wolves. Ye shall know them by their fruits."[12] Jesus described the sheepskin garment worn by the shepherd and warned us that a man could dress like a shepherd and not be a shepherd. Elijah's mantle was a garment of hair,[13] and the sheepskin mantle became the characteristic dress of the prophets. It distinguished the prophet from other men, but it was sometimes worn by false prophets, who taught that what they said was a message direct from God. Jesus said, "Ye shall know them by their fruits." In other words, the false prophet may wear the right clothes and use the right words, but his basic motive is self-interest. He teaches for personal gain and prestige, and he teaches *his own version of the truth.* The real test of a man's message is its fruit: Is it divisive or does it reconcile?

The function of true religion is *not* to erect middle walls of partition, but to follow Jesus, *who tore them down.* [14] Jesus said, "And other sheep I have, which are not of this fold: them also I must bring, and they shall hear my voice; and there shall be *one fold,* and one shepherd."[15] Religion is meant to bring men closer together, not to split them up into hostile groups. *Any teaching* that declares that a church or sect has exclusive possession of the grace of God is *false teaching:* "Unto every one of us is given grace;"[16] "Grace be unto you, and peace, from Him which is, and which was, and which is to come."[17] It is **God,** *not the church,* who gives grace to *everyone.*

I like to think of grace as God's love in action, the gift of eternal life; and faith as man's love in action, as he accepts that gift.

Peacemakers

"Blessed are the peacemakers; for they shall be called the children of God. Blessed are they which are persecuted for righteousness' sake; for theirs is the kingdom of heaven. Blessed are ye, when men shall revile you, and persecute you, and shall say all manner of evil against you falsely, for my sake."[18] Note that Jesus said "peacemakers," not "peacelovers." Evading an issue is not peace. The peacelover, who avoids strife at any cost, only winds up with a bigger problem when he postpones necessary action. We must struggle to *make* peace by actively facing the issue. Barclay says that Jesus meant that the task of the peacemaker is "to establish right relationships between man and man. . . . There are people who are always at the center of trouble, bitterness, and strife. . . . They are either involved in quarrels themselves, or they cause quarrels between others. . . . They are troublemakers."[19]

Freemasonry, by its very nature, functions as a peacemaker, and teaches its adherents to be peacemakers. It encourages Jews and Christians of all denominations to bond together around the beliefs that they hold in common, and to live and practice what they believe, instead of arguing about the differences in their belief.

VIII ‖ Our Judeo-Christian Heritage

T HE WESTERN MIND CREATES NEW words, new ways of saying things, to explain and define a concept in one word. That word becomes a new symbol for the concept, the dogma, or the doctrine expressed by the new terminology. Yet, there is a resistance to that process, even in the western mind, "Why do they use those big words?" Here it is the common man who acts as a check to the process of symbolization.

The Mysteries were designed to keep the original teaching from being altered. This is precisely what infuriates the ambitious man. He cannot inject his personal ideas into the system, and that is precisely what his ambition drives him to do. It is no longer just the man he regards as his inferior that checks his drive. He thinks that those who are important, in his eyes, have joined forces with the common man to isolate him.

He now has two choices: he can either present new evidence to logically support his position, hoping it will become a new part of the system, or he can accept their judgment and withdraw. The man who is capable and self-confident works within the system. When the man of lesser capability cannot accept the verdict of those he regards as his superiors, his offended pride causes him to strike back at the system that frustrates him, a classic example of sour grapes.

When that frustrated man is also a Minister of the Gospel, he faces the same alternatives, but he has a little more clout to strike back; he can make an alliance with his congregation, the common man, to increase the level of derision. But it's a mighty big world out there. To be really effective, he must be convincing and he must carefully select his target, preferably one that can't or won't hit back; like the robber who preys on helpless victims: women and children, the elderly and the infirm.

We know Carlson's target, and we know why he thought Freemasonry was a helpless victim: Freemasonry has a long tradition of charging the brethren, as an act of common sense and courtesy, not to defend our Order. But Carlson made a serious tactical error. Masons are charged to avoid argument with those who, *through ignorance,* may ridicule it. Carlson's ridicule is not through ignorance; his ridicule is through false witness.

The man who judges sees the law as a criterion that he applies to others, and he sees himself as being responsible for the execution of the law. When a man employs his knowledge of the law in accusing or condemning his brother, then in truth he accuses and condemns the law itself, for he mistrusts it and doubts that it possesses the power of the living word of God to establish itself and to take effect by itself. In making himself the lawgiver and the judge he invalidates the law of God.

"Speak not evil one of another, brethren. He that speaketh evil of his brother, and judgeth his brother, speaketh evil of the law, and judgeth the law: but if thou judge the law, thou art not a doer of the law, but a judge. There is one lawgiver, who is able to save and to destroy: who art thou that judgest another?"[1]

In December of 1982, I went to Israel for a workshop program taught by Dr. James Fleming, professor at Hebrew University, and director of the Jerusalem Center for Biblical Studies. Dr. Fleming took us for a tour of the Holy places and shared some insights gleaned from what he called the *Fifth Gospel.*

The Sea of Galilee is 682 feet below true sea level; the Mount of Beatitudes overlooks its northern shore from a height that Dr. Fleming estimated was 2,000 feet above sea level. Dr. Fleming pointed out that this mountain was at the end of a plateau that offered a view of the coasts of the Decapolis, which overlook the eastern shore. "And there followed Him great multitudes of people from Galilee, and from Decapolis."[2] The Gentiles from Decapolis had walked around the shores of Galilee, across the plateau, to reach the Mount of Beatitudes.

Matthew, a Jew, wrote about the Sermon on the Mount; Luke, a Gentile, wrote about the Sermon on the Plain. Thus, what appears to be a point of conflict between the two Gospels, turns out to be only a difference of perspective, or point of view. Dr. Fleming's Fifth Gospel allowed us to *see* their difference of perspective, and to *understand* that there was only an *apparent conflict,* not a real one. It is not necessary to decide which author is correct: we see that both men are right when we use the Fifth Gospel to see the difference that perspective makes.

The Fifth Gospel

The following section comes from my notes, taken as Dr. Fleming lectured us on his concept of the Fifth Gospel:

> The writers of the four Gospels assume their readers are familiar with the Fifth Gospel. They think that everyone has read the Fifth Gospel—so they don't even mention it. In fact, if you have not read the Fifth Gospel, you are less likely to be able to interpret the four gospels. By the Fifth Gospel I mean the land, I mean its history, I mean its customs, its languages, its hopes and fears. This is all part of the life-world of those who were the first to hear the four gospels. So the writers of the four gospels don't tell you *how* Jesus observed the first Passover, or what He *does* at the Passover meal, because you already know that.
>
> We do not make enough use of the Fifth Gospel; we go immediately from the twentieth century to the first-century Scriptures, often without knowing enough to interpret their words, what was meant and said, in their original context, so history, geography, and archeology are ways of getting back to the first century, to the Fifth Gospel.
>
> Ancient historical sources, such as the Dead Sea scrolls, help us understand what people were reading and thinking, and how they would understand certain words and phrases at the time of Jesus. Archeology helps us make some educated guesses: What does this indicate about this people? How did they live? What was important, and what was unimportant to them?
>
> Historical geography, and the study of the land as we see it today, but with an eye to the past, show where towns were in the Bible, how big they were, what their demographic makeup was: which towns were Jewish, which were Gentile, and which were mixed; and how that helps interpret what happened in those towns. The Fifth Gospel includes the history, customs, and languages of the people of Israel. Its proper use as an interpretive device implies the need to know something of the logic of the languages spoken in the gospel period.[3]

Latin was the language of the Romans. Greek was the business language of the Roman Empire. Aramaic was primarily used by women and children and dated from the Babylonian captivity. Men spoke Hebrew, the language of religion.

The Greek mind is concerned with "What *is* something-within-itself?" This is done in description and form: it describes measure, color, weight, dimension. The Latin mind is concerned with *how*, the method of procedure: "*How* does it work?" *How* questions intrigue the Latin mind. The Hebrew or eastern mind is concerned with function: "What does it *do?*" "What's it *for?*" "Does it leak?" "How long will it last?"

Almost all of the Bible comes from the Hebrew mind. Some scholars say they do not find *one* description in the Bible in the western sense. Because of the Greek and Latin influences on the English language, we read the Bible with our western mind as description, but we usually read *into* it description and form when it is *meaning* function. Description in the Bible is functional and is *only* used as it relates to the story: Saul was chosen as the King because "from his shoulders and upwards he was higher than any of the people." Absalom's hair was described because he died by getting it caught in the branches of a tree, Daniel's statue represents nations, and is not intended as a description in the western sense of description. Even the directions for making the Tabernacle in Exodus 26 are not a description in the western sense; the author wants you to know what you *do* with something and what it's *for*.

The Greek mind speculates on the nature of God. To the Greek, God is metaphysical—beyond the physical. Greek metaphysical categories are adjectives describing God-within-Himself: Omnipotent, Omniscient, Omnipresent. God is Omnipotent. He is Omniscient and Omnipresent. But the Greek categories are likely to be misunderstood because you are going to meet them through the Greek mindset, rather than the Hebrew mind. Once someone is raised to think metaphysically in the Greek categories of thought, he can never suspend them in his mind to think of them in terms of ancient Hebrew thought. We have all sorts of problems in Christian theology, because we think in terms of description and form and these two ways of approaching God didn't even enter the minds of the Biblical writers.

The Bible only speaks of God-in-relation-to-persons, never of God-within-Himself. Almost all of our theology speaks of God-within-Himself—the Greek way, which means the God of the Bible is quite different from the Greek gods. A trip to see holy places had no meaning to the ancient Greeks because the Greek gods were not intimately involved with persons. The difference between the revelatory God of the Bible, and just believing in God, is that the God of the Bible is active with persons in time and places. You are now here and will see the places, and we will be speaking of the times. Adjectives were fine for the Greek gods, but verbs are more appropriate for the Hebrew God, because they only think of God-in-relation-to-persons. God has shown what He is like by what He has done with mankind and therefore with verbs.

Traditional theology is a wedding between theology and metaphysics. Biblical theology is a union of theology and man's view of historical geography—what God has done in time and place—and this is peculiar to the Judeo-Christian heritage. When someone says, "I'd like to know what you believe," Jesus says, "Follow me," or "Understand who I am by what I have done." If we describe God, we have to use adjectives, but if we're talking about a revelatory God, we use verbs. Every word in the Hebrew language is derived from verbs. The three consonants found in every verb form the root of the nouns, adjectives, and adverbs that are derived from it. How do we know what God is like? Not through abstract metaphysics, but from what He has done: "For God so loved the world, that He gave His only begotten Son" (John 3:16). That's how you know God is love.

What is the God of the Bible like? He is like what He does, and the way we understand Him is to look at His acts with mankind in history. To John the Baptist's question, "Are you the One, or should we look for another?" Jesus replied, "Tell John what I have done: You see the lame walk, the blind see, the dead raised, and the good news preached to the poor." What kind of an answer is that? It means that we are to understand who Jesus is by what He has done.[4]

The Logic of the Bible

The Bible says that, from the time Moses led them out of their captivity in Egypt, until their return from the Babylonian captivity, the children of Israel were tempted to serve the pagan gods of their neighbors. It was not until the tragedy of the Babylonian captivity that they could understand, "Hear, O Israel, the Lord our God is *one* God." From the time God told Joshua to make a memorial with twelve stones taken from the dry bed of the Jordan, the children of Israel were taught to know their God *in their history*; what God had done for His Chosen People, at *definite times*, and in *specific places*. So Jewish converts understood God in Christ Jesus by what *He had done*. But Gentile converts came into the church with neither the heritage of the Hebrew people, nor the advantage of their laws and traditions.

The laws and traditions of the Gentiles were radically different, because the Greek gods were not intimately involved with persons. The heritage of the Greek mind was a metaphysical philosophy that defined their pagan beliefs, and described their gods. It was inevitable that they would think in terms of description and form to understand the nature of God in Jesus Christ, because once someone is raised to think metaphysically, in the Greek categories of thought, he can never suspend them in his mind to think in terms of ancient Hebrew functional thought.

If we accept what Dr. Fleming says is the logic of the Bible, this may be one of the reasons the Jews are the Chosen People: Because the Hebrew mind thinks in functional terms, the Jew avoids the mistake of speculating about the nature of God; he does not try to define God. He tries to understand *who He is* by what He *does*. Evangelical churches often have people "give their testimony" for the same reason: to see what God has done in the life of a friend. This is the purest form of worship because it avoids the bias that is a part of descriptive theology.

It is precisely man's efforts to define God that Pike said led, step by step, to idolatry:

To present a visible symbol to the eye of another, does not necessarily inform him of the meaning which that symbol has to you. Hence the philosopher added explanations addressed to the ear, more precise, but less effective and impressive than the painted or sculptured forms that he endeavored to explain. And when philosophy resorted to definitions and formulas, its language was only a more complicated symbolism, attempting to grapple with and picture ideas impossible to be expressed. No word can inform you of the exact meaning that it has to me; and so much of religion and philosophy became disputes as to the meaning of words. Any word for Deity is only a sign or symbol for something beyond our comprehension.

There are dangers inseparable from symbolism. Names that stand for things are confused with them; the interpretation becomes reality, and then symbols come to be seen as truths and persons. Though perhaps a necessary path, they were a dangerous one by which to approach the Deity; in which many, mistaking the sign for the thing signified, fell into a ridiculous superstition.[5]

"For since the creation of the world God's invisible qualities—His eternal power and divine nature—have been clearly seen, being understood from what has been made, so that men are without excuse. For although they knew God, they neither glorified Him as God nor gave thanks to Him, but their thinking became futile and their foolish hearts were darkened. Although they claimed to be wise, they became fools and exchanged the glory of the immortal God for images made to look like mortal man and birds and reptiles."[6]

When I sat down to write this section, my wife had just left to spend the day with her daughter, Pam. Before I could get started, Shirley came back in the house for help; our four-wheel drive vehicle was hung up in a snowdrift in the driveway. Before we could gain enough traction to free it, we had to shovel out the deep snow that suspended the undercarriage. It wasn't much fun, but at least it was easier than freeing the tractor when it was mired down in the muddy swamp; the tractor had to be towed out because there wasn't any solid base under the mud.

It seems to me that getting mired down in the mud is a lot like getting entangled in theological differences. Most of those differences have to do with our assumptions about what the Bible means. Perhaps the following riddle will clarify my point.

A father and son were driving to a ballgame when their car stalled on the railroad tracks. In the distance a train whistle blew a warning. Frantically the father tried to start the engine, but in his panic he couldn't turn the key, and the car was hit by the onrushing train. An ambulance sped to the scene and picked them up. On the way to the hospital the father died. The son was alive but his condition was critical, and he needed immediate surgery. The moment they arrived at the hospital he was wheeled into an emergency operating room, and a surgeon came in, expecting a routine case. On seeing the boy, however, the surgeon blanched and muttered, "I can't operate on this boy—he's my son."

What do you make of this grim riddle? How could it be? Was the surgeon lying or mistaken? No. Was the dead father's soul somehow reincarnated in the surgeon's body? No. Was the surgeon the boy's true father and the dead man the boy's adoptive father? No. What then is the explanation? Think it through until you have figured it out on your own—I insist! You'll know when you've got it, don't worry.

So writes Douglas Hofstadter in the November 1982 issue of *Scientific American,* as he uses this riddle to reveal how "default assumptions" permeate our mental representations and channel our thoughts.

A default assumption is what holds true in what you might say is the "simplest" or "most likely" possible model of whatever situation is under discussion. In this case the default assumption is that the surgeon is a man. The way things are in our society today, that is the most plausible assumption. But the critical thing about default assumptions is that they are made automatically, not as a result of consideration and elimination. Your past experience assigned a sex for you. You were not aware of having made any assumption about the surgeon's sex. If you had been, there would not have been any riddle.

Reliance on default assumptions is usually extremely useful—in fact, indispensable—for we cannot afford to be constantly distracted by all kinds of theoretically possible but unlikely exceptions to the models we have built up by induction from many past experiences. Our every thought is permeated by what amounts to shrewd guesses or assumptions of normalcy.

This ability to ignore the unlikely, without even considering whether or not to ignore it, comes out of the need to be able to size up a situation quickly but accurately. Once in a while, however, this marvelous ability leads us astray. When the surgeon story was first told to Hofstadter, his own reaction and the reaction of his companions surprised him. Most of them had manufactured all kinds of bizarre alternative worlds instead of imagining one in which a surgeon could be a woman.

Since our every thought is channeled by default assumptions, we necessarily rely on our assumptions to understand the Bible. When we read Jesus's cry on the cross, "My God, my God, why hast thou forsaken me?"[7] we may believe that God did forsake Him. But the sin that *separated* man from God was *disobedience;* so why would God, who sent His Son to *reconcile* man with his Creator, forsake Jesus *while He was in the very act of obeying Him?* The most common explanation is that God made Jesus, "who knew no sin, to be sin for us,[8] and because God is holy, He cannot look upon sin, even in His own Son. It seems to me that this is an instance when our default assumptions lead us astray. Our assumptions are: God is holy, He hates sin, Jesus is God, and God cannot lie; and so we reason that God really did forsake Jesus as He hung upon the cross.

Now each and every assumption is true, but we should not overlook some other things the Bible says: Matthew 27:50, Mark 15:37, and Luke 23:46 all say that Jesus cried out with a loud voice. Barclay[9] says that it was not the weak cry of despair; His loud cry was the voice of triumph, "Father, into thy hands I commend my spirit." And so, Jesus's cry, "Why hast thou forsaken me?" really reflects that, in that terrible moment when He became sin for us, he experienced the consequence of sin, man's separation from God. For the first time in all of eternity, Jesus knew, as man, the barrier that sin creates. God did not forsake Him, He accepted His sacrifice, and from the confidence of His unity with God, came His voice of triumph, "It is finished."[10]

IX || Viewpoint

O UR VIEW OF GOD AND truth is always changing. The classic definition of "truth" is conformity of thought with factual reality, and reality is a function of each person's experience. For this reason Freemasonry teaches men to seek more light, a symbolic way of saying that truth is more than a creed; it is a lifelong search. The Order of the Eastern Star uses the symbolism of a journey whose mileposts are the difficulties and trials we face along life's road. Members are taught to keep close to God and His teachings, and to return frequently to the Scriptures for instruction.

EXPERIENCE IS THE BEST TEACHER

The difficulties and trials in one person's life are not the same problems in another's, so that everyone will read the Bible with a different eye of experience. God never changes, but our understanding of God and truth changes with Bible study and experience.

All of us need to pray as the psalmist did: "Teach me thy way, O Lord,"[1] "and lead me in the way everlasting."[2] We need to believe as he did, "I have chosen the way of truth."[3] But if we believe that we know *all* of God's truth; who He is, when and how He created the universe, and how He relates to man, we are mistaken: "O the depth of the riches, both of the wisdom and knowledge, of God! How unsearchable are His judgments, and His ways past finding out! For who hath known the mind of the Lord?"[4]

If we refuse to believe that there is a difference between *the truth as God has revealed it,* and *what we believe about* His revelation, then our mind is closed to a deeper and wider knowledge of God. If we are unable to accept new information, we will refuse to change our view. Our view may be correct, but since His truth is infinite, and we are a finite creation, our experience of truth is limited. This problem can be illustrated by paraphrasing Aesop's fable of the blind men and the elephant.

94

Four blind men fell into an argument, each defending his understanding of the elephant. The first man put his hands on its side, and said, "The elephant is a wall. I will use it to build a house to shelter me, and to guide me, as I run my hand along the wall, while walking about my house." The second man, taking hold of its trunk, said, "The elephant is a snake that could eat the rodents who steal my food; but I fear the snake might hurt me." The third grasped the elephant by its tail, and said , "It's only a rope, and not very useful to a blind man." The fourth man, who passed his arms around one of its legs, said, "The elephant might be useful, if I could just figure out what that column supports." Then a sighted man came along, and explained that each of them had a correct, but extremely limited, view of the truth. There is a lot more elephant than they could understand.

There was no room for compromise in their discussion. The "truth" was not somewhere between their views, because *each man understood the truth from his own experience of the elephant*. Their experience was real, but limited in scope. That is why true knowledge relies upon experimental verification, rather than on the personal experience of any one individual. This fable illustrates a basic principle: Most religious controversy can be avoided, if we understand that another man's view is not necessarily false doctrine. We should have no argument with another man's ideas, but we should resist any attack that seeks to impose those ideas on others. He may be looking at a different aspect of the truth, and Infinite Truth demands more than one aspect of the truth to provide complete understanding.

Warren Weaver provides a persuasive explanation of this principle in his article, "The Religion of a Scientist,"[5] in which he explains how scientific method further effects interpretation.

SCIENTIFIC DETERMINISM AND THE UNCERTAINTY PRINCIPLE

Before 1900 most scientific discoveries were made by observing and measuring the structure, location, and movement of objects large enough to be seen with the naked eye. The effect of measurement on the system being observed was negligible, so physicists regarded Sir Isaac Newton's mechanics as unassailable. The successful prediction of the return of "Halley's Comet" in 1758, and comparable successes in other fields of physics in the nineteenth century, left little reason to doubt the unlimited possibilities and perfection of scientific progress.

With J. J. Thomson's discovery of the electron in 1897, the contributions of Max Planck and Albert Einstein to quantum theory (the theory that energy existed in small quanta or bits) in the early 1900s, and the 1913 Niels Bohr theory of atomic structure, science turned to the study of objects too small to be seen, even with a microscope. The effect of measurement influenced the system being observed, because the energy used to find the location of an elementary particle, such as the electron, changed its velocity, and measuring its velocity changed its position. In 1927 Werner Karl Heisenberg's uncertainty principle showed mathematically that it was impossible to measure both its position and its velocity at the same time.[6] Weaver says, "The recognition of the uncertainty principle made it clear that science *cannot furnish us with a rigidly deterministic theory of events. A precise forecast of the future is excluded if we can have only an inaccurate measurement of present circumstances.*" According to Weaver, Niels Bohr concluded that the information obtained when using two different sets of observational procedures should not be expected to be the same, or even consistent with each other.

THE PRINCIPLE OF COMPLEMENTARITY

No matter how contradictory the two sets of information may appear to be, both must be accepted as equally valid. Accepting two contradictory descriptions, and knowing when each one is appropriate to use, provides a more graphic and convincing total concept than either description alone can supply. Bohr's concept of the valid use of two contradictory viewpoints, now known as the principle of complementarity, marked a change in scientists' philosophy as well as in their view of physics.

In the November 1983 issue of *Discover*, K. C. Cole says that according to Bohr, "It didn't matter that you could not measure both the motion and position of a particle at the same time; you cannot see both sides of a coin at the same time either." Cole gives some simple illustrations of complementarity. If blue and orange lights are separately projected on a screen, the color seen in the area where the colors overlap is white. If you remove blue light from white light, the light leftover is orange. Blue and orange are complementary colors.

Observing an animal's behavior and dissecting it in the lab are complementary ways of exploring nature. The microscope is used to see detail, but loses the view of the whole organism. Complementarity is not a compromise. It is more like a child's toy block, with a different letter on each of its six faces. You can hold the block so that you can only see one letter, or you can turn it to see two letters at the same time, and you can tilt the block to see three letters all at once.

I can understand that Carlson was looking at the letter "a," while I was looking at "a, b, and c"; but Carlson cannot see that "b and c" also exist. Accepting complementarity means accepting that someone else's view of truth is not necessarily heresy. Nobel prize-winner Max Born concluded that the trouble lies in the tendency of philosophy and science to make "final and categorical statements." He wrote that the philosophical importance of quantum theory lies in demonstrating the need for complementary considerations. This relaxing of the rules of thinking seemed to him the greatest blessing modern science had given us. Born said, "The belief that there is only one truth and that oneself is in possession of it seems to me the deepest root of all the evil that is in the world."

The illustrations in this section demonstrate that actions based on complementarity are not new. They also demonstrate the principle of complementarity as a change in philosophy. The need to relax the rules of thinking is a new concept.

COMPLEMENTARITY IN THE BIBLE

In the eyes of some, science is supposed to work inductively: gather the facts and then form theories. By the turn of the century, most scientists began to appreciate the value of deductive reasoning: Form a working theory, see if your observations bear it out, and modify it each time new observations do not support the theory. Over time the theory is adapted until it is supported by the observations, or discarded in favor of a new theory. Our approach to Scripture should be inductive—let the Bible speak to us before we form our interpretation. But there are times when we bring a specific concern to the Bible; we need to look for *all of the verses* that discuss the problem, see what the Scripture says about it and how what we find applies to us. Then we can state the case for our view, and we can also recognize that a different view is not false doctrine, if it has Biblical support. Two opposing views can be correct, depending on what aspect of the problem you are looking at.

One example is the doctrine of Baptism: Those who practice baptism by sprinkling believe it carries on the Old Testament ceremonial cleansing:

"Sprinkle water of purifying upon them;"[7] "Then will I sprinkle clean water upon you, and ye shall be clean; from all your filthiness, and from all your idols, will I cleanse you;"[8] "Arise and be baptized, and wash away thy sins, calling on the name of the Lord;"[9] "For by one Spirit are we all baptized into one body, whether we be Jews or Gentiles."[10]

For those who believe in adult baptism by immersion, it is a symbolic burial and resurrection of the believer in Christ: "Baptism doth also now save us (not the putting away of the filth of the flesh, but by the answer of a good conscience toward God,) by the resurrection of Jesus Christ;"[11] "Therefore we are buried with Him by baptism into death: that like as Christ was raised up from the dead by the glory of the Father, even so we also should walk in newness of life;"[12] "In whom also ye are circumcised with the circumcision made without hands, in putting off the body of the sins of the flesh by the circumcision of Christ: Buried with Him in baptism, wherein ye are risen with Him."[13] This verse also serves as the basis for infant baptism because the child was circumcised when he was eight days old. It is possible that two opposing views will each have scriptural support.

Another example is the doctrine of Salvation: The Bible teaches personal salvation and points to the need to repent and confess sin.[14] It says that "all have sinned and fall short of the glory of God;"[15] that "the wages of sin is death, but the gift of God is eternal life in Christ Jesus our Lord;"[16] that "Ye must be born again;"[17] and "He that believeth on Him is not condemned; but he that believeth not is condemned already."[18] "I write these things to you who believe in the name of the Son of God so that you may know that you have eternal life."[19]

But *The Great Doctrines of the Bible,* published by Moody Press, says, "An extensive revelation deals with the theme of God's plan for the salvation of families. The purpose of God to provide for entire households in His offer of salvation is seen in Genesis 7:1 and Acts 11:14; the words 'thou and all thy house' are found in both the Old Testament and the New Testament. This divine provision of deliverance for entire households extended even to children's children, Psalm 103:17-18."[20] Additional Scripture references on this topic are found in Genesis 18:19, 35:2-4; Exodus 12:3-4; Deuteronomy 5:29; Joshua 2:18-19, 24:15; Psalms 78:5-7, 101:2-7, 103:17-18; Proverbs 22:6; Acts 2:39, 16:31; and 1 Peter 3:1-2.

There are other passages of Scripture concerning salvation, first of the Jews: "For I would not, brethren, that ye should be ignorant of this mystery, lest ye should be wise in your own conceits; that blindness in part is happened to Israel, until the fullness of the Gentiles be come in. And so all Israel shall be saved: as it is written, There shall come out of Zion the Deliverer, and shall turn away ungodliness from Jacob: For this is my covenant unto them, when I shall take away their sins. As concerning the Gospel, they are enemies for your sakes: but as touching the election, they are beloved for the father's sakes. For the gifts and calling of God are without repentance."[21]

There are further Scriptures that concern those who did not hear the law or the gospel: "God will render to every man according to his deeds; To them who by patient continuance in well doing seek for glory and honor and immortality, eternal life. To the Jew first, and also to the Gentile: For there is no respect of persons with God. (For not the hearers of the law are just before God, but the doers of the law shall be justified. For when the Gentiles, which have not the law, do by nature the things contained in the law, these, having not the law, are a law unto themselves: Which show the work of the law written in their hearts, their conscience also bearing witness, and their thoughts the meanwhile accusing or else excusing one another;) In the day when God shall judge the secrets of men by Jesus Christ according to my gospel."[22] "God sent not His Son into the world to condemn the world; but that the world through Him might be saved."[23]

When we study a specific topic in the Bible, we need to look for *all of the verses* that refer to that topic, see what the Scripture says about it, and how what we find applies to our study. Then we can state the case for our view, and we can also recognize that a different view is not false doctrine, if it has Biblical support. All the information is correct, but complementary. The trick is in knowing when to use one view, and when to use the other one.

Telephone calls to my parents are long distance, but we live in the same 216 area code. If I dial 1 + 216 + their number, I hear a recorded voice that says, "We're sorry, your call cannot be completed as dialed, or the number has been disconnected." When I call my son, who lives in Texas, if I do not dial 1 + 214 + his number, I hear a voice that says, "I'm sorry, you have the wrong number." To complete one type of long distance call, I must use all eleven digits, but for the other kind, I have to leave three of them out. In both cases, all the information is correct. The trick is in knowing when to use one method, and when to use the other one, as a means of allowing information to govern our activities.

In my adult Sunday school class, when it becomes necessary, complementary views are presented for discussion. Then we arrive at an understanding of why we support one or the other, or which view applies to a given situation.

COMPLEMENTARITY IN FREEMASONRY

The Bible is too complex to permit the luxury of dogmatism, if we have any honest desire to understand it. Each man has the right to decide issues for himself, but problems start when we find a verse that supports our view and quit looking—the proof-text or "the Bible proves I'm right" argument. In religion we need to respect the other man's view on peripheral issues and stand firmly on the essentials.

Freemasonry is a philosophy that practices complementarity: In *The Builders,* Joseph Fort Newton, speaking of the members of his Lodge, says: "In their churches they could not agree about the teachings of the Bible; in the Lodge they could not disagree, because each one was allowed to interpret it the way his heart liked best, and asked to allow others the same right; a secret almost too simple to be found out."[24] Speaking of Masonry as an organization, Newton says, "While Masonry is not a church, it has religiously preserved some things of highest importance to the church—among them the right of each individual soul to its own religious faith. Holding aloof from separate sects and creeds, it has taught all of them how to respect and tolerate one another; asserting a principle broader than any of them—the sanctity of the soul and the duty of every man to revere, or at least to regard with charity, what is sacred to his fellows."[25]

Those who attack Freemasonry, claiming it is a religion, have a problem accepting any variation from their view of the Bible. They read their "proof-texts" and ignore the context. They overlook any verses that do not support their own tradition about God's truth. They echo the view of those who defended teaching "creation science" in Little Rock, Arkansas, in 1981: "The Bible is the written Word of God, and because we believe it to be inspired throughout, all of its assertions are historically and scientifically true."[26] "Creationists see the Bible as a book of facts, not as a book that can be interpreted in countless ways. And that's the way they see the world."[27]

This is an issue that is particularly important to me. It was precisely because neither scientists nor fundamentalist clergy could accept their complementary views of our origin, that I became an atheist. One of the "facts" that cause creationists to oppose the findings of geology is based on the age of the earth, dated according to James Ussher's chronology.

But it was not until ninety years after The King James Version of the Bible was published in 1611 that the dates given in the margin were added. In *The English Bible From KJV to NIV*, Jack Lewis says that the practice of printing Ussher's chronology a t the top of the reference column, begun in 1701, is one of the most obvious causes for the acute tension between many Bible students, and the claims of geology, since the student assumes that these figures accurately represent the teaching of the Bible on the age of the earth. The Bible does not claim to inform us how old the earth is."[28]

God's revelation to Moses was perfect, but we don't know all we would wish to know about the when, why, and how of creation; because Moses could not put into words what is beyond words, nor describe what is beyond description. We all influence our data, and there's no way to avoid it, especially when we are grappling with ideas that are almost impossible to express in human language. Perception is critical, so discussing religion often becomes a dispute about the meaning of words. The creationist may not realize that it is impossible to read the Bible without interpreting it, so they read into the Bible what they were taught to believe; therefore what they read is only what they believe about His truth, not God's revealed truth.

A. Berkeley Mickelsen, author of *Interpreting the Bible,* says, "The individual who originally acted in the actual historical event should have no grounds to say to the historian: 'You have completely misunderstood my experience or message,' or 'You have introduced elements into my message or my experience that distort the basic facts.' "[29] "Everywhere in Scripture, the revelation, which is the inmost meaning of the event, is hidden until it is revealed by the Spirit of God to the faith of man. . . . The goal of interpreters is to say neither more nor less than the Spirit of God conveyed to those to whom He first disclosed the meaning."[30]

Every man has a different life experience, and can only communicate "Truth" within that experience. He must interpret the Bible within his understanding of revealed truth, and within his limited knowledge of current scientific truth. He can only understand God as He has revealed Himself to him in

Scripture, just as Abraham, Moses, and Jacob only saw God as they could understand Him, not God as He actually is. For instance John's understanding of the battle of Armageddon was accurate, but his description was limited, because he had never experienced modern scientific warfare. John Walvoord, chancellor of Dallas Theological Seminary, says, "Whether these are symbols or the best description John can give of modern warfare, this is an awesome picture of an almost irresistible military force destroying all that opposes it. The terms 'horses,' 'lions,' and 'serpents' all speak of deadly warfare."[31]

Some of these creatures are so unlike any animals known to man, that some people believe that they are demons coming out of Hell itself. But these terms could also imply that John used the names of living creatures to describe the machines of modern warfare. Perhaps he described great numbers of jet planes as a swarm of locusts; helicopters became locusts with breastplates of iron and stings in their tails like scorpions; tanks and armored cars were horses having breastplates of fire, and he saw their guns as fire and smoke and brimstone that issued out of their mouths. John had never seen anything but living creatures that could move with apparent purpose. His picture of modern warfare is accurate, if we make allowance for his lack of any other words to describe what he saw.

Our understanding of God and the truth of His revelation changes with our spiritual experience. It was the experience of scientists in their research that altered their philosophy, and it is our experience in the trials of life that deepens and widens our spiritual experience. This is one of the strong points of Freemasonry that teaches men to spend their lives in pursuit of more light, their way of saying that truth is more than a creed; it is a lifelong search.

X || FREE CHOICE

T HE PURPOSE OF THIS BOOK, stated in the introduction, is to show that most of the charges made by Carlson and other anti-Masons are false, and that in those instances where there may be an honest difference of opinion, to show that there is a sound scriptural basis for a different view.

Most opposition to Freemasonry comes from those who believe that our Order represents a danger to their religious view. The holiness movement considers Masonry to be worldly, and is particularly troubled about secret orders. Masons accept non-Christians as members because it is specifically in the area of freedom of religion that Freemasonry seeks to follow the teaching of Jesus: "Blessed are the peacemakers; for they shall be called the children of God. Blessed are they which are persecuted for righteousness' sake; for theirs is the kingdom of heaven. Blessed are ye, when men shall revile you, and persecute you, and shall say all manner of evil against you falsely, for my sake."[1]

Masons can be seen as worldly or as peacemakers. Although the two views are mutually exclusive, both of them are based on Scripture, and both are doctrinally correct. Which of the two views is appropriate to one's faith is an individual decision.

Freemasonry has never been a secret order *except* when freedom of religion or speech is suppressed, and Masons have been forced to hide their identity.

John J. Robinson, in his *A Pilgrim's Path,* says, "Non-Masons have known the 'secret words' and signals for over two and a half centuries and still enjoy 'revealing' them. What the anti-Masons miss is the overridingly important point that Masons never change their 'secrets,' however many times they are revealed.

"If a battlefield commander even suspects that his password has leaked to the enemy, he immediately changes the password. In a truly secret organization,

103

the revelation of a secret term, a recognition or distress signal, necessitates a prompt change because the secret signs are protecting secret information. They are not symbolic, as they are in Freemasonry, but tools of subversion. The 'secrets' in Freemasonry appear in articles, pamphlets, radio shows, books, and videotapes; yet they are never changed by so much as a syllable or a gesture.

"The Masons do not change these well-known secret signs, passwords, and recognition signals because their uses, in their traditional forms, are 'rites of remembrance.' They well know that all of their traditional secrets are no longer secret."[2]

Our differences in belief are *not* the real issue. Eve *knew* the mind of God but the serpent still found a way to create doubt: "Yea hath God said?" Jesus *had* the mind of God and perfect knowledge of the Scriptures. His temptation shows that the Enemy can be defeated only in union with God and with *His Word*. In both cases, the person being tested was without sin, but their perfect knowledge of Truth did not determine their response. Free choice did. The serpent introduced division. Jesus introduced reconciliation.

Carlson says Freemasonry is apostate. Keep in mind how he fabricated his allegations as you read the transcript of his final summation about Masons, on side B of Carlson's tape.[3]

But if you are a Mason tonight, I conclude with 2 Corinthians, chapter 6, and you must listen to it. Two Corinthians 6, beginning with verse 14: "Do not be bound together with unbelievers, for what partnership have righteousness and lawlessness? Or what fellowship has light with darkness? Or what harmony has Christ with Satan? Or what has a believer in common with an unbeliever? Or what agreement has the Temple of God with idols? For we are the Temple of the living God, just as God said: 'I will dwell in them and walk among them, and I will be their God, and they shall be my people. Therefore, come out from their midst, and be separate,' says the Lord, 'and do not touch what is unclean; and I will welcome you, and I will be a Father to you, and you shall be my sons and daughters,' saith the Lord Almighty."

The word of God, which was given by inspiration of God, says to all Masons tonight, "You have no business being in a Masonic Lodge, if you claim the name of Jesus Christ. If He is your Lord and Savior, you have no business in a pagan Lodge, involved in some of the most pagan, idolatrous practice anybody can imagine." I have given this tonight, not to attack anyone; if you're a Mason here tonight, please understand that. As a minister of the Gospel though, we are commanded in the Old Testament to speak prophetically and to warn people from their ways. My friends, the Masonic Lodge is not of God. It condemns itself. It claims to be the universal religion, it says that you do not need Jesus Christ, it says the Bible is a monstrous absurdity, it has set man up as the Supreme God, involved in the vulgar worship of the male organ; it is the one that's involved in sun worship and astrology.

Heavenly Father, we come before you tonight and we recognize you alone as the Sovereign.[4] You are a personal God. You are a personal God who loves us, who made us. You are not a Pantheistic All. You are not a Generating Principle. You are not Nature. You alone are the Sovereign, over all of nature. You alone are the King of Kings and the Lord of Lords. You alone are worthy of worship. Your revelation, the Bible, is not a monstrous absurdity, as the Masons claim; but it is your inspired word, by which you have revealed to us the truth of how we can know you and have light. The name of Jesus Christ is not meaningless. There is no other name given among men, whereby we must be saved, but that of Jesus Christ. We recognize Jesus Christ tonight alone as our Lord and Savior. He alone is the Light of the world, not the sun, not the moon, not the stars, not the pagan and idolatrous gods of Masonry.

Oh Lord, I pray tonight for any person here, who may have taken those oaths, sealed himself into a pagan, idolatrous organization; that your heart, your Holy Spirit will convict his heart tonight, that he will understand that if he is a Christian, he must come out of the Masonic Lodge, and repent of that sin. If there are any Masons here tonight and they do not know you, I pray that tonight, that they will see that a humanistic generating principle will never save anyone. Good works cannot achieve it in a Masonic Lodge, but salvation comes because of your grace, through faith alone in Jesus Christ. Oh Lord, I pray that you will teach us tonight. Open our hearts and minds and give us understanding. Oh Lord, I pray, if I have ever said anything tonight, if I do not have love in my voice, Oh God, forgive me. I have sought to speak clearly the truth of that which you have revealed. You commanded us to test all things by your word, and hold fast to that which is true and good. Oh God, may we have nothing to do with pagan idols, pagan worship, and pagan religion. May we turn back from that and say, "Not I, but Christ." He alone is worthy. In Jesus precious and holy name, we love you tonight, God Incarnate, second person of the Trinity, our source of light alone. We love you. In Jesus precious name, Amen.

Note that Carlson managed to break both the third and ninth commandments, taking God's name in vain and bearing false witness, and to *condemn himself* as a false prophet and an apostate, all in just three sentences:

> *The word of God, which was given by inspiration of God, says to all Masons tonight,* "You have no business being in a Masonic Lodge, if you claim the name of Jesus Christ. *If He is your Lord and Savior, you have no business in a pagan Lodge, involved in some of the most pagan, idolatrous practice anybody can imagine.*" I have given this tonight, not to attack anyone; if you're a Mason here tonight, please understand that. *As a minister of the Gospel though, we are commanded in the Old Testament to speak prophetically and to warn people from their ways. My friends, the Masonic Lodge is not of God. It condemns itself.*

In Art deHoyos's *The Cloud of Prejudice,* on the page prior to the table of contents, is a copy of a letter to Ron Carlson, dated November 1, 1992. According to Roger Kessinger, the publisher, it was sent by registered mail together with a copy of the book and a request for his comments. The receipt was signed by Carlson himself and as of early February there had been no response. "Warn a divisive person once, and then warn him a second time. After that, have nothing to do with him. You may be sure that such a man is warped and sinful; he is self-condemned."[5] Mr. Carlson, you may consider this your second warning. I do not ask that you agree with the teachings of Freemasonry, but I do ask for you to admit that you lied about our Order, and show us the tolerance demanded in the Bible.[6]

There is a certain vocal minority in the fundamentalist movement whose normal method of preaching is a militant attack on the faith and practice of others. Their lack of love for fellow-believers in Christ leads to attacks on friend and foe alike, a dogmatism of personal ethics and experience, and an anti-intellectual stance. Their oversimplified theology lacks intellectual honesty and their assumed authority to judge others is a divisive spirit of discord. According to the apostle Paul's criteria, their actions are those of false apostles.

Carlson isn't the only one who doesn't let the facts stand in the way when he is attacking Freemasonry. Pat Robertson's book, *The New World Order*, opens with a discussion of the "staged" collapse of communism, and continues with a scenario that links the Federal Reserve Bank,[7] the Council on Foreign Relations,[8] the United Nations,[9] and Freemasonry[10] in a worldwide conspiracy. This sequence implies that Robertson's style of preaching requires a new enemy to keep his "700 Club" united and focused on his ministry. Now I don't know much about the history and principles of banking, but I do know enough about Freemasonry to know that he is careless with the truth.

One example is Robertson's list of quotations from Pike's *Morals and Dogma* "without comment,"[11] quotations taken out of context, and addressed in earlier chapters of this book.

On page 35, Robertson says that on the back of every one-dollar bill is printed the Great Seal of the United States, adopted by Congress in 1782. One face of the seal shows an eye set in a blaze of glory, above an unfinished pyramid. The Roman numerals for 1776, MDCCLXXVI, are inscribed at the base of the pyramid, and below the pyramid is *Novus Ordo Seclorum*, a Latin phrase meaning a "new world order." Robertson says the pyramid has special meaning for Masons, and that this seal was designed by the secretary to the Continental Congress, Charles Thompson [sic], a member of the Masonic order.

The *Encyclopaedia Britannica*[12] says those primarily responsible for the design were William Barton, who had some knowledge of heraldry, and Charles Thomson. It says the eye suggests the eye of providence. Both Coil's *Masonic Encyclopedia*[13] and *Mackey's Revised Encyclopedia of Freemasonry*[14] credit the design to Barton, a non-Mason. They agree that the seal is not a Masonic design, nor does it represent Masonic symbolism. Barton, who engraved the seal, explained that the pyramid signifies strength and duration;

the eye over it "witnesses the many signal interpositions of Providence in favor of the American cause." Contrary to Mr. Robertson's statement, the pyramid has no special meaning for Masons.

Robertson says the "all-seeing eye" does not represent the God of the Bible, but the eye of an ancient Egyptian god, Osiris, "who is revered in the secret high ceremonies and sacred rites of the Masonic Order." He promises to show how the beliefs and practices of the high-degree "mystery cult" affects the new order in a later chapter. To Thompson [sic] and others, the unfinished pyramid implied that under the watchful eye of Osiris, the task of nation building begun in 1776 would, according to their Masonic rituals, bring forth a new world order.[15]

As Chapter VI, "The Boy Who Cried Wolf," points out, the accusation that Freemasonry is a "mystery cult" that reveres the ancient Egyptian deity, Osiris, is based on a misconception of Pike's Chapter XXX, "Knight Kadosh," and on the Leo Taxil hoax, perpetrated in the 1890s. According to Coil, Pike began his work on the Scottish Rite rituals in 1854, and completed them in 1868. Pike's work was nearly completed when he first learned that the Scottish Degrees originated in France in 1837. Pike had read that the degrees came down to us from the Ancient Mysteries and had no reason to doubt it. Pike refused to back off and published his lectures in 1871, as he had written them, under the name *Morals and Dogma.*[16]

Yet Robertson would have us believe that "under the watchful eye of Osiris, the endeavor **begun in 1776** would, according to their Masonic rituals, bring forth a new world order." This anachronism alone is enough to discredit Robertson's theory, his research, and his reputation as a man of truth!

But there is more: Robertson suggests the possibility that the great seal of the United States reveals the plan of a select few. They intended to replace the Christian world order of Europe and America with a new world order under a mystery religion.[17] He says his research causes him to believe that the term "new world order" has one meaning to the general membership of the organizations promoting the new world order, and an entirely different meaning to the small inner circle of leadership.[18]

There is absolutely no doubt in Robertson's mind, that there has been a continuity of policy and leadership in this nation for decades, that operates the same regardless of who sits in the White House.[19] It is his firm belief that the events of public policy are planned, and not the accidents and coincidences we are led to believe. He also believes that normal men and women would not spend a lifetime to unify the world in order to control it. Impulses of that sort spring from the depth of something that is evil, and is neither well intentioned nor benevolent.[20]

Robertson says there is a behind-the-scenes Establishment in this country that determines government policy and has the power to control the results of elections. The most visible expression of the Establishment is the Council on Foreign Relations (CFR).[21] These interests engineered the elections of Woodrow Wilson and Jimmy Carter.[22] Eisenhower, Nixon, and Bush were their candidates.[23]

According to Robertson's scenario, radical Marxism is an important step toward the Establishment's goal of a controlled world economy, so they promoted the communist takeover of Russia, China, and Eastern Europe, as well as parts of Central America and Africa.[24]

Robertson views the CFR, *The Washington Post*, *The New York Times*, and Harvard University as Establishment organizations that run huge banks, multinational corporations, the nation's financial system, the State Department, and the Treasury Department.[25] The CIA has been under CFR control for most of its existence.[26] For the past seventy years, nearly every key national security and foreign adviser of this nation were members of the CFR.[27]

Robertson says the aims of a small Bavarian secret society called the Order of the Illuminati were to overthrow civil government, the church, and private property. Their new world order would be led by a group of handpicked "adepts" or "illumined" ones. In 1782, Adam Weishaupt, founder of the Order, infiltrated the Continental Order of Freemasons and created "Illuminated Freemasonry."[28] Robertson attributes the "satanic carnage" of the French Revolution to the Illuminati and compares it to the bloodbaths and purges in the Soviet Union by the communists under Lenin and Stalin.[29]

Robertson admits that Illuminism had been banned in Germany and was discredited in France, but he claims that it surfaced again in the 1800s through secret revolutionary societies holding to the basic tenets of Illuminism. He says that these societies commissioned Karl Marx and Friedrich Engels to write the *Communist Manifesto*.[30]

Robertson says it is relatively easy to trace the continuity of thought and purpose of our policy elites from Cecil Rhodes, whose fortune rested on

African gold and diamonds; to the Federal Reserve Board; to the English Round Table; to the Council on Foreign Relations; to the United Nations; to Henry Kissinger; to Jimmy Carter; and finally to George Bush.[31]

What the average person cannot understand, is why a Wall Street banker personally transported $20 million in gold to help the new communist government of Russia, or why Lord Milner of the British Round Table provided funds in 1917 to get them started again, or why the Establishment repeatedly assisted them with massive private and governmental aid during the decades that followed.[32]

Robertson alleges that the Establishment flowed from the minds of John Ruskin and his pupil, Cecil Rhodes. Ruskin believed in the rule of the elite. Rhodes left part of his great fortune to found the Rhodes Scholarships at Oxford in order to spread the English ruling-class tradition. Rhodes and other pupils of Ruskin formed a secret society. Rhodes was the leader; Lord Milner and two others were the executive committee. Others were listed as a circle of initiates. An outer circle of initiates was later organized by Lord Milner and called the Round Table.[33]

From 1909–1913, Lord Milner organized semi-secret groups, known as Round Table Groups, in the British dependencies and America. In 1919, they founded the Royal Institute of International Affairs. The Council on Foreign Relations was conceived at the same time by Colonel Edward House, President Woodrow Wilson's key aide, as the United States affiliate of the Royal Institute of International Affairs and the various Round Table Groups. The American branch of this organization, sometimes called the "Eastern Establishment," has since played a very significant role in the United States.[34]

Robertson says the power of the Masonic Order was extraordinary, and in England it quickly spread among the highest classes. From 1737 to 1907 about sixteen English princes of royal blood joined the order. This background of royal power associated with Freemasonry causes Robertson to believe that "the powerful Cecil Rhodes and his secret society" had some involvement with the Freemasons of England or those on the Continent.[35]

There is not a shred of evidence connecting these societies, except for innuendo, and Robertson's claim that they had similar goals.

Robertson says he understands that in the initation for the 32nd Degree, the candidate is told that he must strike back at the three assassins of Hiram, the builder of Solomon's temple, which are, thanks to the Illuminati, "government, organized religion, and private property."[36]

First of all, it is not in the 32nd Degree, but in Pike's 30th Degree. Secondly, the candidate is told that there is a far more barbarous and bloody tragedy than the murder of Hiram to avenge, and that he is bound to assist by the destruction of "arbitrary and irresponsible power, of tyranny over the conscience, of bigotry and intolerance, and by the establishment everywhere of well-ordered liberty."[37] This is to be attained by "the Love of God and Love of our Neighbor."[38] Third, the candidate is told the history of the destruction of the Knights Templar, and of the burning of its Grand Master, Jacques de Molay, at the stake, by Pope Clement V, and King Philip of France, with the connivance of the Knights Hospitallers.[39] The three assassins are identified as Regal Tyranny, Sacerdotal Usurpation by whatever Church, and Corporate Monopolies and abuses vested in Privileged Orders.[40] Finally, the candidate is told that the power of Truth is the only true vengeance.[41] "Such is the Masonry of the true Kadosch: Love for the people; hatred of Tyranny; sacred regard for the rights of free thought, free speech, and free conscience; and detestation of intolerance, bigotry and priestly arrogance and usurpation; respect and regard for Labour, which makes human nature noble, and contempt and disgust for all monopolies and laziness."[42]

But Robertson says, "It is self-evident that Masonic beliefs and rituals flow from the occult. . . . The New Age religions, the beliefs of the Illuminati, and Illuminated Freemasonry all seem to move along parallel tracks with world communism and world finance. Their appeals vary somewhat, but essentially they are striving for the same very frightening vision."[43]

In 1884, Pope Leo XIII's papal bull, *Humanum Genus,* divided the human race into two groups, the Kingdom of God on earth and the Kingdom of Satan. John Robinson points out that "its major theme is an argument against the idea of democracy, and against the theory of separation of the Catholic church from temporal authority over every state. . . . In that respect, *Humanum Genus* was every bit as much a condemnation of the Constitution of the United States, as it was of Freemasonry, as comes out in a catalog of sins of which Masonry is accused:"[44] "It condemns Masonic teachings of the separation of the church and state, government by the people, civil marriage, and teaching of children by laymen rather than priests, but none of these things is specifically espoused by Freemasonry, which leaves choices in such matters entirely to the individual members. The pope simply confused Freemasonry with all non-Catholics. In any event, *Humanum Genus* contributes nothing in the way of evidence of Masonic devil worship."[45]

Taxil's hoax was inspired by *Humanum Genus*. Anti-Masons read about his hoax, find apparent confirmation in Pike's *Morals and Dogma*, and quote it as if it were factual. They begin with a preconceived idea and quit looking when they find "support" for their ideas, hence their attacks.

Make no mistake about it; the enemies of Freemasonry will not change their minds because of this book. Nor would 10,000 more books with absolute proof that they are lying. In fact, it won't even embarrass them. They are absolutely convinced that they have the mind of God. They are suspicious of anyone who disproves their charges, and become angry when they are shown the true facts. As already stated, they begin with a preconceived idea and quit looking when they find support for their ideas. They will deliberately use anything they find in print, without respect for context, logic, or truth. They expect and even look for opposition. To their way of thinking, counterattacks are the works of Satan, and "prove" that they are God's messenger. The extreme form of this manner of thinking is shown by what happened at Waco and Jonestown. These extremists have a "Masada complex" and will become "martyrs" rather than back down.

So why bother to write this book? The answer lies in the history of our Order. Freemasonry has always had enemies; we should heed the lessons our history teaches, and assume that it will always be under attack. The best that we can hope for is to make the current wave of attacks counterproductive. There is a need to disclose the facts to those who believe the lies of our detractors. Some will only be angry at Masons for facing them with the truth, but there will be others who will listen and be persuaded. Many will ask for a petition to our Order. In this sense, perhaps we should thank our protagonists, because the publicity they have given us is counterproductive to their cause, and will cause a resurgence in our numbers. With what measure they have judged us they will be rewarded!

FUTURE CHOICES

Freemasonry stands at a fork in the road and must choose which path to follow. I believe it was a wise decision to "break silence," and address the allegations made by our accusers, but I also believe we could win the battle and lose the war. We are sending potential candidates a mixed message when we defend our traditions and modify them at the same time.

Is it really necessary to consider action to water down or eliminate our obligations, or are we becoming self-conscious about them in response to our detractors? The Grand Lodge of Ohio requires a statement to be read to the candidate prior to receiving each degree, that informs the candidate that the only penalties imposed are reprimand, suspension, or expulsion; all other references are symbolic in nature.

This statement serves as an ideal model for handling any apparent need for changes in our traditions. We should maintain the integrity of our proven teaching methods, trusting them to do what they always have: make a good man into a better man. We can continue to emphasize man's genuine need for Brotherhood, Relief, and Truth; or we can put our primary attention on declining membership.

Membership *is* a genuine cause for concern. We can either take polls, change our obligations to pacify our detractors, and change the requirements for membership; or we can let our membership be measured by quality, not numbers. I believe we need to take a long hard look at educating our brethren about the basic principles of our Order. As they learn the meaning behind the symbols and allegories, there will be a corresponding growth in their zeal.

Our Lodge has a Monitorial Breakfast that meets once a month to discuss a topic taken from each degree. We bring in well-informed brethren from other Lodges to make a fifteen minute presentation, followed by a discussion period. We are now forming a smaller group composed of brothers who regularly attend, to get more deeply involved in some of the topics that have generated the most interest. There is a renewed sense of what it means to be a Mason, more fellowship, and a lot of new ideas are becoming a part of our Lodge programs and business activities. Our breakfasts have also made it possible to increase our Lodge contributions to charity, and provide cash for our temple fund.

We can continue to focus on our present vicious enemies or we can again turn the other cheek, and let them meet their just end: they will be judged (by God, and by the American public), by the same measure in which they have judged us. This could turn out to be a blessing in disguise, because as they become discredited, the attention they have created could provide a strong boost to our membership rolls.

NOTES

Introduction

1. 2 Corinthians 10:8, NIV. Scripture quotations are from the King James Version, except those marked: (NIV), the New International Version; (NKJV), the New King James Version; or (RSV), the Revised Standard Version.

2. 11:3–4, 13–15, NIV.

3. Galatians 2:14.

Chapter I

1. Pages 194–195.

2. Psalm 14:1; 53:1.

3. Jeremiah 29:23.

4. Page 230.

5. Luke 10:25–37.

6. John 4:9.

7. Matthew 5:43–48, NIV.

8. Matthew 23:24, NIV.

9. Matthew 25:31–46, NIV.

10. Galatians 5:6, NIV.

11. James 2:14–18, NIV.

12. Matthew 12:1–14.

13. Matthew 12:22–14.

14. Matthew 9:10–11.

Chapter II

1. Pietism, *The New International Dictionary of the Christian Church.*

2. Barker, William P. *Who's Who in Church History.*

3. Bryan received the Master Mason Degree in Lincoln Lodge No. 19, Nebraska, on April 15, 1902, and later affiliated with Temple Lodge No. 247, Miami, Florida. See Allen E. Roberts's *Freemasonry in American History.*

4. See Scopes Trial, *Encyclopaedia Britanicca.* Also see entry on Bryan in Barker's *Who's Who in Church History.*

5. See "Biblical Criticism" in Zondervan's *Pictorial Encyclopedia of the Bible,* and in *The Illustrated Bible Dictionary.*

Chapter III

1. Side A, index 003.
2. Side A, index 010.
3. Side A, index 050.
4. Side A, index 309.
5. Pike, page 216.
6. Page iv.
7. James 1:27.
8. Isaiah 58:6.
9. Side A, index 362.
10. Side B, index 026.
11. Isaiah 60:20–21.

Chapter IV

1. Side A, index 253.
2. Matthew 5:34, 36.
3. Jeremiah 29:23: "Because they . . . have spoken lying words in my name, which I have not commanded them; *even I know, and am a witness, saith the Lord.*"
4. Exodus 20:7; Leviticus 19:12.
5. Leviticus 5:5–9; 6:4–7.
6. Pages 133–135.
7. Matthew 26:62–64; Daniel 7:13–14; Meyer, pages 481–482.
8. Matthew 26:63.
9. Pages 158–162.
10. Matthew 5:33.
11. Matthew 5:34–37.
12. Matthew 26:63–64.
13. 2 Corinthians 1:23, RSV.
14. Galatians 1:20, RSV.
15. Genesis 26:28; Ezekiel 16:59; 17:13–19; Hosea 10:4.
16. NIV.
17. Genesis 50:24; Psalms 89:19–37, 49; 110:1–4.
18. Acts 2:29–31; 2 Corinthians 1:18–22; Hebrews 7:14–22.
19. Exodus 22:9–11; Numbers 5:11–31.
20. Genesis 17:11.
21. Romans 1:4; Colossians 2:13–15.
22. 2 Chronicles 15:14–15.
23. 1 Samuel 20:42.
24. Genesis 22:16–18; Psalms 110:4; Hebrews 6:13.
25. Numbers 23:19.
26. Genesis 22:16; Isaiah 45:23; Amos 6:8.
27. Ezekiel 17:19.
28. Jeremiah 44:26.
29. Amos 4:2.
30. Genesis 15:7–21.
31. Jeremiah 34:18–20, NIV.
32. Genesis 17:11–14.
33. Colossians 2:9–15, NIV.
34. Galatians 3:13–14.
35. Deuteronomy 21:22–23.
36. Colossians 2:9–15; Galatians 3:13–14.

Chapter V

1. Page 691.
2. Side A, index 463.
3. Page 72.
4. Page 23.
5. Here Pike parallels Dr. Jim Tresner's thought in the February 1993 issue of *The Scottish Rite Journal:* "Masonry tries very hard to raise questions, and to help its members acquire the tools for thought—but we do not try to give answers" (page 18).
6. Page 19.
7. Page 20.
8. Page 624.

Chapter VI

1. Appendix A, pages 128-129.
2. Side A, index 512.
3. Matthew 13:10-11.
4. Isaiah 6:9-10.
5. Matthew 13:13-16.
6. Matthew 13:34-35; Psalm 78:2.
7. Mark 4:33-34, NIV.
8. Page 359.
9. Page 820.
10. *Born in Blood*, pages 136, 138.
11. Page 818.
12. Pages 814-15.
13. Bracketed notes within the text in this chapter are in the original text.

14. Pages 815-817.
15. Page 818.
16. Appendix A, page 136.
17. Page 1013.
18. Barker, *Who's Who in Church History*, pages 227-28.
19. Pages 1013-1017.
20. 13:951.
21. Pages 107-108, n. 84.
22. Page 69.
23. Side A, index 309.
24. *Bartlett's Familiar Quotations*, page 523, n.9.
25. *Bartlett's Familiar Quotations*, page 524, n.10.

Chapter VII

1. John 21:17.
2. 2 Corinthians 5:2-5.
3. Matthew 4:1-11.
4. Luke 12:14, NIV.
5. Job 42:7.
6. Matthew 7:1-2, NIV.
7. John 3:17, 19.
8. Matthew 18:15-17; Galatians 6.
9. Matthew 7:24.
10. Vol. 1, pages 291-292.
11. James 1:22.
12. Matthew 7:15-16.

13. 2 Kings 1:8, NIV.

14. Ephesians 2:14.

15. John 10:16.

16. Ephesians 4:7.

17. Revelation 1:4.

18. Matthew 5:9–11.

19. Barclay, pages 108–110.

Chapter VIII

1. James 4:11–12.

2. Matthew 4:25.

3. "The Fifth Gospel," lecture of December 5, 1982.

4. "The Hebrew Mind," lecture of December 18, 1982.

5. *Morals and Dogma*, page 62.

6. Romans 1:20–23, NIV.

7. Matthew 27:46; Mark 15:34.

8. 2 Corinthians 5:21.

9. Vol. 2, pages 367–369.

10. John 19:30.

Chapter IX

1. 27:11.

2. 139:24.

3. 119:30.

4. Romans 11:33–34.

5. In *Religions of America*, edited by Leo Rosten.

6. Quantum Mechanics, *Encyclopaedia Britannica.*

7. Numbers 8:7.

8. Ezekiel 36:25.

9. Acts 22:16.

10. 1 Corinthians 12:13.

11. 1 Peter 3:21.

12. Romans 6:4.

13. Colossians 2:11–12.

14. Luke 15:21, 18:13; 1 John 1:9.

15. Romans 3:23.

16. Romans 6:23.

17. John 3:3.

18. John 3:18.

19. 1 John 5:13.

20. Pages 298–99.

21. Romans 11:25–29.

22. Romans 2:6–7, 10–11, 13–16.

23. John 3:17.

24. Page xvii.

25. Page 236.

26. James Gorman, *Discover,* February 1982.

27. Sarah Boxer, *Discover,* March 1987.

28. Page 53.

29. Page 62.

30. Pages 64–65.

31. *Revelation,* page 167.

Chapter X

1. Matthew 5:9–11, NIV.
2. Page 125.
3. Appendix A, page 141.
4. Side B, index 580.
5. Titus 3:10–11, NIV.
6. Matthew 9:10; Mark 9:38, 39; Luke 9:49, 50; Acts 10:28; Phillipians 1:17, 18; 1 Corinthians 12:3–7, 14, 24, 25.
7. Pages 8, 32, 65–67, 96, 100–103, 109, 178.
8. Pages 6, 8, 66–67, 96, 98–102, 109, 112–113, 135–140.
9. Pages 8, 90–92, 101–102, 143, 176–179.
10. Pages 35–37, 67–73, 170, 176–185.
11. Pages 183–184.
12. Vol. 20, page 128.
13. Page 618.
14. Page 1364.
15. Page 35.
16. Pages 472–475.
17. Page 36.
18. Page 37.
19. Page 8.
20. Page 9.
21. Page 96.
22. Pages 64, 103, 125.
23. Pages 67, 100–101.
24. Page 97.
25. Page 98.
26. Page 99.
27. Page 67.
28. Pages 67, 68, 177–185.
29. Page 68.
30. Pages 68–69.
31. Page 8.
32. Page 73.
33. Pages 110–111, 137.
34. Pages 111–112.
35. Page 179.
36. Page 185.
37. *The Magnum Opus,* page XXX . . . 3.
38. Ibid, XXX . . . 6.
39. Ibid, XXX . . . 9–14.
40. Ibid, XXX . . . 15.
41. Ibid, XXX . . . 16–18.
42. Ibid, XXX . . . 18.
43. Page 185.
44. *Born in Blood,* page 308. For a complete rendition of *Humanum Genus,* in English, see pages 345–359.
45. Page 311.

BIBLIOGRAPHY

Adams, Jay E. *The Use of the Scriptures in Counseling*. Grand Rapids: Baker, 1975.

Aesop. *Aesop for Children*. New York: Checkerboard Press, 1947.

Barclay, William. *The Gospel of Matthew*, rev. Philadelphia: Westminster, 1975.

Barker, William P. *Who's Who in Church History*. Grand Rapids: Baker, 1969.

Biblical Criticism. *The Zondervan Pictorial Encyclopedia of the Bible*, vol. 1. Grand Rapids: Zondervan, 1975.

Bonhoeffer, Dietrich. *Ethics*. New York: Macmillan, 1955.

Boxer, Sarah, ed. "Up Front." *Discover*, 1987 8(3): 6.

Bryan, William Jennings. *Encyclopaedia Britannica*, vol 4. Chicago: 1967.

Cairns, Earle E. *Christianity through the Centuries: A History of the Christian Church*. Grand Rapids: Zondervan, 1954, 1981.

Coil, Henry W. *Coil's Masonic Encyclopedia*. New York: Macoy, 1961.

Cole, K.C. "Natural Complements." *Discover*. 1983, 4(11): 62–63.

Dake, Finis Jennings. *Dake's Annotated Reference Bible*. Atlanta: Dake Bible Sales, 1963.

deHoyos, Art. *The Cloud of Prejudice: A Study in Anti-Masonry*. Kita, MT: Kessinger, 1992.

Evans, William. *The Great Doctrines of the Bible*. Chicago: Moody Press, 1974.

Fleming, James. "The Fifth Gospel." Lecture presented at the Jerusalem Center for Biblical Studies, Jerusalem, Israel, December 5, 1982.

——. "The Hebrew Mind." Lecture, December 18, 1982.

Gorman, James. "Judgement Day for Creationism." *Discover*, 1982 3(2), 14–18.

Gould, Stephen Jay. "Darwinism Defined: The Difference Between Fact and Theory." *Discover*, 1987, 8(1): 64.

Harris, Thomas A. *I'm OK—You're OK*. New York: Harper & Row, 1967.

Hofstadter, Douglas R. " 'Default Assumptions' and Their Effects on Writing and Thinking." *Scientific American*, 1982 247(11): 18–22.

Interlinear Bible, The. Hebrew/English. Grand Rapids, MI: Baker, 1981.

Lewis, Jack P. *The English Bible: From KJV to NIV*. Grand Rapids, MI: Baker, 1981.

Lincoln, Abraham. In *Bartlett's Familiar Quotations*. Boston: Little, Brown and Company, 1980.

Mackey, Albert G. *Mackey's Revised Encyclopedia of Freemasonry.* Chicago: The Masonic History Company, 1946.

Meyer, H. A. W. *Commentary on the New Testament: Matthew.* Translated and edited by F. Crombie and W. Stewart. Peabody, MA: Hendrickson, 1983. (Originally published, 1883.)

Mickelsen, A. Berkeley. *Interpreting the Bible.* Grand Rapids: Eerdmans, 1963.

The New International Dictionary of the Christian Church. Grand Rapids: Zondervan, 1974, 1978.

Newton, Joseph Fort. *The Builders.* Lexington, MA: Supreme Council, AASR, Northern Masonic Jurisdiction, 1973.

Oath. *The New Bible Commentary,* rev. Grand Rapids: Eerdmans, 1970.

Oath. *The Zondervan Pictorial Encyclopedia of the Bible,* vol. 4. Grand Rapids: Zondervan, 1975.

Oaths. *The Illustrated Bible Dictionary.* Wheaton, IL: Inter-Varsity Press, 1980.

Oaths. *The Interpreter's Dictionary of the Bible.* Nashville: Abingdon, 1962.

Patterson, Bob E. *Carl F. H. Henry.* (Makers of the Modern Theological Mind). Waco, TX: Word Books, 1983.

Pietism, *The New International Dictionary of the Christian Church.*

Pike, Albert. *Morals and Dogma.* Richmond, VA: L.H. Jenkins, 1914.

Pike, Albert. *The Magnum Opus Reprint.* Kita, MT: Kessinger, 1992.

Quantum Mechanics, *Encyclopaedia Britannica* vol. 18. Chicago, 1967.

Roberts, Allen E. *The Craft and Its Symbols.* Richmond, VA: Macoy, 1974.

Roberts, Allen E. *Freemasonry in American History.* Richmond, VA: Macoy, 1985.

Robertson, Pat. *The New World Order.* Dallas: Word Publishing, 1991.

Robinson, John J. *Born in Blood: The Lost Secrets of Freemasonry.* New York: M. Evans, 1989.

Robinson, John J. *A Pilgrim's Path: One Man's Road to the Masonic Temple.* New York: M. Evans, 1993.

Scopes Trial, *Encyclopaedia Britannica* vol. 20. Chicago: 1967.

Tresner, Jim. "Conscience and the Craft." *The Scottish Rite Journal,* 1993, *101*(2): 13–25.

Tyndale New Testament Commentaries: The Gospel According to St. Matthew. Grand Rapids: Eerdmans, 1961.

Walvoord, John F. *The Revelation of Jesus Christ.* Chicago: Moody Press, 1966.

Weaver, Warren. "The Religion of a Scientist." In L. Rosten, ed. *Religions of America.* New York: Simon & Schuster, 1975.

Webster's Dictionary of Synonyms. Springfield, MA: G. & C. Merriam, 1951.

Webster's Ninth New Collegiate Dictionary. Springfield, MA: Merriam-Webster, 1991.

Webster's Third New International Dictionary. Springfield, MA: G. & C. Merriam, 1966.

World Almanac & Book of Facts, 1993, The. New York: Pharos Books, 1992.

APPENDIX A

TRANSCRIPT OF

CARLSON'S TAPE

PPENDIX A IS A TRUE and complete transcript of an audiocassette of Carlson's anti-Masonic lecture. Index numbers locate corresponding positions on Carlson's tape. An ellipsis (". . .") shows where portions of Pike's text were omitted by Carlson. Parentheses ( ) enclose Carlson's words where they were substituted for Pike's. Asterisks mark a page number, *218*, to reveal his source, where Carlson added selected phrases to those found on the page he cited. All pages cited from Albert Pike's *Morals and Dogma*, either by Carlson or myself, are reproduced as Appendix B for comparison. *Italics* within Pike's text are those that Pike used.

Index 003: Ron Carlson, lecturer in Conservative Religion, has studied at seven Universities, including working on and specializing in non-Christian Cults in Eastern philosophy. He has traveled extensively in over thirty countries and many major universities.

Index 010: It is good to have you here tonight, as we deal with a very timely and important subject to deal with. Tonight we want to speak on the subject of Freemasonry and the Masonic Lodge, the Shriners. I have prayed much about tonight's message. I know that this message tonight touches very close to home to many people. I know that it affects many of you that are here today who have husbands or fathers or brothers or relatives. I know that we have Masons here this evening. It is our purpose tonight not to attack or tear down any individual. I have no quarrel with Masons as people. I have a great love for them. My quarrel

121

tonight though, is with an organization, which claims to be the supreme universal religion, and denies Jesus Christ, our Lord. We are commanded in 1 Thessalonians 5:21 to test all things, hold fast to that which is true and good. Hebrews 4:12 tells us that the Word of God is sharper than any two-edged sword, and we must test all things by it. That is what we want to do this evening.

Index 050: This message is a combination of eighteen months of research. I have not gone to anti-Masonic writers, but rather to the authoritative works of Masonry. What I am going to say tonight is from their own source books, from the authorities of Masonry, including Albert Pike, his *Morals and Dogma*, of which all Masons have a copy of; including Albert G. Mackey, his *Encyclopedia of Freemasonry*, *History of Freemasonry*, his other works; including a variety of other 33rd Degree Masons. I have spent hours interviewing across this country, talking with some of the leading authorities in Masonic Law. To give you some background as to what we're dealing with tonight, Masons claim to have a membership, somewhere around five million worldwide today. Of those about three and a half million are here in the United States. Of those three and a half million Masons, there are about one million Shriners, who have achieved a 32nd degree of the Scottish Rite, which is the highest degree except for the 33rd degree, honorary degree of Masonry. Of those Shriners, we have here in the state of Minnesota about twenty thousand, in the Twin Cities about twelve thousand Shriners or 32nd Degree Masons. When most of you think about Freemasonry or the Masonic Lodge, the thing that comes to your mind is not some secret esoteric doctrine, that we're gonna look at tonight, but rather you think usually of some secret organization which you're not quite sure what it is. You've heard about the Shrine hospitals, about the Home for Elderly Masons. We have the Shrine circus in town right now. But these things, as we're going to see tonight, are all a thin veneer. They are the outer wrapping of the package which the public sees. Tonight we wanna tear away the outer wrapping of the package, the veil of secrecy, and discover what the content and essence of the package is. If you grasp one-tenth of what I will say tonight, I guarantee you that you will understand more about Masonry than does one in ten thousand Masons.

Index 119: Most Masons do not understand what they are involved in. Why do they go into it? As I've interviewed hundreds of Masons across this country, you soon discover that they go into it, not because of the religious teachings, but rather they go into it out of peer pressure, because of their friends are in it. Some go into it because of business advantage, that they think that they can obtain by becoming a Mason. Some people view it as a social club or a mutual-aid society. There are a few who are attracted by the lure of secret, mystic ritual. Some go into it seeking self-development or philanthropy. Some go into it because of their pride, seeking to save themselves through good works, and becoming a Master Mason appeals to their pride, that people will call them Worshipful Masters. For whatever reason Masons go into it, one in ten thousand Masons does not understand what is going on. It is deliberately hid from them, as we're gonna see tonight, because the adepts, the leaders of Freemasonry, as we're gonna discover, do not want the average Mason to understand the pagan idolatry that he is involved in.

Index 152: Freemasonry claims to be a very ancient practice. The institution of Freemasonry actually began in England in the year 1717 A.D. You have today in Masonry what is known as the Blue Lodge. All Masons go through the Blue Lodge, which is the first three degrees of Masonry. In order to go into a Masonic Lodge you must first be initiated. You'll be initiated into the first three degrees, the first being that of Entered Apprentice, then into the second degree of the Fellowcraft, and then into the Master Degree, the third degree. Once you have achieved the Blue Lodge, then you have the choice either to go into the Scottish Rite, which has 32 degrees, leading to becoming a Shriner; or you can go into the York Rite or American Rite, which leads to the Knights Templar degree after 13 degrees. If you go through 32 degrees of Freemasonry of the Scottish Rite, then you will become part of, if you choose to be, what has come to be known as the Shrine, known as the Ancient and Arabic Order of Nobles of the Mystic Shrine. Here in Minnesota, you will get your hat representing the Shrine Temple of Minnesota.

Index 188: Tonight we want to examine what goes on within the Masonic Temple, in the Masonic Lodge, what is their teaching, what are men actually participating in that they do not understand, and ask ourselves, "Is it something that a Christian should be involved in?" What is the decision? First of all, to enter in the Masonic Lodge, you must first be initiated. Now they have a variety of very interesting initiation ceremonies. When a person enters into the first degree, the Entered Apprentice Degree, the usual initiation is very similar to what I'm gonna read right now. The typical initiation ceremony, the candidate is first divested of his jacket and his collar and tie, also of any money or metal articles. His left trouser leg is rolled up above the knee, his shirt is opened to expose his left breast and his right shoe is removed and replaced by a slipper. The ritual effect is the explanation for these practices. He is also blindfolded. In the Masonic parlance, it's known as hoodwinked. It demonstrates his state of darkness. A leather noose or cable-tow is placed around his neck. After the lodge has been formally opened, he is led to the outer door by the Tyler or doorkeeper. At the threshold, he is confronted by the inner guard, who holds the point of a dagger to his bare breast, barring his way. He is then led before the Worshipful Master, the chief officer of the Lodge. The Worshipful Master recites a prayer for the Supreme Governor of the Universe. He puts a series of ritual questions to the candidate who is required to answer according to a prescribed formula without a slip of the tongue. Kneeling in front of the Worshipful Master's pedestal, with his right foot formed in a square and the point of a pair of compasses touching his breast, the candidate then swears not to reveal any part of the secrets of Masonry. Should he do so, he accepts the penalty of, quote, "Having my throat cut across, my tongue torn out by its roots, and buried in the sand of the sea at the low watermark." When you enter the second degree, you're then required to take a second oath, which includes the following: "Binding myself under no less a penalty than that of having my left breast torn open, my heart plucked out, and given to the prey of the world, the beasts of the sea, or the fowls of the air." When you enter the third degree, the Master Mason Degree, the oath that you must take includes, quote, "Binding myself under no less a penalty than that of having my body severed in twain, my bowels taken from thence and burned in ashes, et cetera, et cetera." All Masons have gone through these rituals.

Index 253: What does the Bible say about things like this, even taking of an oath? If you have your Bibles, I'd like you to turn with me to Matthew 5:34–37. Jesus says, "But I say to you, 'Make no oath at all, either by heaven, for it is the throne of God, or by the earth, for it is the footstool of His feet, or by Jerusalem, for it is the city of the Great King; nor shall you make an oath by your head, for you cannot make one hair white or black; so let your statements be yes or no, and anything beyond this is of evil.' " Turn with me to James 5:12: "But above all, my brethren, do not swear, either by heaven or by earth, or of any other oath; but let your yes be yes, your no be no, so that you may not fall under the judgment." 1 Corinthians 3:16–17: "Do you not know that you are the temple of God, and that the Spirit of God dwells in you? If any man destroys the temple of God, God will destroy him, for the temple of God is holy and that is what you are." My friends, to take an oath as a Mason, to swear an oath that you will rip your body to shreds if you should reveal any of the secrets, have your throat cut across, your tongue ripped out; God says, as a Christian, you should have no part of it. After the oaths are taken, the Mason is then told what he is to believe. It's interesting to me that Masons are sworn to secrecy on the oath of death, before they are told anything about what is going on inside the Masonic Lodge. Because they are sworn to secrecy, many don't want to talk, so tonight I will talk for them. We will reveal the secrets tonight of Freemasonry, of which they take oaths to hide.

Index 309: To begin with, one of the things that you will hear from Masons is they will tell you that Masonry is not a religion. They say, "Oh, I'm not in it for religion, I'm in it for the social advantage, the business advantage." The Mason simply does not understand what he is involved in. Tonight I would like to quote from their authoritative works, mainly from the book which all masons have, that of Albert Pike's book, *Morals and Dogma*. Tonight when I quote a reference, a page number, it will be from *Morals and Dogma*, unless I otherwise specify. To begin with, in Albert Pike's *Morals and Dogma*, I'll quote the page numbers, so you can go home and look them up, if anyone questions what I am saying. Beginning on page 213, Pike says, quote, "Every Masonic Lodge is a temple of religion, and its teachings are instructions in religion." Page 210, quote, "Masonry is from the earliest times the custodian and depository of the great . . . religious truths, unknown to the world at large, and handed down from age to age by an unbroken current of tradition, embodied in symbols, emblems, and allegories." Page 219, quote, *218* "Much of the Masonic secret manifests itself, . . . *219* to him who even partially comprehends all of the Degrees in proportion as he receives them; and particularly to those who advance to the highest degrees of the Ancient and Accepted Scottish Rite. That Rite raises a corner of the veil, even in the Degree of (Entered) Apprentice; for it (is there declared) that Masonry is a worship. Masonry . . . is the universal, . . . religion, . . . in the heart of universal humanity. . . . The ministers of this religion are all Masons . . . its sacrifices to God are good works, . . . and perpetual efforts to attain to all the moral perfection of which man is capable." Unquote.

Albert Pike, their leading authority, says, first of all, that the Masonic Lodge is a temple of religion, that Masonry is a worship, it is a universal religion, that all Masons are ministers of this religion, its sacrifices to God are good works and perpetual moral efforts of man. We now understand what we're dealing with. We're dealing with a religion which claims to be the universal worship of man.

Index 362:   What is this universal religion that Masons are the ministers of? I quote Albert Pike's *Morals and Dogma*, page 311: "In all religions, there is a basis of Truth; in all there is pure Morality. . . . all teachers and reformers of mankind we admire and revere. Masonry . . . has her mission to perform. . . . she invites all men of all religions to enlist under her banners . . ." Page 226, quote, "Masonry, around whose altars (the Hebrew, the Christian), the Moslem, the Brahmin, the followers of Confucius, (of) Zoroaster, can assemble as brethren and unite in prayer . . ." Page 276: "In no other way could Masonry possess its character of Universality; . . . which enables two kings, worshipers of different Deities, to sit together as Master (Mason)s, . . . and to sit . . . in the same Lodge as brethren." We wouldn't have to go any farther tonight. Albert Pike goes on, page 525: "(Masonry) reverences all the great reformers. It sees in Moses, the Lawgiver of the Jews, in Confucius, (in) Zoroaster, (in Buddha), in Jesus of Nazareth, in the Arabian Iconoclast, Great Teachers of Morality, and Eminent Reformers, . . . Masonry is a worship; but one in which all . . . men can unite; . . ." Here they reduce Jesus Christ to nothing but a moral teacher, equal in status with Buddha, Confucius, Zoroaster, and every other pagan teacher. Page 277: "The first Masonic (Teacher) whose memory is preserved to us (in) history was Buddha, who, about a thousand years before the Christian era, reformed the religion of Manous. He called to the priesthood all men, without distinction of caste, who felt themselves inspired by God to instruct men."

Index 400: Page 166: "Masonry wisely requires no more than a belief in One Great All-Powerful Deity, . . . Preserver of the Universe. Therefore it . . . teaches . . . that toleration is one of the chief duties of every good Mason, . . . *167* for in every faith there are excellent moral precepts." Page 226: "The Mason . . . considers that if there were no written revelation, he could safely rest the hopes that animate him and the principles that guide him, on the deductions of reason and the convictions of instinct and consciousness. He can find a sure foundation for his religious belief in these deductions of the intellect . . ." Here Masons reduce Jesus Christ to nothing but a moral teacher, teach that all religions are summed up in Masonry, and that you don't need any revelation from God because the Mason's own intellect is a basis for a firm foundation of faith. Little do they understand what Jeremiah 17 says, when it says the heart of man is deceitful and desperately wicked, that all are sinners and all fall short of the kingdom of God. They go on, page 708: "Thus we . . . are in communion with the great (philosophy) . . . and . . . the religions which cover the earth, and all repose on the sacred foundation of natural religion; . . . that religion which reveals to us the natural light given to all men, without the aid of (any) particular revelation. . . . *715* (Beautiful), above the great white chaos of human errors, shines the calm, clear light of natural human religion, . . . the Universe, (is) the Great Bible of God. Material nature is (the) Old Testament, . . . Human Nature is the New Testament . . ." The material was and has been the element of communion between man and God. Nature is full of religious lessons to the Mason. Here we find what the true basis of Masonic religion is, as we're gonna see in a moment, that of natural religion, nature worship. The universe is God, the natural world is the Old Testament, human nature is the New Testament. You do not need any revelation, you do not need the revelation of Jesus Christ because your own intellect and nature will lead you to the path.

What we find summed up then, is that this universal religion, which all Masons claim to be Ministers of, is a universalism of morality, it's a syncretism of all religion, taking a little from everything, mixing it in a blender, and coming up with Freemasonry. It worships all gods and deities. It doesn't matter which god you worship, you can sit as a brother in the Masonic Temple. Jesus is only a teacher of morality. Buddha was the first Masonic teacher. You don't need a revelation, your own intellectual deduction will lead you to nature worship.

What is this nature worship? Nature worship, we find, is summed up in the ancient mysteries of Freemasonry. Freemasonry prides itself on holding the mysteries of the universe, that all the mysteries are summed up in Freemasonry.

Index 463: Albert Pike, *Morals and Dogma*, page 352: "Among most of the Ancient Nations there was, in addition to their public worship, a private one styled, the Mysteries; to which (only those who were admitted by initiation and ceremonies could be welcomed)." Page 353: "Where the Mysteries originated is not known. It is supposed that they came from India, by . . . way of Chaldea, into Egypt, and then were carried into Greece. Wherever they arose, they were practiced (by) all the ancient nations; . . ." Page 22: "Masonry, successor of the Mysteries, still follows the ancient manner of teaching. . . . *23* Masonry is identical with the ancient Mysteries, . . ."

The powers revealed in the Mysteries were all, in reality, nature gods. The Mysteries taught that doctrine of the Divine Oneness. Here we get into the fact that Freemasonry claims to be identical to the ancient Mysteries, that the Mysteries revered Nature and the Nature God, and held to the pantheistic Divine One as their god.

Index 483: "Zoroaster, . . . Confucius, (Buddha), Socrates, and Plato (taught their esoteric doctrine). They did not communicate them to the people at large, but only to a favored few; and as they were communicated in Egypt, (in) India, in Persia, (in) Phoenicia, in Greece . . . to the Initiates. The communication of this knowledge and (the) other secrets, some of which (perhaps are) lost, constituted, under other names, what we now call Masonry, or (Frank or Freemasonry)," page 207.

The Mysteries, like the symbols of Masonry, are but the image of Nature. The Mysteries embrace the three Great Doctrines of the ancient theosophies. They treated God, man, and nature in symbolic form. The Mysteries exhibited the Divine Universal One. Here we see Freemasonry claims to follow the ancient Mysteries, that they are exact representations of what the Mysteries taught. Now as we get into what the Mysteries are, these secrets which Masons are sworn to secrecy on, they say that you cannot know the Mysteries unless you're a Mason. The problem is, most Masons don't know them themselves. These Mysteries, which are the basis of true Masonry, are hidden even from the

Masons. Now this is one of the things which, as I talked with Masons, they do not understand themselves; that the leaders of Freemasonry, and the authorities, are consciously lying and seeking to mislead the average Mason, so that he does not understand what he is involved in.

Index 512: Let me read for you, their authority, Albert Pike, *Morals and Dogma*, page 104, I quote: "Masonry, like all the Religions, all the Mysteries, . . . conceals its secrets from all except the Adepts and Sages, . . . and uses false (interpretations) and misinterpretations of its symbols."

Page 359: "The rites of initiation became progressively more complicated. Signs and tokens were invented by which the Children of Light could with facility make themselves known to each other. Different Degrees were invented, as the number of Initiates enlarged, in order that there might be . . . (an) . . . inner apartment of the Temple, a favored few, to whom alone the more valuable secrets were entrusted, . . . All persons were initiated into the lesser Mysteries, but few attained the greater, in which the true spirit of them, and most of their secret doctrines were hidden. The veil of secrecy was impenetrable, sealed by oaths and penalties the most (treacherous) and appalling."

Page 819, Albert Pike: "The Blue Degrees (which are the first three degrees of Masonry, that all go through), The Blue Degrees are but the outer court . . . of the Temple. Part of (its) symbols are displayed there to the Initiate, but he is intentionally misled by false interpretations. It is not intended that he shall understand them; . . . Their true explication is reserved for the Adepts, the Princes of Masonry. The whole body of the Royal and Sacerdotal Art was hidden so carefully, centuries since, in the High Degrees, . . . It is well enough"—listen to this—"it is well enough for the mass of those (so) called Masons, to imagine that all is contained in the Blue Degrees; . . ." What the Chiefs of the Order really believed and taught is indicated only to the Adepts by hints contained only in the High Degrees of Freemasonry.

What they're saying to you, if you're a Mason, is that you are consciously being misled. Now this is not Ron Carlson speaking, this is Albert Pike, *Morals and Dogma*. Albert Pike is telling you that when you go into Masonry, they are consciously misleading you, so that you do not understand, they do not want you to understand, what you are practicing, because of its pagan, idolatrous nature, as we're gonna see in a moment. So not only are you swearing oaths to keep secret, but then you have them lying to you and deceiving you.

Page 545: "All the (Mysteries) should be kept concealed, . . . (The Mason) sins against God, who divulges to the unworthy the Mysteries confided to him. The danger is not merely in violating truth, but in telling truth, . . ." How different this is from the Gospel of Jesus Christ. The danger is not simply telling the truth, but revealing the truth. He who sins against God is he who reveals the truth. My friends, as Christians, we're told to go into all the world and proclaim the good news!

Jesus said, "I am the truth and the truth will set you free," not enslaving you to pagan oaths and initiations to be kept secret. You are consciously misled: page 304: "The Masonry of the Blue Lodge, (which all Masons have gone through), finds symbolic meaning within the Temple), . . . the whole structure . . . (of the Temple represents) the Universe, . . . *305* the . . . grand principle of (the) occult philosophy veiled under the name 'Kabalah,' and indicated by all the sacred hieroglyphs of the Ancient Sanctuaries, and of the rites, so little understood by the mass of . . . Initiates of the Ancient and Modern Freemasonry."

This is where he begins to go into the occult philosophy as Albert Pike himself calls it, that once you've been misled, from the true teachings, then they begin to indoctrinate you into the occult philosophy of the Kabalah, which was the ancient Jewish mystical rites of theosophy, mysticism, magic, and a variety of other pagan teachings. What is this philosophy of the Masonic religion, which all Masons are following? Stay with me, it might get a little complicated; we'll try and make it simple.

Index 587:   Page 208, Albert Pike, *Morals and Dogma*, quote: "The Temple of Solomon presented a symbolic image of the Universe; and resembled, in its arrangements and furniture, all the temples of the ancient nations that practiced the Mysteries. The system of numbers was intimately connected with their religion and worship, and has come down to us in (Free)Masonry; . . . (through) the esoteric meaning with which the numbers used by us are pregnant (with meaning) . . . *209* The Holy of Holies of the Temple formed a cube; . . . It corresponded with the number four, by which the ancients presented Nature. . . (the) nature and . . . attributes (are God), . . . (are) written by Him upon the leaves of the great Book of Universal Nature, . . . Masonry has in all ages been the interpreter, . . . (of this religion). . . . And so (it is) in our day every Masonic Lodge represents the Universe." Listen to this, "Every Masonic Lodge today represents the Universe. . . . In it are represented the sun, (the) moon, . . . (the) stars; (the) three great torches in the East, West, and South, forming a triangle, give it light. . . . These three great lights . . . represent *210* the great mystery of the three principles of creation, . . . destruction, and . . . regeneration, . . ." (The Temple of Solomon was symbolic in its astrological symbols. The signs of the Zodiac were evident today even in our own Masonic Lodge.) Page 411, "The images of the Sun, Moon, and Mercury (are) represented (in the Temple); and they are still the three lights of (the) Masonic Lodge; except . . . for Mercury, the Master of the Lodge has been absurdly substituted."

A lot of Master Masons don't understand what Pike says about them. Page 486, "The Ancient Astronomers saw all the great Symbols of Masonry in the Stars. . . . The Sun is still symbolized by the point within a Circle;" (which's a very famous Masonic symbol), "the Moon and Mercury . . . are the three Great Lights of the Lodge. . . . *487* The veneration paid to (the) numbers (in Masonry) . . . (finds) its source (here)." (Astrology was practiced among all the ancient Masons. In Egypt, the book of Astrology was borne reverently in a religious procession. In China, astrology was taught as in Arabia. In Egypt, it was called the feast of fire and light. Astrology is also found in the passover, when the lamb was slain and eaten among the Jews.) When you get into their teachings, what he is saying, is that the Masonic Lodge represents the Universe, the lights of the Temple which shine and give truth, are the sun, the moon, the stars. Even the Passover Lamb, which foreshadowed the coming of Jesus Christ, as the Eternal Lamb of God, the Masons say is actually a sign of the Zodiac. He goes on, "There is no more striking proof," page 460, "There is no more striking proof of the universal adoration paid to the stars . . . than the arrangement of the Hebrew camp in the Desert, and . . . the twelve tribes of Israel, . . . (which represented the twelve signs of the Zodiac in astrology.)" Unquote.

When you get into the teaching, and we can't go into it all, all of Masonry is summed up in the practice of Astrology: in venerating the stars, the sun, the moon; the tribes of Israel were Zodiac signs; the Passover Lamb was a sign of Astrology in the Zodiac. If you turn with me to Deuteronomy 4, you see what God says about this. Not only were they involved in Astrology, but also in

Numerology, part of this Kabalah and the Occult of Jewish Mysticism. Deuteronomy 4:15: "So watch yourself carefully, since you did not see any form on the day the Lord spoke to you at Horeb from the midst of the fire." Verse 19: "Beware lest you lift up your eyes to heaven and see the sun and the moon and the stars and all the host of heaven and be drawn away and worship and serve them." Deuteronomy 17:2: "If there is found in your midst, in any of your towns, which the Lord your God has given you, a man or a woman who does what is evil in the sight of the Lord your God, by transgressing His Covenant, and has gone and served other gods and worshiped them or the sun or the moon or any of the heavenly host, which I have not commanded, if it is told you, and you have heard of it, then you shall inquire thoroughly, and behold if it is true, and it seems certain that this detestable thing has been done in Israel, then you shall bring out that man or that woman who has done this evil deed to your gates, that is this man or woman, and you shall stone them to death." [Carlson is apparently reading from the Revised Standard Version.]

Israel at this time was a theocracy, a government ruled by God. He said it was such an abomination to practice Astrology, to follow the sun and moon and stars, that people were to be put to death for. If you read 2 Kings 21, you see what happened to a king of Judah, who followed the sun and moon and stars, and God destroyed the nation of Judah because of it. This is what the Masonic Lodge is intimately involved in. They go on teaching, page 473, Albert Pike, *Morals and Dogma*, "The universal Soul of the World, . . . exercises its creative energy chiefly through the medium of the Sun, . . ." Page 474: "all through the great body of the world are disseminated portions of the Universal Soul, . . ." Page 393: "All soul is part of the Universal Soul, . . . The human soul is itself . . . a God within the mind, capable through its own power . . . of making itself immortal by the practice of the good, . . . Man descended from the elemental Forces . . . who fed on the body of the Pantheistic Deity creating the Universe . . . Death is the inseparable antecedent of life; the seed dies in order to produce the plant, . . . Hence the (significance) of the phallus, or . . . its inoffensive substitute, the obelisk, rising as an emblem of resurrection . . ."

Here you get into the Masonic teaching of nature worship, of Pantheism, that everything is part of the universal soul, that all men are part of this universal soul, and they can achieve immortality by creating this generating process of life, that we're going to see in a moment.

This concludes Side A. Please turn your cassette over for Side B.

Index 026: What you soon discover, as you get into Freemasonry, is that the god of Freemasonry, in nature worship, of the Universal Pantheistic All, underneath it all is the philosophy of the generating principle of life. I quote Albert Pike, *Morals and Dogma*, page 13: "The Sun is the ancient symbol of the life-giving . . . generative power of the Deity. . . . The Moon was the symbol of the passive capacity of nature to produce the female, of which the life-giving power and energy was the male. . . . The Master of Light and Life, the Sun and the Moon, are symbolized in every Lodge . . . The Sun and Moon," . . . "represent the two grand principles of all generations, the active and passive, the male and . . . female. The Sun represents the *14* actual light. He pours upon the Moon his . . . (impregnating) rays; both shed their light upon their offspring, the Blazing Star, (known as) . . . HORUS (within the Masonic Lodge), and the three form the great Equilateral Triangle, in the center of which is the omnific letter of the Kabalah, by which creation is said to have been effected."

Page 15: "In the East of the Lodge, over the Master, inclosed in . . . (the) triangle, is the Hebrew letter YOD (Y-O-D). In the English and American Lodges the Letter (capital) G is substituted for this, as the initial of the word GOD, . . . YOD is, in the Kabalah, the symbol of Unity, . . . To understand its mystic meanings, you must open the pages of the Sohar . . . and other kabalistic (occult) books, . . . it is the Creative Energy . . . represented as a point, and that point in the center of the Circle . . . the symbol of that unmanifested Deity, the Absolute, who has no name."

What am I saying? In all Masonic Lodges, you will see a triangle. In that triangle, representing the sun, the moon, and Horus, the shining star, you will see the letter G. You can drive by a Masonic Temple, and often times on top of the Masonic Temple is a big letter G. That represents their Masonic god. Now, who is that Masonic god, the capital G of which you see on Masonic Lodges?

For the kabalist, the sun and moon, emblems of the two divine sexes and the two creative forces. "In the Mysteries . . . (were) taught the division of the Universal Cause into . . . (the) Active and . . . Passive Cause, of which two, Osiris and Isis, the (heaven and earth) were symbols. . . . These two Divinities, . . . were commonly symbolized by the generative parts of man and woman; . . ."—this is page 401, Albert Pike—"These two Divinities, . . . were commonly symbolized by the generative parts of man and woman; to which, in remote ages, no idea of indecency was attached; . . . (the male and female sex organs), emblems of generation and production, and which, as such, appeared in the Mysteries. . . . the (Masonic) point within a circle, . . . (expresses) the . . . philosophical idea as to the Union of these two great Causes . . ." (They are male and female, of which the phallus, or male sex organ, is the generative organ.) *402* "Not only the Egyptians, . . . but every other people that conse-crate this symbol (of the Phallus), deem that they thereby do honor to the Active Force of the (universe) generation of all living things." The ancients—let me stop here.

Index 121: What the Masons teach, as the basis of their philosophy, is a natural religion of nature worship. In this nature worship, they see two great principles, male and female, represented by the sun and the moon in all Lodges. It is also represented in the Lodge by a point within a circle, the point being the male, the circle being the female.

Page 476, Albert Pike, quote: "the Egyptians pictured . . . Osiris, (who is the Sun in the Egyptian allegory), united with the Moon, (communicating) to her the seeds of fruitfulness which she poured upon the air, . . . the Sun or Osiris, when in union with Isis . . . the Moon, (concurs) with her in provok-ing everything that lives (in) generation." (Osiris, this generating principle, is the symbol of the eye in Masonry, known as, quote), "the All-Seeing Eye in our Lodges."

You have in Masonry this All-Seeing Eye. You're probably all carrying one with you on the back of your dollar bill. The one dollar bill has the Masonic symbol of the Egyptian pyramid. On top of it is the All-Seeing Eye. This is the Masonic symbol that was placed there by George Washington, Alexander Hamilton, and Ben Franklin, who were Masons, and you all have it on the back of your dollar bill. In Egyptian mythology, the pyramid is the building which Masons are seeking to finish. Overseeing that is this All-Seeing Eye, which is represented by the sun, or Osiris. Let me go on and we'll clear things up in just a moment—it gets worse.

I quote Albert Mackey, *Symbolism of Freemasonry*, page 353, and I might say before we do this, one of the main allegories that Freemasonry is based upon, you find it in all their books, the main allegory is that of Osiris and Isis, representing also the allegory of Hiram Abif. They are very similar. In the allegory of Osiris and Isis, which every Mason is taught, in the Egyptian legend of the third degree, Osiris, the chief deity, or sun god of Egypt, is said to have been treacherously slain by his brother Typhon. His body was cut into fourteen different pieces, and buried or concealed in as many different places. Isis, or nature, the wife of Osiris, in her search for the mutilated body of her husband, is supposed to have found all the parts but one, the organ, of generation. For this she made a factitious representation, which Masonic textbooks assure us was in the shape of a sculptured column, made of wood and surrounded by a circle at its base, representing the female generative organ, and this she set up in the temple of Isis, that divine honor might be paid to it. You have in Masonic Lodges and Temples this broken pillar, the point within a circle representing these sexual organs.

Mackey, *Symbolism of Freemasonry*, page 353, says, quote, "The point within a circle is derived from sun worship and is in reality of phallic origin." "The point within a circle"—this is Mackey, *Manual of the Lodge*, page 156—"The point within a circle is an interesting and important symbol in Freemasonry, but it has been debased in the interpretation of it in the modern lectures, and the sooner that interpretation is forgotten by the Masonic student, the better he will be. This symbol is really a symbol of sun worship and introduces us for the first time in Masonry to that symbol, known to the ancients, which was the worship of the phallus or male sex organ." Unquote.

Albert Mackey, *Symbolism of Freemasonry*, page 352: "The phallus, representation of the virile member, or the male sex organ, which was venerated as a religious symbol, has universally been held by the ancients. The Masonic point within a circle is undoubtedly of phallic origin."

Albert Mackey, *Manual of the Lodge*, page 56, "The phallus was an imitation of the male generative organ. The union of the phallus with the female, active or male principle in the passive or female principle." Now, I could go on. I have hundreds of pages of documentation. Let me explain what's going on.

Index 219: Simply put, the great god of Masonry is this all-pervasive nature worship, the Universal Soul, of which the two active parts are the male and female, which conceive to generate nature. When Masons claim to believe in immortality, what they are meaning is that immortality occurs through the generating principle of sexually bearing more children. The god which they worship, according to Albert Mackey and Albert Pike, is the symbol of the point within the circle, or the phallic symbol, ancient veneration of the male organ. You find this in India.

When Cal and I were in India, in Katmandu, Nepal, you see this on the Hindu Temple, on the Buddhist Temple, the symbol of the male sexual organ. This is why you find Albert Pike, on page 470, or 407, says, "(The ancients had their) religious initiation; (into the worship of the sun god, represented by Osiris), one of the principle ceremonies of which consisted in clothing the Initiate with the skin of (the) white lamb. And in this we see the origin of the apron of (the) white sheepskin, used (today) in (Free)Masonry." Now all Masons have what is a Masonic apron and when they go into the Masonic Lodge, they will put this apron on, and they wear this when they are in the Lodge. Albert Pike, when you get into his teaching, says that this is in order to cover the generative male organ, which is Osiris, the sun god, which is the great "G," the generative principle, the god which they worship. The flap in the "V," Pike says, represents the female parts and the Masons cover over their parts because that is what they venerate as their god, the generating principle of life.

A lot of Masons don't understand and this is why they conceal it to the Masons in the Blue Lodge. Albert Pike says you are consciously misled and only a few understand what is going on. What is going on is that you are involved in ancient sun worship, you are involved in Pantheism, in Dualism, in Gnosticism, in Astrology, in Numerology, worshiping the generative principle of life, which is the male sex organ. Albert Pike, before he died, finally addressed, on July 14th, 1889, gave his final instructions to the twenty-three supreme councils of the world.

Let me quote Albert Pike, the leading authority as to what is going on. I quote, "That which we must say to the crowd is, 'We worship a God and it is the God that one adores without superstition.' To you sovereign grand inspectors general, we say this, that you may repeat it to the brethren of the 32nd, to the 31st, and to the 30th degrees, 'The Masonic religion should be, by all of its initiates of the high degrees, maintained in the purity of the Luciferian Doctrine. Yes, Lucifer is God, the God we worship, and the pure philosophic religion is the belief in Lucifer.'" Unquote.

To sum up, my friends, and I have for eighteen months, gone through every piece of authoritative work of Freemasonry, I have hundreds and hundreds of pages of documentation, to simply sum it up, my friends, the religion of Freemasonry is this, that if one could take all of the idolatrous religions of the world, combine it with the blasphemous philosophies of the Occult, mix it with the pagan teachings of the non-Christian cults, blend in the darkness of Satan, what you would come up with, my friends, is Freemasonry and the Masonic Lodge.

Now, I understand tonight that most Masons do not understand this. Most Masons are in it today out of peer pressure or because they think they're in it for business reasons, but this is the religion of Masonry. Let me skip over and as we conclude look at what Masonry says about the Bible and Jesus Christ, for this is all important.

What place does the Bible have in Freemasonry? I might just put this up to show you what is going on. First of all, you have three symbols in the Lodge. Masons will tell me, "But we've got the Bible on our altar, and on top of the Bible are two symbols, the compass and the square."

Let me read for you what Albert Pike, in *Morals and Dogma*, says in the 32nd degree, concerning the square and the compass, page 851, *Morals and Dogma:* "Returning now to the degrees of Blue Masonry," and remember, this is not taught until the 32nd degree, *850* "(Returning) now, . . . to the Degrees of . . . Blue Masonry (the first three degrees), and for your last lesson, receive the explanation of . . . (the) Symbols. The SQUARE, . . . is a natural and appropriate Symbol of (the) Earth . . . The COMPASS is a . . . (equal and natural) . . . Symbol of the Heavens, . . . The Heavens and . . . Earth were personified as Deities, . . . *851* The EARTH, therefore, the great PRODUCER, . . . (is) represented as . . . female, . . . the procreative and generative (agent), . . . (was) regarded as male; . . . the (generator impregnates) the Earth and (causes) it to produce. . . . The Compass, therefore, is the . . . Symbol of the Creative Deity, and the Square (is) the productive Earth or Universe."

You find this symbol on Masonic Lodges, of the square and compass with the letter G. Some Masons will even wear it on their lapel. When you get to the 32nd degree, Albert Pike says that this means that the square is the female being receptive to the male compass coming down upon her, and the G in the center is the generative principle, the god of Masonry, the male sex organ. You see, this is why females cannot be members of the Masonic Lodge. Now, they have created the Eastern Star and Rainbow Girls, but women cannot be Masons, for the simple reason that they are not the generating power of the universe, which the Masons have set themselves up in this humanistic philosophy, deifying man and deifying his generative organ, Albert Pike, page 851.

Index 355:   Well, what about the Bible? I quote Albert Pike, *Morals and Dogma*, page 11, "The Holy Bible, Square, and Compasses, are not only styled the Great Lights in Masonry, but they are also technically called the Furniture of the Lodge; . . . The Bible is an indispensable part of the furniture of a Christian Lodge, only because it is the sacred book of the Christian . . . The Hebrew Pentateuch in a Hebrew Lodge, and the Koran in a (Moslem Lodge, these) belong on the Altar; . . . The obligation of the candidate is (to always) be taken on the sacred book or books of his (own) religion, . . ." Page 17, quote: "The Holy Scriptures (were) an entirely modern addition to the . . . (Lodge), like the terrestrial and celestial globes on the columns . . . (which you see in the Masonic Lodge). Thus the ancient symbol has been denaturalized by (incongruitous) additions, . . ."

Albert Pike, the leading authority, says that the Bible is simply a piece of furniture in the Lodge, that it's actually a modern addition, which shouldn't even be there. Let me go further. Albert Pike, *Morals and Dogma*, page 744, I quote, "The Bible, with all the allegories it contains, expresses, in an incomplete and veiled manner only, the religious science of the Hebrews. The doctrine of Moses and the Prophets, identical at bottom with that of the Ancient (Egyptian Mysteries), also had its outward meaning and its veils. The Hebrew books were written only to recall to memory the traditions; and they were written in Symbols unintelligible to the Profane. *745* The Pentateuch and the prophetic poems were merely elementary books of doctrine, morals, (and) liturgy; and the true secret and traditional philosophy was only written afterward, under veils still less transparent. Thus was a second Bible born, (the New Testament), unknown to, or rather uncomprehended by, . . . Christians; a collection, . . . of monstrous absurdities; . . ." Unquote.

So, according to Albert Pike, the leading Masonic authority, he says the Old Testament is nothing but Egyptian Mysteries and the New Testament is a monstrous absurdity. If you're a Christian and you're a Mason, you'd better listen to what Albert Pike says. He says it's a piece of furniture that doesn't even belong there and is a monstrous absurdity.

Well, what does he say about Jesus Christ, and the cross? I quote Albert Pike, *Morals and Dogma*, page 525, quote, "(Masonry) reverences all the great reformers. It sees in Moses, in Confucius, (in) Zoroaster, (in Buddha), in Jesus, in the Arabian Iconoclast, Great Teachers of Morality, and Eminent Reformers, . . . *524* (Masonry does) . . . not tell the sincere Christian that Jesus of Nazareth was but a man like us, or His history but the unreal revival of an older legend. Masonry, . . . belongs to all time; of no one religion, . . ." Jesus is a man, who is not God Incarnate, he is simply a moral reformer, along with Buddha, Zoroaster, Confucius, and everybody else. The history of Masonry, page 540, quote, "The history of Masonry is the history of Philosophy. . . . None can deny that Christ taught a lofty morality. . . . The early Christians followed in His footsteps. . . . *541* Their sole object was to make men better, by bringing them back to a simple worship, of which universal morality was (its) basis; . . ."

The whole basis of Masonry, when you get into it, was a morality, a system of morality, to achieve your own salvation. I was speaking recently to one of the leading heads of the Shrine, here in the Twin Cities. I finally asked him, I said "Sir, if you were to stand before God tonight and He should ask you, 'Why should I let you into my heaven,' " I said, "What would you say to Him?" He put his head down, and for twenty seconds he thought, and then he looked up at me, and he said, "Well, I guess I would have to tell Him I was a good Mason." You see, they have no place for Jesus Christ, they have no place for God's revelation, the Bible.

What about the cross? Albert Pike, page 290, "The Cross has been a sacred symbol from the earliest Antiquity. It is found upon all the enduring monuments of the world, in Egypt, in Assyria, in (India), in Persia, and on the Buddhist towers . . . Buddha was said to have died upon (one). . . . Krishna (of India, also died upon one). . . . To us therefore (the cross) is (merely a) symbol of Life- . . . *291* (Its great secret is found in) Nature, (and) that of universal regeneration." Pike, page 483, "Our (Masonic) ceilings (in the Temple) still glitter with the greater and lesser luminaries of the Heavens, and our lights, in their number and arrangements, (all) have (astrological reference). In all churches and chapels, . . . in all Pagan temples and pagodas, the Altar is in the East; . . . (I'm thankful this church has its Altar in the west) "Even the cross"— listen to this—"Even the cross . . . (was a symbol of astrology and had its origin in the Zodiac)."

Index 453: Let me quote for you Manley Hall, in his book, *Lost Keys of Freemasonry*—he is a 33rd degree honorary Mason— page 54, he says, quote, "The true disciple of Ancient Masonry has given up"—now listen to this—"The true disciple of Ancient Masonry has given up forever the worship of personalities. With his greater insight, he realizes that all forms of their position in the material affairs are of no importance to him, compared to the life which is evolving within. The true Mason realizes that behind every diverse form, there is one connected life principle, the spark of God in all living things: it's nature worship, Pantheism. The true Mason is not creed bound. He realizes with the divine illumination of his Lodge, that as a Mason, his religion must be universal. Christ, Buddha, or Mohammed, the name means little, for he recognizes only the life he worships at every shrine. He bows before altar, whether in temple, mosque, cathedral, or pagoda. No true Mason can be narrow, for his Lodge is the divine expression of all broadness." Unquote.

He says the name of Christ is meaningless. It doesn't matter whether it's Buddha, Christ, Mohammed. They're all the same. How different from what God has revealed to us.

In Acts 4:12 we read, "There is no other name given among men, whereby we must be saved, but that of Jesus Christ." John 1:12 says, "But as many as received Him, to them He gave the right to become children of God, even to those who believe on His name." Jesus said, "I am the way, the truth, and the life. No man comes unto the Father but by me." But they both, quote, "No true Mason can be narrow, for his Lodge is a divine expression of all broadness."

Turn with me to Matthew, chapter 7, to see what Jesus says about that. Matthew 7:13, 14: "Enter by the narrow gate, for the gate is wide and the way is broad, that leads to destruction, and many are those who enter by it, for the gate is small and the way is narrow that leads to life, and few are those who find it." They boast in their broadness, but Jesus said, "Broad is the way that leads to destruction. Narrow is the way." Proverbs 14, turn there with me, Proverbs 14:12: "There is a way which seems right to man, but its end is the way of death." Verse 15: "The naive believes everything, but the prudent man considers his ways." A wise man is cautious and turns from evil.

They say universal morality will achieve salvation. Turn to Titus, chapter 3, Titus 3:4–7: "But when the kindness of God, our Savior, and His love for mankind appeared, He saved us, not on the basis of deeds which we have done in righteousness, but according to His mercy, by the washing of regeneration, and by renewing by the Holy Spirit, which He poured out richly upon us through Jesus Christ our Savior;"

They say the Bible is a monstrous absurdity. Two Timothy 3:16 says, "All scripture was given by inspiration of God, and is profitable for reproof, for correction, for training in righteousness."

My friends, if you are a Mason, here tonight, I understand that you do not know what is going on. Albert Pike says you have been misled, consciously, because they do not want you to understand the pagan, idolatrous practice that you are following. But if you are a Mason tonight, I conclude with 2 Corinthians, chapter 6, and you must listen to it. Two Corinthians 6, beginning with verse 14: "Do not be bound together with unbelievers, for what partnership have righteousness and lawlessness? Or what fellowship has light with darkness? Or what harmony has Christ with Satan? Or what has a believer in common with an unbeliever? Or what agreement has the Temple of God with idols? For we are the Temple of the living God, just as God said: 'I will dwell in them and walk among them, and I will be their God, and they shall be my people. Therefore, come out from their midst, and be separate,' says the Lord, 'and do not touch what is unclean; and I will welcome you, and I will be a Father to you, and you shall be my sons and daughters,' saith the Lord Almighty."

The word of God, which was given by inspiration of God, says to all Masons tonight, "You have no business being in a Masonic Lodge, if you claim the name of Jesus Christ. If He is your Lord and Savior, you have no business in a pagan Lodge, involved in some of the most pagan, idolatrous practice anybody can imagine."

I have given this tonight, not to attack anyone; if you're a Mason here tonight, please understand that. As a minister of the Gospel though, we are commanded in the Old Testament to speak prophetically and to warn people from their ways. My friends, the Masonic Lodge is not of God. It condemns itself. It claims to be the universal religion, it says that you do not need Jesus Christ, it says the Bible is a monstrous absurdity, it has set man up as the Supreme God, involved in the vulgar worship of the male organ; it is the one that's involved in sun worship and astrology.

If you turn to Exodus 20, we'll see what God says about this. Exodus 20:3,4: "You shall have no other gods before me. You shall not make for yourself an idol, or any likeness of what is in heaven above, or on the earth beneath, or under the water. You shall not worship them or serve them, for I the Lord your God am a jealous God, visiting the iniquity of the fathers unto the children unto the third and fourth generations of those who hate me;"

Look at Exodus, chapter 23, Exodus 23, verse 24: "You shall not worship their gods nor serve them, nor do according to their deeds, but you shall utterly overthrow them and break their sacred pillars in pieces." Verse 32: "You shall make no covenant with them, or with their gods. They shall not live in your land, lest they make you sin against me. For if you serve their gods, it will surely be a snare to you."

Index 580: Heavenly Father, we come before you tonight and we recognize you alone as the Sovereign. You are a personal God. You are a personal God who loves us, who made us. You are not a Pantheistic All. You are not a Generating Principle. You are not Nature. You alone are the Sovereign, over all of nature. You alone are the King of Kings and the Lord of Lords. You alone are worthy of worship. Your revelation, the Bible, is not a monstrous absurdity, as the Masons claim; but it is your inspired word, by which you have revealed to us the truth of how we can know you and have light. The name of Jesus Christ is not meaningless. There is no other name given among men, whereby we must be saved, but that of Jesus Christ. We recognize Jesus Christ tonight, alone as our Lord and Savior. He alone is the Light of the world, not the sun, not the moon, not the stars, not the pagan and idolatrous gods of Masonry. Oh Lord, I pray tonight for any person here, who may have taken those oaths, sealed himself into a pagan, idolatrous organization; that your heart, your Holy Spirit will convict his heart tonight, that he will understand that if he is a Christian, he must come out of the Masonic Lodge, and repent of that sin. If there are any Masons here tonight and they do not know you, I pray that tonight, that they will see that a humanistic generating principle will never save anyone. Good works cannot achieve it in a Masonic Lodge, but salvation comes because of your grace, through faith alone in Jesus Christ. Oh Lord, I pray that you will teach us tonight. Open our hearts and minds and give us understanding. Oh Lord, I pray, if I have ever said anything tonight, if I do not have love in my voice, Oh God, forgive me. I have sought to speak clearly the truth of that which you have revealed. You commanded us to test all things by your word, and hold fast to that which is true and good. Oh God, may we have nothing to do with pagan idols, pagan worship, and pagan religion. May we turn back from that and say, "Not I, but Christ." He alone is worthy. In Jesus precious and holy name, we love you tonight, God Incarnate, second person of the Trinity, our source of light alone. We love you. In Jesus precious name, Amen.

Index 721: *For more information concerning Ron Carlson's Ministry, or for our free catalogue of other tapes, write to us. Our address is: Liberation Tapes, P.O. Box 6044, Lubbock, Texas 79413.*

Appendix B
Selected Pages
from Pike's
Morals and Dogma

MORALS AND DOGMA

OF THE

ANCIENT AND ACCEPTED SCOTTISH RITE

OF

FREEMASONRY

PREPARED FOR THE

SUPREME COUNCIL OF THE THIRTY-THIRD DEGREE,

FOR THE

SOUTHERN JURISDICTION OF THE UNITED STATES,

AND

PUBLISHED BY ITS AUTHORITY.

CHARLESTON.
A∴ M∴ 5641

Manufactured by
L. H. Jenkins, Richmond, Va.
March, 1914

PREFACE.

THE following work has been prepared by authority of the Supreme Council of the Thirty-third Degree, for the Southern Jurisdiction of the United States, by the Grand Commander, and is now published by its direction. It contains the Lectures of the Ancient and Accepted Scottish Rite in that jurisdiction, and is specially intended to be read and studied by the Brethren of that obedience, in connection with the Rituals of the Degrees. It is hoped and expected that each will furnish himself with a copy, and make himself familiar with it; for which purpose, as the cost of the work consists entirely in the printing and binding, it will be furnished at a price as moderate as possible. No *individual* will receive pecuniary profit from it, except the agents for its sale.

It has been copyrighted, to prevent its republication elsewhere, and the copyright, like those of all the other works prepared for the Supreme Council, has been assigned to Trustees for that Body. Whatever profits may accrue from it will be devoted to purposes of charity.

The Brethren of the Rite in the United States and Canada will be afforded the opportunity to purchase it, nor is it *forbidden* that other Masons shall; but they will not be solicited to do so.

In preparing this work, the Grand Commander has been about equally Author and Compiler; since he has extracted quite half its contents from the works of the best writers and most philosophic or eloquent thinkers. Perhaps it would have been better and more acceptable, if he had extracted more and written less.

Still, perhaps half of it is his own; and, in incorporating here

the thoughts and words of others, he has continually changed
and added to the language, often intermingling, in the same sentences, his own words with theirs. It not being intended for the
world at large, he has felt at liberty to make, from all accessible
sources, a Compendium of the Morals and Dogma of the Rite, to
re-mould sentences, change and add to words and phrases, combine them with his own, and use them as if they *were* his own,
to be dealt with at his pleasure and so availed of as to ·make the
whole most valuable for the purposes intended. He claims, therefore, little of the merit of authorship, and has not cared to distinguish his own from that which he has taken from other sources,
being quite willing that every portion of the book, in turn, may
be regarded as borrowed from some old and better writer.

The teachings of these Readings are not sacramental, so far as
they go beyond the realm of Morality into those of other domains
of Thought and Truth. The Ancient and Accepted Scottish Rite
uses the word "Dogma" in its true sense, of *doctrine,* or *teaching;*
and is not *dogmatic* in the odious sense of that term. Every one
is entirely free to reject and dissent from whatsoever herein may
seem to him to be untrue or unsound. It is only required of him
that he shall weigh what is taught, and give it fair hearing and
unprejudiced judgment. Of course, the ancient theosophic and
philosophic speculations are not embodied as part of the *doctrines*
of the Rite; but because it is of interest and profit to know what
the Ancient Intellect thought upon these subjects, and because
nothing so conclusively proves the radical difference between our
human and the animal nature, as the capacity of the human
mind to entertain such speculations in regard to itself and the
Deity. But as to these opinions themselves, we may say, in the
words of the learned Canonist, Ludovicus Gomez: " *Opiniones
secundùm varietatem temporum senescant et intermoriantur,
aliæque diversæ vel prioribus contrariæ renascantur et deinde
pubescant.*"

into seven steps or stages, to each of which was a gate, and at the summit an eighth one, that of the fixed stars. The symbol was the same as that of the seven stages of Borsippa, the Pyramid of vitrified brick, near Babylon, built of seven stages, and each of a different color. In the Mithraic ceremonies, the candidate went through seven stages of initiation, passing through many fearful trials—and of these the high ladder with seven rounds or steps was the symbol.

You see the Lodge, its details and ornaments, by its Lights. You have already heard what these Lights, the greater and lesser, are said to be, and how they are spoken of by our Brethren of the York Rite.

The *Holy Bible, Square, and Compasses,* are not only styled the Great Lights in Masonry, but they are also technically called the *Furniture* of the Lodge; and, as you have seen, it is held that there is no Lodge without them. This has sometimes been made a pretext for excluding Jews from our Lodges, because they cannot regard the New Testament as a holy book. The Bible is an indispensable part of the furniture of a *Christian* Lodge, only because it is the sacred book of the Christian religion. The Hebrew Pentateuch in a Hebrew Lodge, and the Koran in a Mohammedan one, belong on the Altar; and one of these, and the Square and Compass, properly understood, are the Great Lights by which a Mason must walk and work.

The obligation of the candidate is always to be taken on the sacred book or books of his religion, that he may deem it more solemn and binding; and therefore it was that you were asked of what religion you were. We have no other concern with your religious creed.

The Square is a right angle, formed by two right lines. It is adapted only to a plane surface, and belongs only to geometry, earth-measurement, that trigonometry which deals only with planes, and with the earth, which the ancients supposed to be a plane. The Compass describes circles, and deals with spherical trigonometry, the science of the spheres and heavens. The former, therefore, is an emblem of what concerns the earth and the body; the latter of what concerns the heavens and the soul. Yet the Compass is also used in plane trigonometry, as in erecting perpendiculars; and, therefore, you are reminded that, although in this Degree both points of the Compass are under the Square, and

Rite is not told. Nor does the Moon in any sense rule the night with regularity.

The Sun is the ancient symbol of the life-giving and generative power of the Deity. To the ancients, light was the cause of life; and God was the source from which all light flowed; the *essence* of Light, the *Invisible* Fire, developed as Flame *manifested* as light and splendor. The Sun was His manifestation and visible image; and the Sabæans worshipping the Light—God, *seemed* to worship the Sun, in whom they saw the manifestation of the Deity.

The Moon was the symbol of the passive capacity of nature to produce, the female, of which the life-giving power and energy was the male. It was the symbol of Isis, Astarte, and Artemis, or Diana. The *"Master of Life"* was the Supreme Deity, above both, and manifested through both; Zeus, the Son of Saturn, become King of the Gods; Horus, son of Osiris and Isis, become the Master of Life; Dionusos or Bacchus, like Mithras, become the author of Light and Life and Truth.

*   *   *   *   *   *

The Master of Light and Life, the Sun and the Moon, are symbolized in every Lodge by the Master and Wardens: and this makes it the duty of the Master to dispense light to the Brethren, by himself, and through the Wardens, who are his ministers.

"Thy sun," says ISAIAH to Jerusalem, "shall no more go down, neither shall thy moon withdraw itself; for the LORD shall be thine everlasting light, and the days of thy mourning shall be ended. Thy people also shall be all righteous; they shall inherit the land forever." Such is the type of a free people.

Our northern ancestors worshipped this tri-une Deity; ODIN, the Almighty FATHER; FREA, his wife, emblem of universal matter; and THOR, his son, the mediator. But above all these was the Supreme God, " the author of everything that existeth, the Eternal, the Ancient, the Living and Awful Being, the Searcher into concealed things, the Being that never changeth." In the Temple of Eleusis (a sanctuary lighted only by a window in the roof, and representing the Universe), the images of the Sun, Moon, and Mercury, were represented.

"The Sun and Moon," says the learned Bro.·. DELAUNAY, " represent the two grand principles of all generations, the active and passive, the male and the female. The Sun represents the actual light. He pours upon the Moon his fecundating rays; both shed their light upon their offspring, the Blazing Star, or HORUS, and the three form the great Equilateral Triangle, in the centre of which is the omnific letter of the Kabalah, by which creation is said to have been effected."

The ORNAMENTS of a Lodge are said to be "the Mosaic Pavement, the Indented Tessel, and the Blazing Star." The Mosaic Pavement, chequered in squares or lozenges, is said to represent the ground-floor of King Solomon's Temple; and the Indented Tessel "that beautiful tesselated border which surrounded it." The Blazing Star in the centre is said to be "an emblem of Divine Providence, and commemorative of the star which appeared to guide the wise men of the East to the place of our Saviour's nativity." But "there was no stone seen" within the Temple. The walls were covered with planks of cedar, and the floor was covered with planks of fir. There is no evidence that there was such a pavement or floor in the Temple, or such a bordering. In England, anciently, the Tracing-Board was surrounded with an indented border; and it is only in America that such a border is put around the Mosaic pavement. The tesseræ, indeed, are the squares or lozenges of the pavement. In England, also, "the indented or denticulated border" is called "tesselated," because it has four "tassels," said to represent Temperance, Fortitude, Prudence, and Justice. It was termed the Indented Trassel; but this is a misuse of words. It is a *tesserated* pavement, with an indented border round it.

The pavement, alternately black and white, symbolizes, whether so intended or not, the Good and Evil Principles of the Egyptian and Persian creed. It is the warfare of Michael and Satan, of the Gods and Titans, of Balder and Lok; between light and shadow, which is darkness; Day and Night; Freedom and Despotism; Religious Liberty and the Arbitrary Dogmas of a Church that thinks for its votaries, and whose Pontiff claims to be infallible, and the decretals of its Councils to constitute a gospel.

The edges of this pavement, if in lozenges, will necessarily be indented or denticulated, toothed like a saw; and to complete and finish it a bordering is necessary. It is completed by tassels as ornaments at the corners. If these and the bordering have any symbolic meaning, it is fanciful and arbitrary.

To find in the BLAZING STAR of five points an allusion to the

Divine Providence, is also fanciful; and to make it commemorative
of the Star that is said to have guided the Magi, is to give it a
meaning comparatively modern. Originally it represented SIRIUS,
or the Dog-star, the forerunner of the inundation of the Nile; the
God ANUBIS, companion of ISIS in her search for the body of
OSIRIS, her brother and husband. Then it became the image of
HORUS, the son of OSIRIS, himself symbolized also by the Sun,
the author of the Seasons, and the God of Time; Son of ISIS, who
was the universal nature, himself the primitive matter, inexhaustible source of Life, spark of uncreated fire, universal seed of all
beings. It was HERMES, also, the Master of Learning, whose
name in Greek is that of the God Mercury. It became the sacred
and potent sign or character of the Magi, the PENTALPHA, and is
the significant emblem of Liberty and Freedom, blazing with a
steady radiance amid the weltering elements of good and evil of
Revolutions, and promising serene skies and fertile seasons to the
nations, after the storms of change and tumult.

In the East of the Lodge, over the Master, inclosed in a triangle, is the Hebrew letter YŌD [' or ʰʰ]. In the English and
American Lodges the Letter G.'. is substituted for this, as the
initial of the word GOD, with as little reason as if the letter D.,
initial of DIEU, were used in French Lodges instead of the proper
letter. YŌD is, in the Kabalah, the symbol of Unity, of the
Supreme Deity, the first letter of the Holy Name; and also a
symbol of the Great Kabalistic Triads. To understand its mystic
meanings, you must open the pages of the Sohar and Siphra de
Zeniutha, and other kabalistic books, and ponder deeply on their
meaning. It must suffice to say, that it is the Creative Energy of
the Deity, is represented as a *point,* and that point in the centre of
the *Circle* of immensity. It is to us in this Degree, the symbol of
that unmanifested Deity, the Absolute, who has no name.

Our French Brethren place this letter YŌD in the centre of the
Blazing Star. And in the old Lectures, our ancient English
Brethren said, "The Blazing Star or Glory in the centre refers
us to that grand luminary, the Sun, which enlightens the earth,
and by its genial influence dispenses blessings to mankind." They
called it also in the same lectures, an emblem of PRUDENCE. The
word *Prudentia* means, in its original and fullest signification,
Foresight; and, accordingly, the Blazing Star has been regarded
as an emblem of Omniscience, or the All-seeing Eye, which to the

It would be a waste of time to comment upon this. Some writers have imagined that the parallel lines represent the Tropics of Cancer and Capricorn, which the Sun alternately touches upon at the Summer and Winter solstices. But the tropics are not perpendicular lines, and the idea is merely fanciful. If the parallel lines ever belonged to the ancient symbol, they had some more recondite and more *fruitful* meaning. They probably had the same meaning as the twin columns Jachin and Boaz. That meaning is not for the Apprentice. The adept may find it in the Kabalah. The JUSTICE and MERCY of God are in equilibrium, and the result is HARMONY, because a Single and Perfect Wisdom presides over both.

The Holy Scriptures are an entirely modern addition to the symbol, like the terrestrial and celestial globes on the columns of the portico. Thus the ancient symbol has been denaturalized by incongruous additions, like that of Isis weeping over the broken column containing the remains of Osiris at Byblos.

*   *   *   *   *   *

Masonry has its decalogue, which is a law to its Initiates. These are its Ten Commandments:

I. ⊕∴ God is the Eternal, Omnipotent, Immutable WISDOM and Supreme INTELLIGENCE and Exhaustless LOVE.
Thou shalt adore, revere, and love Him!
Thou shalt honor Him by practising the virtues!

II. O∴ Thy religion shall be, to do good because it is a pleasure to thee, and not merely because it is a duty.
That thou mayest become the friend of the wise man, thou shalt obey his precepts!
Thy soul is immortal! Thou shalt do nothing to degrade it!

III. ⊕∴ Thou shalt unceasingly war against vice!
Thou shalt not do unto others that which thou wouldst not wish them to do unto thee!
Thou shalt be submissive to thy fortunes, and keep burning the light of wisdom!

IV. O∴ Thou shalt honor thy parents!
Thou shalt pay respect and homage to the aged!
Thou shalt instruct the young!
Thou shalt protect and defend infancy and innocence!

V. ⊕∴ Thou shalt cherish thy wife and thy children!
Thou shalt love thy country, and obey its laws!

II.

THE FELLOW-CRAFT.

In the Ancient Orient, all religion was more or less a mystery and there was no divorce from it of philosophy. The popular theology, taking the multitude of allegories and symbols for realities, degenerated into a worship of the celestial luminaries, of imaginary Deities with human feelings, passions, appetites, and lusts, of idols, stones, animals, reptiles. The Onion was sacred to the Egyptians, because its different layers were a symbol of the concentric heavenly spheres. Of course the popular religion could not satisfy the deeper longings and thoughts, the loftier aspirations of the Spirit, or the logic of reason. The first, therefore, was taught to the initiated in the Mysteries. There, also, it was taught by symbols The vagueness of symbolism, capable of many interpretations, reached what the palpable and conventional creed could not. Its indefiniteness acknowledged the abstruseness of the subject: it treated that mysterious subject mystically: it endeavored to illustrate what it could not explain; to excite an appropriate *feeling*, if it could not develop an adequate *idea;* and to make the image a mere subordinate conveyance for the conception, which itself never became obvious or familiar.

Thus the knowledge now imparted by books and letters, was of old conveyed by symbols; and the priests invented or perpetuated a display of rites and exhibitions, which were not only more attractive to the eye than words, but often more suggestive and more pregnant with meaning to the mind.

Masonry, successor of the Mysteries, still follows the ancient manner of teaching. Her ceremonies are like the ancient mystic shows,—not the reading of an essay, but the opening of a problem, requiring research, and constituting philosophy the arch-expounder. Her symbols are the instruction she gives. The lectures are endeavors, often partial and one-sided, to interpret these symbols. He who would become an accomplished Mason must not be content merely to hear, or even to understand, the lectures; he

22

must, aided by them, and they having, as it were, marked out the way for him, study, interpret, and develop these symbols for himself.

*   *   *   *   *   *   *   *

Though Masonry is identical with the ancient Mysteries, it is so only in this qualified sense: that it presents but an imperfect image of their brilliancy, the ruins only of their grandeur, and a system that has experienced progressive alterations, the fruits of social events, political circumstances, and the ambitious imbecility of its improvers. After leaving Egypt, the Mysteries were modified by the habits of the different nations among whom they were introduced, and especially by the religious systems of the countries into which they were transplanted. To maintain the established government, laws, and religion, was the obligation of the Initiate everywhere; and everywhere they were the heritage of the priests, who were nowhere willing to make the common people co-proprietors with themselves of philosophical truth.

Masonry is not the Coliseum in ruins. It is rather a Roman palace of the middle ages, disfigured by modern architectural improvements, yet built on a Cyclopæan foundation laid by the Etruscans, and with many a stone of the superstructure taken from dwellings and temples of the age of Hadrian and Antoninus.

Christianity taught the doctrine of FRATERNITY; but repudiated that of political EQUALITY, by continually inculcating obedience to Cæsar, and to those lawfully in authority. Masonry was the first apostle of EQUALITY. In the Monastery there is *fraternity* and *equality*, but no *liberty*. Masonry added that also, and claimed for man the three-fold heritage, LIBERTY, EQUALITY, and FRATERNITY.

It was but a development of the original purpose of the Mysteries, which was to teach men to know and practice their duties to themselves and their fellows, the great practical end of all philosophy and all knowledge.

Truths are the springs from which duties flow; and it is but a few hundred years since a new Truth began to be distinctly seen; that MAN IS SUPREME OVER INSTITUTIONS, AND NOT THEY OVER HIM. Man has *natural* empire over *all* institutions. They are for him, according to his development; not he for them. This seems to us a very simple statement, one to which all men, everywhere, ought to assent. But once it was a great new Truth,—not

III.

THE MASTER.

*   *   *   *   *   *

To understand literally the symbols and allegories of Oriental books as to ante-historical matters, is willfully to close our eyes against the Light. To translate the symbols into the trivial and commonplace, is the blundering of mediocrity.

All religious expression is symbolism; since we can *describe* only what we *see,* and the true objects of religion are THE SEEN. The earliest instruments of education were symbols; and they and all other religious forms differed and still differ according to external circumstances and imagery, and according to differences of knowledge and mental cultivation. All language is symbolic, so far as it is applied to mental and spiritual phenomena and action. All *words* have, primarily, a *material* sense, however they may afterward get, for the ignorant, a spiritual *non-*sense. "To retract," for example, is to *draw back,* and when applied to a *statement,* is symbolic, as much so as a picture of an arm drawn back, to express the same thing, would be. The very word *"spirit"* means *"breath,"* from the Latin verb *spiro, breathe.*

To present a visible symbol to the eye of another, is not necessarily to inform him of the meaning which that symbol has to you. Hence the philosopher soon superadded to the symbols explanations addressed to the ear, susceptible of more precision, but less effective and impressive than the painted or sculptured forms which he endeavored to explain. Out of these explanations grew by degrees a variety of narrations, whose true object and meaning were gradually forgotten, or lost in contradictions and incongruities. And when these were abandoned, and Philosophy resorted to definitions and formulas, its language was but a more complicated symbolism, attempting in the dark to grapple with and picture ideas impossible to be expressed. For as with the visible symbol, so with the word: to utter it to you does not inform you of the *exact* meaning which it has to *me;* and thus religion and philosophy became to a great extent disputes as to the meaning of words. The most abstract expression for Deity, which language can supply, is but a *sign* or *symbol* for an object beyond our comprehension, and not more truthful and adequate than the images of Osiris and Vishnu, or their names, except as being less sensuous and explicit. We avoid sensuousness, only by .resorting to simple negation. We come at last to define spirit by saying that it is not matter. Spirit is—spirit.

A single example of the symbolism of *words* will indicate to you one branch of Masonic study. We find in the English Rite this phrase: "I will always *hail*, ever conceal, and never reveal;" and in the Catechism, these:

Q.·. *"I hail."*

A.·. *"I conceal;"*

and ignorance, misunderstanding the word *"hail,"* has interpolated the phrase, "From whence do you *hail?"*

But the word is really *"hele,"* from the Anglo-Saxon verb Þelan, *helan,* to *cover, hide,* or *conceal.* And this word is rendered by the Latin verb *tegere,* to *cover* or *roof over.* "That ye fro me no thynge woll hele," says Gower. "They *hele* fro me no priuyte," says the Romaunt of the Rose. "To *heal* a house," is a common phrase in Sussex; and in the west of England, he that covers a house with slates is called a *Healer.* Wherefore, to *"heal"* means the same thing as to *"tile,"*—itself symbolic, as meaning, primarily, to *cover* a house with *tiles,*—and means to *cover, hide,* or *conceal.* Thus language too is symbolism, and words are as much misunderstood and misused as more material symbols are.

Symbolism tended continually to become more complicated; and all the powers of Heaven were reproduced on earth, until a web of fiction and allegory was woven, partly by art and partly by the ignorance of error, which the wit of man, with his limited means of explanation, will never unravel. Even the Hebrew Theism became involved in symbolism and image-worship, borrowed probably from an older creed and remote regions of Asia,—the worship of the Great Semitic Nature-God Al or Els and its symbolical representations of Jehovah Himself were not even confined to poetical or illustrative language. The priests were monotheists: the people idolaters.

There are dangers inseparable from symbolism, which afford an impressive lesson in regard to the similar risks attendant on the use of language. The imagination, called in to assist the reason, usurps its place or leaves its ally helplessly entangled in its web. Names which stand for things are confounded with them; the means are mistaken for the end; the instrument of interpretation for the object; and thus symbols come to usurp an independent character as truths and persons. Though perhaps a necessary path, they were a dangerous one by which to approach the Deity; in which many, says PLUTARCH, "mistaking the sign for the thing signified, fell into a ridiculous superstition; while others, in avoiding one extreme, plunged into the no less hideous gulf of irreligion and impiety."

It is through the Mysteries, CICERO says, that we have learned the first principles of life; wherefore the term "initiation" is used with good reason; and they not only teach us to live more happily and agreeably, but they soften the pains of death by the hope of a better life hereafter.

The Mysteries were a Sacred Drama, exhibiting some legend significant of nature's changes, of the visible Universe in which the Divinity is revealed, and whose import was in many respects as open to the Pagan as to the Christian. Nature is the great Teacher of man; for it is the Revelation of God. It neither dogmatizes nor attempts to tyrannize by compelling to a particular creed or special interpretation. It presents its symbols to us, and adds nothing by way of explanation. It is the text without the commentary; and, as we well know, it is chiefly the commentary and gloss that lead to error and heresy and persecution. The earliest instructors of mankind not only adopted the lessons of Nature, but as far as possible adhered to her method of imparting them. In the Mysteries, beyond the current traditions or sacred and enigmatic recitals of the Temples, few explanations were given to the spectators, who were left, as in the school of nature, to make inferences for themselves. No other method could have suited every degree of cultivation and capacity. To employ nature's universal symbolism instead of the technicalities of language, rewards the humblest inquirer, and discloses its secrets to every one in proportion to his preparatory training and his power to comprehend them. If their philosophical meaning was above the comprehension of some, their moral and political meanings are within the reach of all.

These mystic shows and performances were not the reading of a lecture, but the opening of a problem. Requiring research, they were calculated to arouse the dormant intellect. They implied no hostility to Philosophy, because Philosophy is the great expounder of symbolism; although its ancient interpretations were often ill-founded and incorrect. The alteration from symbol to dogma is fatal to beauty of expression, and leads to intolerance and assured infallibility.

*   *   *   *   *   *

If, in teaching the great doctrine of the divine nature of the Soul, and in striving to explain its longings after immortality, and in proving its superiority over the souls of the animals, which have no aspirations Heavenward, the ancients struggled in vain to express the *nature* of the soul, by comparing it to FIRE and LIGHT, it will be well for us to consider whether, with all our boasted knowledge, we have any better or clearer idea of its nature, and whether we have not despairingly taken refuge in having none at all. And if they erred as to its original place of abode, and understood literally the mode and path of its descent, these were but the accessories of the great Truth, and probably, to the Initiates, mere allegories, designed to make the idea more palpable and impressive to the mind.

They are at least no more fit to be smiled at by the self-conceit of a vain ignorance, the wealth of whose knowledge consists solely in words, than the *bosom* of Abraham, as a home for the *spirits* of the just dead; the gulf of actual fire, for the eternal torture of *spirits;* and the City of the New Jerusalem, with its walls of jasper and its edifices of pure gold like clear glass, its foundations of precious stones, and its gates each of a single pearl. "I knew a man," says PAUL, "caught up to the third Heaven;....that he was caught up into Paradise, and heard ineffable words, which it is not possible for a man to utter." And nowhere is the antagonism and conflict between the spirit and body more frequently and forcibly insisted on than in the writings of this apostle, nowhere the Divine nature of the soul more strongly asserted. "With the mind," he says, "I serve the law of God; but with the flesh the law of sin....As many as are led by the Spirit of God, are the sons of God.... The earnest expectation of the created waits for the manifestation of the sons of God.... The created shall be delivered from the bondage of corruption, of the flesh liable to decay, into the glorious liberty of the children of God."

*   *   *   *   *   *

Two forms of government are favorable to the prevalence of

sonified rays: first, *Teutates* or *Teuth,* the same as the *Thoth* of the Egyptians, the Word, or the Intelligence formulated; then Force and Beauty, whose names varied like their emblems. Finally, they completed the sacred Septenary by a mysterious image that represented the progress of the dogma and its future realizations. This was a young girl veiled, holding a child in her arms; and they dedicated this image to "The Virgin who will become a mother;—*Virgini parituræ.*"

Hertha or Wertha, the young Isis of Gaul, Queen of Heaven, the Virgin who was to bear a child, held the spindle of the Fates, filled with wool half white and half black; because she presides over all forms and all symbols, and weaves the garment of the Ideas.

One of the most mysterious pantacles of the Kabalah, contained in the Enchiridion of Leo III., represents an equilateral triangle reversed, inscribed in a double circle. On the triangle are written, in such manner as to form the prophetic Tau, the two Hebrew words so often found appended to the Ineffable Name, אלהם and צבאות, ALOHAYIM, or the Powers, and TSABAOTH, or the Starry Armies and their guiding spirits; words also which symbolize the Equilibrium of the Forces of Nature and the Harmony of Numbers. To the three sides of the triangle belong the three great Names יהוה, אדני, and אגלא, IAHAVEH, ADONAÏ, and AGLA. Above the first is written in Latin, *Formatio,* above the second *Reformatio,* and above the third, *Transformatio.* So Creation is ascribed to the FATHER, Redemption or Reformation to the SON, and Sanctification or Transformation to the HOLY SPIRIT, answering unto the mathematical laws of Action, Reaction, and Equilibrium. IAHAVEH is also, in effect, the Genesis or Formation of dogma, by the elementary signification of the four letters of the Sacred Tetragram; ADONAÏ is the realization of this dogma in the Human Form, in the Visible LORD, who is the Son of God or the perfect Man; and AGLA (formed of the initials of the four words *Ath Gebur Laulaïm Adonaï*) expresses the synthesis of the whole dogma and the totality of the Kabalistic science, clearly indicating by the hieroglyphics of which this admirable name is formed the Triple Secret of the Great Work.

Masonry, like all the Religions, all the Mysteries, Hermeticism and Alchemy, *conceals* its secrets from all except the Adepts and Sages, or the Elect, and uses false explanation*s* and misinterpretations of its symbols to mislead those who deserve only to be misled; to conceal the Truth, which it calls Light, from them, and to draw them away from it. Truth is not for those who are unworthy or unable to receive it, or would pervert it. So God Himself incapacitates many men, by color-blindness, to distinguish colors, and leads the masses away from the highest Truth, giving them the power to attain only so much of it as it is profitable to them to know. Every age has had a religion suited to its capacity.

The Teachers, even of Christianity, are, in general, the most ignorant of the true meaning of that which they teach. There is no book of which so little is known as the Bible. To most who read it, it is as incomprehensible as the Sohar.

So Masonry jealously conceals its secrets, and intentionally leads conceited interpreters astray. There is no sight under the sun more pitiful and ludicrous at once, than the spectacle of the Prestons and the Webbs, not to mention the later incarnations of Dullness and Commonplace, undertaking to "explain" the old symbols of Masonry, and adding to and "improving" them, or inventing new ones.

To the Circle inclosing the central point, and itself traced between two parallel lines, a figure purely Kabalistic, these persons have added the superimposed Bible, and even reared on that the ladder with three or nine rounds, and then given a vapid interpretation of the whole, so profoundly absurd as actually to excite admiration.

8

that he is both sane and honest. *And yet he is both.* His reason is as perfect as mine, and he is as honest as I.

The fancies of a lunatic are realities, *to him.* Our dreams are realities *while they last;* and, in the Past, no more *un*real than what we have acted in our waking hours. No man can say that he hath as sure possession of the truth as of a chattel. When men entertain opinions diametrically opposed to each other, and each is honest, who shall decide which hath the Truth; and how can either say with certainty that *he* hath it? We know not what *is* the truth. That we ourselves believe and feel absolutely certain that our own belief is true, is in reality not the slightest proof of the fact, seem it never so certain and incapable of doubt to us. No man is responsible for the rightness of his faith; but only for the *up*rightness of it.

Therefore no man hath or ever had a right to persecute another for his belief; for there cannot be two antagonistic rights; and if one can persecute another, because he himself is satisfied that the belief of that other is erroneous, the other has, for the same reason, equally as certain a right to persecute him.

The truth comes to us tinged and colored with our prejudices and our preconceptions, which are as old as ourselves, and strong with a divine force. It comes to us as the image of a rod comes to us through the water, bent and distorted. An argument sinks into and convinces the mind of one man, while from that of another it rebounds like a ball of ivory dropped on marble. It is no merit in a man to have a particular faith, excellent and sound and philosophic as it may be, when he imbibed it with his mother's milk. It is no more a merit than his prejudices and his passions.

The sincere Moslem has as much right to persecute us, as we to persecute him; and therefore Masonry wisely requires no more than a belief in One Great All-Powerful Deity, the Father and Preserver of the Universe. Therefore it is she teaches her votaries that toleration is one of the chief duties of every good Mason, a component part of that charity without which we are mere hollow images of true Masons, mere sounding brass and tinkling cymbals.

No evil hath so afflicted the world as intolerance of religious opinion. The human beings it has slain in various ways, if once and together brought to life, would make a nation of people; left to live and increase, would have doubled the population of the civilized portion of the globe; among which civilized portion it chiefly is that religious wars are waged. The treasure and the human labor thus lost would have made the earth a garden, in which, but for his evil passions, man might now be as happy as in Eden.

No man truly obeys the Masonic law who *merely* tolerates those whose religious opinions are opposed to his own. Every man's opinions are his own private property, and the rights of all men to maintain each his own are perfectly equal. Merely to *tolerate,* to *bear with* an opposing opinion, is to assume it to be heretical; and assert the *right* to persecute, if we would; and claim our *toleration* of it as a merit. The Mason's creed goes farther than that. No man, it holds, has any right in any way to interfere with the religious belief of another. It holds that each man is absolutely sovereign as to his own belief, and that belief is a matter absolutely foreign to all who do not entertain the same belief; and that, if there were any right of persecution at all, it would in all cases be a mutual right; because one party has the same right as the other to sit as judge in his own case; and God is the only magistrate that can rightfully decide between them. To that great Judge, Masonry refers the matter; and opening wide its portals, it invites to enter there and live in peace and harmony, the Protestant, the Catholic, the Jew, the Moslem; every man who will lead a truly virtuous and moral life, love his brethren, minister to the sick and distressed, and believe in the ONE, *All-Powerful, All-Wise, everywhere-Present* GOD, *Architect, Creator,* and *Preserver of all things,* by whose universal law of Harmony ever rolls on this universe, the great, vast, infinite circle of successive Death and Life:—to whose INEFFABLE NAME let all true Masons pay profoundest homage! for whose thousand blessings poured upon us, let us feel the sincerest gratitude, now, henceforth, and forever!

We may well be tolerant of each other's creed; for in every faith there are excellent moral precepts. Far in the South of Asia, Zoroaster taught this doctrine: "On commencing a journey, the Faithful should turn his thoughts toward Ormuzd, and confess him, in the purity of his heart, to be King of the World; he should love him, do him homage, and serve him. He must be upright and charitable, despise the pleasures of the body, and avoid pride and haughtiness, and vice in all its forms, and especially falsehood, one of the basest sins of which man can be guilty. He resented the general ignorance of the true nature and attributes of God, the proneness of the people of Judah and Israel to worship other deities, and their low and erroneous and dishonoring notions of the Grand Architect of the Universe, which all shared except a few favored persons; for even Solomon built altars and sacrificed to Astarat, the goddess of the Tsidunim, and Malcûm, the Aamûnite god, and built high places for Kamûs, the Moabite deity, and Malec the god of the Beni-Aamûn. The true nature of God was unknown to them, like His name; and they worshipped the calves of Jeroboam, as in the desert they did that made for them by Aarûn.

The mass of the Hebrews did not believe in the existence of one only God until a late period in their history. Their early and popular ideas of the Deity were singularly low and unworthy. Even while Moses was receiving the law upon Mount Sinai, they forced Aarûn to make them an image of the Egyptian god Apis, and fell down and adored it. They were ever ready to return to the worship of the gods of the Mitzraim; and soon after the death of Joshua they became devout worshippers of the false gods of all the surrounding nations. "Ye have borne," Amos, the prophet, said to them, speaking of their forty years' journeying in the desert, under Moses, "the tabernacle of your Malec and Kaiûn your idols, the star of your god, which ye made to yourselves."

Among them, as among other nations, the conceptions of God formed by individuals varied according to their intellectual and spiritual capacities; poor and imperfect, and investing God with the commonest and coarsest attributes of humanity, among the ignorant and coarse; pure and lofty among the virtuous and richly gifted. These conceptions gradually improved and became purified and ennobled, as the nation advanced in civilization—being lowest in the historical books, amended in the prophetic writings, and reaching their highest elevation among the poets.

Among *all* the ancient nations there was one faith and one idea of Deity for the enlightened, intelligent, and educated, and another for the common people. To this rule the Hebrews were no exception. Yehovah, to the mass of the people, was like the gods of the nations around them, except that he was the *peculiar* God, first of the family of Abraham, of that of Isaac, and of that of Jacob, and afterward the *National* God; and, as they believed, *more powerful* than the other gods of the same nature worshipped

by their neighbors—"Who among the Baalim is like unto thee, O
Yehovah?"—expressed their whole creed.

The Deity of the early Hebrews talked to Adam and Eve in the
garden of delight, as he walked in it in the cool of the day; he
conversed with Kayin; he sat and ate with Abraham in his tent;
that patriarch required a visible token, before he would believe in
his positive promise; he permitted Abraham to expostulate with
him, and to induce him to change his first determination in regard
to Sodom; he wrestled with Jacob; he showed Moses his person,
though not his face; he dictated the minutest police regulations
and the dimensions of the tabernacle and its furniture, to the
Israelites; he insisted on and delighted in sacrifices and burnt-
offerings; he was angry, jealous, and revengeful, as well as waver-
ing and irresolute; he allowed Moses to reason him out of his
fixed resolution utterly to destroy his people; he commanded the
performance of the most shocking and hideous acts of cruelty and
barbarity. He hardened the heart of Pharaoh; he repented of
the evil that he had said he would do unto the people of Nineveh;
and he did it not, to the disgust and anger of Jonah.

Such were the popular notions of the Deity; and either the
priests had none better, or took little trouble to correct these notions; or the popular intellect was not enough enlarged to enable
them to entertain any higher conceptions of the Almighty.

But such were not the ideas of the intellectual and enlightened
few among the Hebrews. It is certain that *they* possessed a
knowledge of the true nature and attributes of God; as the same
class of men did among the other nations—Zoroaster, Menu, Confucius, Socrates, and Plato. But their doctrines on this subject
were esoteric; they did not communicate them to the people at
large, but only to a favored few; and as they were communicated
in Egypt and India, in Persia and Phœnicia, in Greece and Samothrace, in the greater mysteries, to the Initiates.

The communication of this knowledge and other secrets, some
of which are perhaps lost, constituted, under other names, what
we now call *Masonry*, or *Free* or *Frank-Masonry*. That knowledge was, in one sense, *the Lost Word*, which was made known to
the Grand Elect, Perfect, and Sublime Masons. It would be folly
to pretend that the *forms* of Masonry were the same in those ages
as they are now. The present name of the Order, and its titles,
and the names of the Degrees now in use, were not then known.

Even Blue Masonry cannot trace back its *authentic* history, *with its present Degrees,* further than the year 1700, *if so far.* But, by whatever *name* it was known in this or the other country, Masonry existed as it now exists, the same in spirit and at heart, not only when Solomon builded the temple, but centuries before—before even the first colonies emigrated into Southern India, Persia, and Egypt, from the cradle of the human race.

The Supreme, Self-existent, Eternal, All-wise, All-powerful, Infinitely Good, Pitying, Beneficent, and Merciful Creator and Preserver of the Universe was the same, by whatever name he was called, to the intellectual and enlightened men of all nations. The name was nothing, if not a symbol and representative hieroglyph of his nature and attributes. The name AL represented his remoteness *above* men, his *inaccessibility;* BAL and BALA, his *might;* ALOHIM, his various *potencies;* IHUH, *existence* and the *generation* of things. None of his names, among the Orientals, were the symbols of a divinely infinite love and tenderness, and all-embracing mercy. As MOLOCH or MALEK he was but an omnipotent *monarch,* a tremendous and irresponsible *Will;* as ADONAÏ, only an arbitrary LORD and *Master;* as AL *Shadaï, potent* and a DESTROYER.

To communicate true and correct ideas in respect of the Deity was one chief object of the mysteries. In them, Khūrūm the King, and Khūrūm the Master, obtained their knowledge of him and his attributes; and in them that knowledge was taught to Moses and Pythagoras.

Wherefore nothing forbids you to consider the whole legend of this Degree, like that of the Master's, an allegory, representing the perpetuation of the knowledge of the True God in the sanctuaries of initiation. By the subterranean vaults you may understand the places of initiation, which in the ancient ceremonies were generally under ground. The Temple of Solomon presented a symbolic image of the Universe; and resembled, in its arrangements and furniture, all the temples of the ancient nations that practised the mysteries. The system of numbers was intimately connected with their religions and worship, and has come down to us in Masonry; though the esoteric meaning with which the numbers used by us are pregnant is unknown to the vast majority of those who use them. Those numbers were especially employed that had a reference to the Deity, represented his attributes, or figured in the frame-work of the world, in time and space, and formed more or less the bases of that frame-work. These were universally regarded as sacred, being the expression of order and intelligence, the utterances of Divinity Himself.

The Holy of Holies of the Temple formed a cube; in which, drawn on a plane surface, there are $4 + 3 + 2 = 9$ *lines* visible, and three sides or faces. It corresponded with the number *four,* by which the ancients presented *Nature,* it being the number of substances or corporeal forms, and of the elements, the cardinal points and seasons, and the *secondary* colors. The number *three* everywhere represented the Supreme Being. Hence the name of the Deity, engraven upon the *triangular* plate, and that sunken into the *cube* of agate, taught the ancient Mason, and teaches us, that the true knowledge of God, of His nature and His attributes, is written by Him upon the leaves of the great Book of Universal Nature, and may be read there by all who are endowed with the requisite amount of intellect and intelligence. This knowledge of God, so written there, and of which Masonry has in all ages been the interpreter, is *the Master Mason's Word.*

Within the Temple, all the arrangements were mystically and symbolically connected with the same system. The vault or ceiling, starred like the firmament, was supported by twelve columns, representing the twelve months of the year. The border that ran around the columns represented the zodiac, and one of the twelve celestial signs was appropriated to each column. The brazen sea was supported by twelve oxen, three looking to each cardinal point of the compass.

And so in our day every Masonic Lodge represents the Universe. Each extends, we are told, from the rising to the setting sun, from the South to the North, from the surface of the Earth to the Heavens, and from the same to the centre of the globe. In it are represented the sun, moon, and stars; three great torches in the East, West, and South, forming a triangle, give it light; and, like the Delta or Triangle suspended in the East, and inclosing the Ineffable Name, indicate, by the mathematical equality of the angles and sides, the beautiful and harmonious proportions which govern in the aggregate and details of the Universe; while those sides and angles represent, by their number, three, the Trinity of Power, Wisdom, and Harmony, which presided at the building of this marvellous work. These three great lights also represent the great mystery of the three principles, of creation, dissolution or destruction, and reproduction or regeneration, consecrated by all creeds in their numerous Trinities.

The luminous pedestal, lighted by the perpetual flame within, is a symbol of that light of *Reason,* given by God to man, by which he is enabled to read in the Book of Nature the record of the thought, the revelation of the attributes of the Deity.

The three Masters, Adoniram, Joabert, and Stolkin, are types of the True Mason, who seeks for knowledge from pure motives, and that he may be the better enabled to serve and benefit his fellow-men; while the discontented and presumptuous Masters who were buried in the ruins of the arches represent those who strive to acquire it for unholy purposes, to gain power over their fellows, to gratify their pride, their vanity, or their ambition.

The Lion that guarded the Ark and held in his mouth the key wherewith to open it, figuratively represents Solomon, the Lion of the Tribe of Judah, who preserved and communicated the key to the true knowledge of God, of His laws, and of the profound mysteries of the moral and physical Universe.

ENOCH [חנוך, Khanôc], we are told, walked with God three hundred years, after reaching the age of sixty-five—"walked with God, and he was no more, for God had taken him." His name signified in the Hebrew, INITIATE or INITIATOR. The legend of the columns, of granite and brass or bronze, erected by him, is probably symbolical. That of bronze, which survived the flood, is supposed to symbolize the mysteries, of which Masonry is the legitimate successor—from the earliest times the custodian and depository of the great philosophical and religious truths, unknown to the world at large, and handed down from age to age by an unbroken current of tradition, embodied in symbols, emblems, and allegories.

The legend of this Degree is thus, partially, interpreted. It is of little importance whether it is in anywise historical. For its value consists in the lessons which it inculcates, and the duties which it prescribes to those who receive it. The parables and allegories of the Scriptures are not less valuable than history. Nay, they are more so, because ancient history is little instructive, and truths are concealed in and symbolized by the legend and the myth.

There are profounder meanings concealed in the symbols of this Degree, connected with the philosophical system of the Hebrew

to see and welcome these many-handed coadjutors, to the great and good cause. The oracles of God do not speak from the pulpit alone.

There is also a religion of society. In business, there is much more than sale, exchange, price, payment; for there is the sacred faith of man in man. When we repose perfect confidence in the integrity of another; when we feel that he will not swerve from the right, frank, straightforward, conscientious course, for any temptation; his integrity and conscientiousness are the image of God to us; and when we believe in *it*, it is as great and generous an act, as when we believe in the rectitude of the Deity.

In gay assemblies for amusement, the good affections of life gush and mingle. If *they* did not, these gathering-places would be as dreary and repulsive as the caves and dens of outlaws and robbers. When friends meet, and hands are warmly pressed, and the eye kindles and the countenance is suffused with gladness, there is a religion between their hearts; and each loves and worships the True and Good that is in the other. It is not policy, or self-interest, or selfishness that spreads such a charm around that meeting, but the halo of bright and beautiful affection.

The same splendor of kindly liking, and affectionate regard, shines like the soft overarching sky, over all the world; over all places where men meet, and walk or toil together; not over lovers' bowers and marriage-altars alone, not over the homes of purity and tenderness alone; but over all tilled fields, and busy work-shops, and dusty highways, and paved streets. There is not a worn stone upon the sidewalks, but has been the altar of such offerings of mutual kindness; nor a wooden pillar or iron railing against which hearts beating with affection have not leaned. How many soever other elements there are in the stream of life flowing through these channels, *that* is surely here and everywhere; honest, heartfelt, disinterested, inexpressible affection.

Every Masonic Lodge is a temple of religion; and its teachings are instruction in religion. For here are inculcated disinterestedness, affection, toleration, devotedness, patriotism, truth, a generous sympathy with those who suffer and mourn, pity for the fallen, mercy for the erring, relief for those in want, Faith, Hope, and Charity. Here we meet as brethren, to learn to know and love each other. Here we greet each other gladly, are lenient to each other's faults, regardful of each other's feelings, ready to relieve

Appendix B

each other's wants. This is the true religion revealed to the ancient patriarchs; which Masonry has taught for many centuries, and which it will continue to teach as long as time endures. If unworthy passions, or selfish, bitter, or revengeful feelings, contempt, dislike, hatred, enter here, they are intruders and not welcome, strangers uninvited, and not guests.

Certainly there are many evils and bad passions, and much hate and contempt and unkindness everywhere in the world. We cannot refuse to see the evil that is in life. But *all* is not evil. We still see God in the world. There is good amidst the evil. The hand of mercy leads wealth to the hovels of poverty and sorrow. Truth and simplicity live amid many wiles and sophistries. There are good hearts underneath gay robes, and under tattered garments also.

Love clasps the hand of love, amid all the envyings and distractions of showy competition; fidelity, pity, and sympathy hold the long night-watch by the bedside of the suffering neighbor, amidst the surrounding poverty and squalid misery. Devoted men go from city to city to nurse those smitten down by the terrible pestilence that renews at intervals its mysterious marches. Women well-born and delicately nurtured nursed the wounded soldiers in hospitals, before it became fashionable to do so; and even poor lost women, whom God alone loves and pities, tend the plague-stricken with a patient and generous heroism. Masonry and its kindred Orders teach men to love each other, feed the hungry, clothe the naked, comfort the sick, and bury the friendless dead. Everywhere God finds and blesses the kindly office, the pitying thought, and the loving heart.

There is an element of good in all men's lawful pursuits and a divine spirit breathing in all their lawful affections. The ground on which they tread is holy ground. There is a natural religion of life, answering, with however many a broken tone, to the religion of nature. There is a beauty and glory in Humanity, in man, answering, with however many a mingling shade, to the loveliness of soft landscapes, and swelling hills, and the wondrous glory of the starry heavens.

Men may be virtuous, self-improving, and religious *in* their employments. Precisely for that, those employments were made. All their social relations, friendship, love, the ties of family, were made to be holy. They may be religious, not by a kind of protest and

tions have left upon the earth; for it is the handwriting of the Almighty.

A Mason's great business with life is to read the book of its teaching; to find that life is not the doing of drudgeries, but the hearing of oracles. The old mythology is but a leaf in that book; for it peopled the world with spiritual natures; and science, many-leaved, still spreads before us the same tale of wonder.

We shall be just as happy hereafter, as we are pure and upright, and no more, just as happy as our character prepares us to be, and no more. Our moral, like our mental character, is not formed in a moment; it is the habit of our minds; the result of many thoughts and feelings and efforts, bound togther by many natural and strong ties. The great law of Retribution is, that all coming experience is to be affected by every present feeling; every future moment of being must answer for every present moment; one moment, sacrificed to vice, or lost to improvement, is *forever* sacrificed and lost; an hour's delay to enter the right path, is to put us back so far, in the everlasting pursuit of happiness; and every sin, even of the best men, is to be thus answered for, if not according to the full measure of its ill-desert, yet according to a rule of unbending rectitude and impartiality.

The law of retribution presses upon every man, whether he thinks of it or not. It pursues him through all the courses of life, with a step that never falters nor tires, and with an eye that never sleeps. If it were not so, God's government would not be impartial; there would be no discrimination; no moral dominion; no light shed upon the mysteries of Providence.

Whatsoever a man soweth, that, and not something else, shall he reap. That which we are doing, good or evil, grave or gay; that which we do to-day and shall do to-morrow; each thought, each feeling, each action, each event; every passing hour, every breathing moment; all are contributing to form the character, according to which we are to be judged. Every particle of influence that goes to form that aggregate,—our character,—will, in that future scrutiny, be sifted out from the mass; and, particle by particle, with ages perhaps intervening, fall a distinct contribution to the sum of our joys or woes. Thus every idle word and idle hour will give answer in the judgment.

Let us take care, therefore, what we sow. An evil temptation comes upon us; the opportunity of unrighteous gain, or of unhal-

XIV.

GRAND ELECT, PERFECT, AND SUBLIME MASON.

[Perfect Elu.]

IT is for each individual Mason to discover the secret of Masonry, by reflection upon its symbols and a wise consideration and analysis of what is said and done in the work. Masonry does not *inculcate* her truths. She *states* them, once and briefly; or hints them, perhaps, darkly; or interposes a cloud between them and eyes that would be dazzled by them.. *"Seek, and ye shall find,"* knowledge and the truth.

The practical object of Masonry is the physical and moral amelioration and the intellectual and spiritual improvement of individuals and society. Neither can be effected, except by the dissemination of truth. It is falsehood in doctrines and fallacy in principles, to which most of the miseries of men and the misfortunes of nations are owing. Public opinion is rarely right on any point; and there are and always will be important truths to be substituted in that opinion in the place of many errors and absurd and injurious prejudices. There are few truths that public opinion has not at some time hated and persecuted as heresies; and few errors that have not at some time seemed to it truths radiant from the immediate presence of God. There are moral maladies, also, of man and society, the treatment of which requires not only boldness, but also, and more, prudence and discretion; since they are more the fruit of false and pernicious doctrines, moral, political, and religious, than of vicious inclinations.

Much of the Masonic secret manifests itself, without speech

revealing it, to him who even partially comprehends all the Degrees in proportion as he receives them; and particularly to those
who advance to the highest Degrees of the Ancient and Accepted
Scottish Rite. That Rite raises a corner of the veil, even in the
Degree of Apprentice; for it there declares that Masonry is a
worship.

Masonry labors to improve the social order by enlightening
men's minds, warming their hearts with the love of the good, in-
spiring them with the great principle of human fraternity, and
requiring of its disciples that their language and actions shall con-
form to that principle, that they shall enlighten each other, control their passions, abhor vice, and pity the vicious man as one
afflicted with a deplorable malady.

It is the universal, eternal, immutable religion, such as God
planted it in the heart of universal humanity. No creed has ever
been long-lived that was not built on this foundation. It is the
base, and they are the superstructure. "Pure religion and undefiled before God and the Father is this, to visit the fatherless and
widows in their affliction, and to keep himself unspotted from the
world." "Is not *this* the fast that I have chosen? to loose the
bands of wickedness, to undo the heavy burdens, and to let the
oppressed go free, and that ye break every yoke?" The ministers
of this religion are all Masons who comprehend it and are devoted
to it; its sacrifices to God are good works, the sacrifices of the
base and disorderly passions, the offering up of self-interest on the
altar of humanity, and perpetual efforts to attain to all the moral
perfection of which man is capable.

To make honor and duty the steady beacon-lights that shall
guide your life-vessel over the stormy seas of time; to do that
which it is right to do, not because it will insure you success, or
bring with it a reward, or gain the applause of men, or be "the
best policy," more prudent or more advisable; but because it *is*
right, and therefore *ought* to be done; to war incessantly against
error, intolerance, ignorance, and vice, and yet to pity those who
err, to be tolerant even of intolerance, to teach the ignorant, and
to labor to reclaim the vicious, are some of the duties of a Mason.

A good Mason is one that can look upon death, and see its face
with the same countenance with which he hears its story; that
can endure all the labors of his life with his soul supporting his
body, that can equally despise riches when he hath them and

when he hath them not; that is not sadder if they are in his neighbor's exchequer, nor more lifted up if they shine around about his own walls; one that is not moved with good fortune coming to him, nor going from him; that can look upon another man's lands with equanimity and pleasure, as if they were his own; and yet look upon his own, and use them too, just as if they were another man's; that neither spends his goods prodigally and foolishly, nor yet keeps them avariciously and like a miser; that weighs not benefits by weight and number, but by the mind and circumstances of him who confers them; that never thinks his charity expensive, if a worthy person be the receiver; that does nothing for opinion's sake, but everything for conscience, being as careful of his thoughts as of his acting in markets and theatres, and in as much awe of himself as of a whole assembly; that is bountiful and cheerful to his friends, and charitable and apt to forgive his enemies; that loves his country, consults its honor, and obeys its laws, and desires and endeavors nothing more than that he may do his duty and honor God. And such a Mason may reckon his life to be the life of a man, and compute his months, not by the course of the sun, but by the zodiac and circle of his virtues.

The whole world is but one republic, of which each nation is a family, and every individual a child. Masonry, not in anywise derogating from the differing duties which the diversity of states requires, tends to create a new people, which, composed of men of many nations and tongues, shall all be bound together by the bonds of science, morality, and virtue.

Essentially philanthropic, philosophical, and progressive, it has for the basis of its dogma a firm belief in the existence of God and his providence, and of the immortality of the soul; for its object, the dissemination of moral, political, philosophical, and religious truth, and the practice of all the virtues. In every age, its device has been, "Liberty, Equality, Fraternity," with constitutional government, *law, order, discipline,* and *subordination* to legitimate authority—*government* and not *anarchy.*

But it is neither a political party nor a religious sect. It embraces all parties and all sects, to form from among them all a vast fraternal association. It recognizes the dignity of human nature, and man's right to such freedom as he is fitted for; and it knows nothing that should place one man below another, except

XVIII.

KNIGHT ROSE CROIX.

[Prince Rose Croix.]

EACH of us makes such applications to his own faith and creed, of the symbols and ceremonies of this Degree, as seems to him proper. With these special interpretations we have here nothing to do. Like the legend of the Master Khūrūm, in which some see figured the condemnation and sufferings of Christ; others those of the unfortunate Grand Master of the Templars; others those of the first Charles, King of England; and others still the annual descent of the Sun at the winter Solstice to the regions of darkness, the basis of many an ancient legend; so the ceremonies of this Degree receive different explanations; each interpreting them for himself, and being offended at the interpretation of no other.

In no other way could Masonry possess its character of Universality; that character which has ever been peculiar to it from its origin; and which enables two Kings, worshippers of different Deities, to sit together as Masters, while the walls of the first temple arose; and the men of Gebal, bowing down to the Phœnician Gods, to work by the side of the Hebrews to whom those Gods were abomination; and to sit with them in the same Lodge as brethren.

You have already learned that these ceremonies have one general significance, to every one, of every faith, who believes in God, and the soul's immortality.

The primitive men met in no Temples made with human hands. "God," said Stephen, the first Martyr, "dwelleth not in Temples made with hands." In the open air, under the overarching mysterious sky, in the great World-Temple, they uttered their vows and thanksgivings, and adored the God of Light; of that Light that was to them the type of Good, as darkness was the type of Evil.

All antiquity solved the enigma of the existence of Evil, by supposing the existence of a Principle of Evil, of Demons, fallen Angels, an Ahriman, a Typhon, a Siva, a Lok, or a Satan, that, first falling themselves, and plunged in misery and darkness, tempted man to his fall, and brought sin into the world. All believed in a future life, to be attained by purification and trials; in a state or successive states of reward and punishment; and in a Mediator or Redeemer, by whom the Evil Principle was to be overcome, and the Supreme Deity reconciled to His creatures. The belief was general, that He was to be born of a Virgin, and suffer a painful death. The Indians called him Chrishna; the Chinese, Kioun-tse; the Persians, Sosiosch; the Chaldeans, Dhouvanai; the Egyptians, Har-Oeri; Plato, Love; and the Scandinavians, Balder.

Chrishna, the Hindoo Redeemer, was cradled and educated among Shepherds. A Tyrant, at the time of his birth, ordered all the male children to be slain. He performed miracles, say his legends, even raising the dead. He washed the feet of the Brahmins, and was meek and lowly of spirit. He was born of a Virgin; descended to Hell, rose again, ascended to Heaven, charged his disciples to teach his doctrines, and gave them the gift of miracles.

The first Masonic Legislator whose memory is preserved to us by history, was Buddha, who, about a thousand years before the Christian era, reformed the religion of Manous. He called to the Priesthood all men, without distinction of caste, who felt themselves inspired by God to instruct men. Those who so associated themselves formed a Society of Prophets under the name of Samaneans. They recognized the existence of a single uncreated God, in whose bosom everything grows, is developed and trans-

tirpation of vice, the purification of man, the development of the arts and sciences, and the relief of humanity.

None admit an adept to their lofty philosophical knowledge, and mysterious sciences, until he has been purified at the altar of the symbolic Degrees. Of what importance are differences of opinion as to the age and genealogy of the Degree, or variance in the practice, ceremonial and liturgy, or the shade of color of the banner under which each tribe of Israel marched, if all revere the Holy Arch of the symbolic Degrees, first and unalterable source of Free-Masonry; if all revere our conservative principles, and are with us in the great purposes of our organization?

If, anywhere, brethren of a particular religious belief have been excluded from this Degree, it merely shows how gravely the purposes and plan of Masonry may be misunderstood. For whenever the door of any Degree is closed against him who believes in one God and the soul's immortality, on account of the other tenets of his faith, that Degree is Masonry no longer. No Mason has the right to interpret the symbols of this Degree for another, or to refuse him its mysteries, if he will not take them with the explanation and commentary superadded.

Listen, my brother, to *our* explanation of the symbols of the Degree, and then give them such further interpretation as you think fit.

The *Cross* has been a sacred symbol from the earliest Antiquity. It is found upon all the enduring monuments of the world, in Egypt, in Assyria, in Hindostan, in Persia, and on the Buddhist towers of Ireland. Buddha was said to have died upon it. The Druids cut an oak into its shape and held it sacred, and built their temples in that form. Pointing to the four quarters of the world, it was the symbol of universal nature. It was on a cruciform tree, that Chrishna was said to have expired, pierced with arrows. It was revered in Mexico.

But its peculiar meaning in this Degree, is that given to it by the Ancient Egyptians. *Thoth* or *Phtha* is represented on the oldest monuments carrying in his hand the *Crux Ansata*, or *Ankh*. [a Tau cross, with a ring or circle over it]. He is so seen on the double tablet of Shufu and Noh Shufu, builders of the greatest of the Pyramids, at Wady Meghara, in the peninsula of Sinai. It was the hieroglyphic for *life,* and with a triangle prefixed meant *life-giving.* To us therefore it is the symbol of *Life*—of that life that emanated from the Deity, and of that Eternal Life for which we all hope; through our faith in God's infinite goodness.

The ROSE was anciently sacred to Aurora and the Sun. It is a symbol of *Dawn*, of the resurrection of Light and the renewal of life, and therefore of the dawn of the first day, and more particularly of the resurrection: and the Cross and Rose together are therefore hieroglyphically to be read, *the Dawn of Eternal Life* which all Nations have hoped for by the advent of a Redeemer.

The *Pelican* feeding her young is an emblem of the large and bountiful beneficence of Nature, of the Redeemer of fallen man, and of that humanity and charity that ought to distinguish a Knight of this Degree.

The *Eagle* was the living Symbol of the Egyptian God *Mendes* or *Menthra*, whom *Sesostris-Ramses* made one with *Amun-Re*, the God of Thebes and Upper Egypt, and the representative of the Sun, the word RE meaning *Sun* or *King*.

The *Compass* surmounted with a *crown* signifies that notwithstanding the high rank attained in Masonry by a Knight of the Rose Croix, equity and impartiality are invariably to govern his conduct.

To the word INRI, inscribed on the Crux Ansata over the Master's Seat, many meanings have been assigned. The Christian Initiate reverentially sees in it the initials of the inscription upon the cross on which Christ suffered—*Iesus Nazarenus Rex Iudæorum*. The sages of Antiquity connected it with one of the greatest secrets of Nature, that of universal regeneration. They interpreted it thus, *Igne Natura renovatur integra;* [entire nature is renovated by fire] : The Alchemical or Hermetic Masons framed for it this aphorism, *Igne nitrum roris invenitur*. And the Jesuits are charged with having applied to it this odious axiom, *Justum necare reges impios*. The four letters are the initials of the Hebrew words that represent the four elements—*Iammim*, the seas or water; *Nour*, fire; *Rouach*, the air, and *Iebeschah*, the dry earth. How we read it, I need not repeat to you.

The CROSS, **X**, was the Sign of the Creative Wisdom or Logos, the Son of God. Plato says, "He expressed him upon the Universe in the figure of the letter X. The next Power to the Supreme God was decussated or figured in the shape of a Cross on the Universe." Mithras signed his soldiers on the forehead with a

exhibited by animals that think, dream, remember, argue from cause to effect, plan, devise, combine, and communicate their thoughts to each other, so as to act rationally in concert,—if their love, hate, and revenge, can be conceived of as results of the organization of matter, like color and perfume, the resort to the hypothesis of an immaterial Soul to explain phenomena of the same kind, only more perfect, manifested by the *human* being, is supremely absurd. That organized matter can think or even *feel*, at all, is the great insoluble mystery. "Instinct" is but a word without a meaning, or else it means inspiration. It is either the animal itself, or God *in* the animal, that thinks, remembers, and reasons; and instinct, according to the common acceptation of the term, would be the greatest and most wonderful of mysteries,— no less a thing than the direct, immediate, and continual promptings of the Deity,—for the animals are not machines, or automata moved by springs, and the ape is but a dumb Australian.

Must we *always* remain in this darkness of uncertainty, of doubt? Is there *no* mode of escaping from the labyrinth except by means of a blind faith, which explains nothing, and in many creeds, ancient and modern, sets Reason at defiance, and leads to the belief either in a God without a Universe, a Universe without a God, or a Universe which is itself a God?

We read in the Hebrew Chronicles that Schlomoh the wise King caused to be placed in front of the entrance to the Temple two huge columns of bronze, one of which was called YAKAYIN and the other BAHAZ; and these words are rendered in our version *Strength* and *Establishment*. The Masonry of the Blue Lodges gives no explanation of these symbolic columns; nor do the Hebrew Books advise us that they were symbolic. If not so intended as symbols, they were subsequently understood to be such.

But as we are certain that everything *within* the Temple was symbolic, and that the whole structure was intended to represent the Universe, we may reasonably conclude that the columns of the portico also had a symbolic signification. It would be tedious to repeat all the interpretations which fancy or dullness has found for them.

The key to their true meaning is not undiscoverable. The perfect and eternal distinction of the two primitive terms of the creative syllogism, in order to attain to the demonstration of their harmony by the analogy of contraries, is the second grand principle of that occult philosophy veiled under the name *"Kabalah,"* and indicated by all the sacred hieroglyphs of the Ancient Sanctuaries, and of the rites, so little understood by the mass of the Initiates, of the Ancient and Modern Free-Masonry.

The Sohar declares that everything in the Universe proceeds by the mystery of "the Balance," that is, of Equilibrium. Of the Sephiroth, or Divine Emanations, Wisdom and Understanding, Severity and Benignity, or Justice and Mercy, and Victory and Glory, constitute pairs.

Wisdom, or the Intellectual Generative *Energy,* and Understanding, or the *Capacity* to be impregnated by the Active Energy and produce intellection or thought, are represented symbolically in the Kabalah as male and female. So also are Justice and Mercy. Strength is the intellectual Energy or Activity; Establishment or Stability is the intellectual Capacity to produce, a passivity. They are the POWER of *generation* and the CAPACITY of *production.* By WISDOM, it is said, God creates, and by UNDERSTANDING establishes. These are the two Columns of the Temple, contraries like the Man and Woman, like Reason and Faith, Omnipotence and Liberty, Infinite Justice and Infinite Mercy, Absolute Power or Strength to do even what is most unjust and unwise, and Absolute Wisdom that makes it impossible to do it; Right and Duty. They were the columns of the intellectual and moral world, the monumental hieroglyph of the antinomy necessary to the grand law of creation.

There must be for every Force a Resistance to support it, to every light a shadow, for every Royalty a Realm to govern, for every affirmative a negative.

For the Kabalists, Light represents the Active Principle, and Darkness or Shadow is analogous to the Passive Principle. Therefore it was that they made of the Sun and Moon emblems of the two Divine Sexes and the two creative forces; therefore, that they ascribed to woman the Temptation and the first sin, and then the first labor, the maternal labor of the redemption, because it is from the bosom of the darkness itself that we see the Light born again. The Void attracts the Full; and so it is that the abyss of poverty and misery, the Seeming Evil, the seeming empty nothingness of life, the temporary rebellion of the creatures, eternally attracts the overflowing ocean of being, of riches, of pity, and of

qually guided, sometimes toward abundance and sometimes toward barrenness, though ever advancing, is illuminated by the primitive ideas, the rays that emanate from the Divine Intelligence, whenever it ascends toward the Sublime Treasures. When, on the contrary, it descends, and is barren, it falls within the domain of those Intelligences that are termed Angels. . . for, when the soul is deprived of the light of God, which leads it to the knowledge of things, it no longer enjoys more than a feeble and secondary light, which gives it, not the understanding of things, but that of words only, as in this baser world. . . ."

". . . Let the narrow-souled withdraw, having their ears sealed up! We communicate the divine mysteries to those only who have received the sacred initiation, to those who practise true piety, and who are not enslaved by the empty pomp of words, or the doctrines of the pagans. . . ."

". . . O, ye Initiates, ye whose ears are purified, receive this in your souls, as a mystery never to be lost! Reveal it to no Profane! Keep and contain it within yourselves, as an incorruptible treasure, not like gold or silver, but more precious than everything besides; for it is the knowledge of the Great Cause, of Nature, and of that which is born of both. And if you meet an Initiate, besiege him with your prayers, that he conceal from you no new mysteries that he may know, and rest not until you have obtained them! For me, although I was initiated in the Great Mysteries by Moses, the Friend of God, yet, having seen Jeremiah, I recognized him not only as an Initiate, but as a Hierophant; and I follow his school."

We, like him, recognize all Initiates as our Brothers. We belong to no one creed or school. In all religions there is a basis of Truth; in all there is pure Morality. All that teach the cardinal tenets of Masonry we respect; all teachers and reformers of mankind we admire and revere.

Masonry also has her mission to perform. With her traditions reaching back to the earliest times, and her symbols dating further back than even the monumental history of Egypt extends, she invites all men of all religions to enlist under her banners and to war against evil, ignorance, and wrong. You are now her knight, and to her service your sword is consecrated. May you prove a worthy soldier in a worthy cause!

21

XXIII.

CHIEF OF THE TABERNACLE.

AMONG most of the Ancient Nations there was, in addition to their public worship, a private one styled the Mysteries; to which those only were admitted who had been prepared by certain ceremonies called initiations.

The most widely disseminated of the ancient worships were those of Isis, Orpheus, Dionusos, Ceres, and Mithras. Many barbarous nations received the knowledge of the Mysteries in honor of these divinities from the Egyptians, before they arrived in Greece; and even in the British Isles the Druids celebrated those of Dionusos, learned by them from the Egyptians.

The Mysteries of Eleusis, celebrated at Athens in honor of Ceres, swallowed up, as it were, all the others. All the neighboring nations neglected their own, to celebrate those of Eleusis; and in a little while all Greece and Asia Minor were filled with the Initiates. They spread into the Roman Empire, and even beyond its limits, "those holy and august Eleusinian Mysteries," said Cicero, "in which the people of the remotest lands are initiated." Zosimus says that they embraced the whole human race; and Aristides termed them the common temple of the whole world.

There were, in the Eleusinian feasts, two sorts of Mysteries, the great, and the little. The latter were a kind of preparation for the former; and everybody was admitted to them. Ordinarily there was a novitiate of three, and sometimes of four years.

Clemens of Alexandria says that what was taught in the great Mysteries concerned the Universe, and was the completion and perfection of all instruction; wherein things were seen as they were, and nature and her works were made known.

The ancients said that the Initiates would be more happy after death than other mortals; and that, while the souls of the Profane on leaving their bodies, would be plunged in the mire, and remain buried in darkness, those of the Initiates would fly to the Fortunate Isles, the abode of the Gods.

CHIEF OF THE TABERNACLE.   353

Plato said that the object of the Mysteries was to re-establish the soul in its primitive purity, and in that state of perfection which it had lost. Epictetus said, "whatever is met with therein has been instituted by our Masters, for the instruction of man and the correction of morals."

Proclus held that initiation elevated the soul, from a material, sensual, and purely human life, to a communion and celestial intercourse with the Gods; and that a variety of things, forms, and species were shown Initiates, representing the first generation of the Gods.

Purity of morals and elevation of soul were required of the Initiates. Candidates were required to be of spotless reputation and irreproachable virtue. Nero, after murdering his mother, did not dare to be present at the celebration of the Mysteries: and Antony presented himself to be initiated, as the most infallible mode of proving his innocence of the death of Avidius Cassius.

The Initiates were regarded as the only fortunate men. "It is upon us alone," says Aristophanes, "shineth the beneficent daystar. We alone receive pleasure from the influence of his rays; we, who are initiated, and who practise toward citizen and stranger every possible act of justice and piety." And it is therefore not surprising that, in time, initiation came to be considered as necessary as baptism afterward was to the Christians; and that not to have been admitted to the Mysteries was held a dishonor.

"It seems to me," says the great orator, philosopher, and moralist, Cicero, "that Athens, among many excellent inventions, divine and very useful to the human family, has produced none comparable to the Mysteries, which for a wild and ferocious life have substituted humanity and urbanity of manners. It is with good reason they use the term *initiation*; for it is through them that we in reality have learned the first principles of life; and they not only teach us to live in a manner more consoling and agreeable, but they soften the pains of death by the hope of a better life hereafter."

Where the Mysteries originated is not known. It is supposed that they came from India, by the way of Chaldæa, into Egypt, and thence were carried into Greece. Wherever they arose, they were practised among all the ancient nations; and, as was usual, the Thracians, Cretans, and Athenians each claimed the honor of in-because both the most virtuous as well as the most learned and philosophic of the ancients speak of them in the loftiest terms. That they ultimately became degraded from their high estate, and corrupted, we know.

The rites of initiation became progressively more complicated. Signs and tokens were invented by which the Children of Light could with facility make themselves known to each other. Different Degrees were invented, as the number of Initiates enlarged, in order that there might be in the inner apartment of the Temple a favored few, to whom alone the more valuable secrets were entrusted, and who could wield effectually the influence and power of the Order.

Originally the Mysteries were meant to be the beginning of a new life of reason and virtue. The initiated or esoteric companions were taught the doctrine of the One Supreme God, the theory of death and eternity, the hidden mysteries of Nature, the prospect of the ultimate restoration of the soul to that state of perfection from which it had fallen, its immortality, and the states of reward and punishment after death. The uninitiated were deemed Profane, unworthy of public employment or private confidence, sometimes proscribed as Atheists, and certain of everlasting punishment beyond the grave.

All persons were initiated into the lesser Mysteries; but few attained the greater, in which the true spirit of them, and most of their secret doctrines were hidden. The veil of secrecy was impenetrable, sealed by oaths and penalties the most tremendous and appalling. It was by initiation only, that a knowledge of the Hieroglyphics could be obtained, with which the walls, columns, and ceilings of the Temples were decorated, and which, believed to have been communicated to the Priests by revelation from the celestial deities, the youth of all ranks were laudably ambitious of deciphering.

The ceremonies were performed at dead of night, generally in apartments under-ground, but sometimes in the centre of a vast pyramid, with every appliance that could alarm and excite the candidate. Innumerable ceremonies, wild and romantic, dreadful and appalling, had by degrees been added to the few expressive symbols of primitive observances, under which there were instances in which the terrified aspirant actually expired with fear.

The pyramids were probably used for the purposes of initiation,

And in this sense, as presiding over life and death, Dionusos is
in the highest sense *the* LIBERATOR: since, like Osiris, he frees the
soul, and guides it in its migrations beyond the grave, preserving
it from the risk of again falling under the slavery of matter or
of some inferior animal form, the purgatory of Metempsychosis;
and exalting and perfecting its nature through the purifying discipline of his Mysteries. "The great consummation of all philosophy," said Socrates, professedly quoting from traditional and
mystic sources, "is *Death:* He who pursues philosophy aright, *is
studying how to die.*"

All soul is part of the Universal Soul, whose totality is Dionusos;
and it is therefore he who, as Spirit of Spirits, leads back the
vagrant spirit to its home, and accompanies it through the purifying processes, both real and symbolical, of its earthly transit. He
is therefore emphatically the *Mystes* or Hierophant, the great
Spiritual Mediator of Greek religion.

The human soul is itself δαιμονιος, a God *within* the mind,
capable through its own power of rivalling the canonization of the
Hero, of making itself immortal by the practice of the good, and
the contemplation of the beautiful and true. The removal to the
Happy Islands could only be understood mythically; everything
earthly must die; Man, like Œdipus, is wounded from his birth,
his real elysium can exist only beyond the grave. Dionusos died
and descended to the Shades. His passion was the great Secret of
the Mysteries; as Death is the Grand Mystery of existence. His
death, typical of Nature's Death, or of her periodical decay and
restoration, was one of the many symbols of the *palingenesia* or
second birth of man.

Man descended from the elemental Forces or Titans [Elohim],
who fed on the body of the Pantheistic Deity creating the Universe
by self-sacrifice, commemorates in sacramental observance this
mysterious passion; and while partaking of the raw flesh of the
victim, seems to be invigorated by a fresh draught from the foun-
tain of universal life, to receive a new pledge of regenerated existence. Death is the inseparable antecedent of life; the seed dies in
order to produce the plant, and earth itself is rent asunder and
dies at the birth of Dionusos. Hence the significancy of the
phallus, or of its inoffensive substitute, the obelisk, rising as an
emblem of resurrection by the tomb of buried Deity at Lerna or
at Sais.

to him whom it was wished to instruct in her secrets and initiate in her mysteries; and Clemens of Alexandria might well say that initiation was a real physiology.

So Phanes, the Light-God, in the Mysteries of the New Orphics, emerged from the egg of chaos: and the Persians had the great egg of Ormuzd. And Sanchoniathon tells us that in the Phœnician theology, the matter of chaos took the form of an egg; and he adds: "Such are the lessons which the Son of Thabion, first Hierophant of the Phœnicians, turned into allegories, in which physics and astronomy intermingled, and which he taught to the other Hierophants, whose duty it was to preside at orgies and initiations; and who, seeking to excite the astonishment and admiration of mortals, faithfully transmitted these things to their successors and the Initiates."

In the Mysteries was also taught the division of the Universal Cause into an Active and a Passive cause; of which two, Osiris and Isis,—the heavens and the earth were symbols. These two First Causes, into which it was held that the great Universal First Cause at the beginning of things divided itself, were the two great Divinities, whose worship was, according to Varro, inculcated upon the Initiates at Samothrace. "As is taught," he says, "in the initiation into the Mysteries at Samothrace, Heaven and Earth are regarded as the two first Divinities. They are the potent Gods worshipped in that Island, and whose names are consecrated in the books of our Augurs. One of them is male and the other female; and they bear the same relation to each other as the soul does to the body, humidity to dryness." The Curetes, in Crete, had builded an altar to Heaven and to Earth; whose Mysteries they celebrated at Gnossus, in a cypress grove.

These two Divinities, the Active and Passive Principles of the Universe, were commonly symbolized by the generative parts of man and woman; to which, in remote ages, no idea of indecency was attached; the *Phallus* and *Cteis*, emblems of generation and production, and which, as such, appeared in the Mysteries. The Indian Lingam was the union of both, as were the boat and mast, and the point within a circle: all of which expressed the same philosophical idea as to the Union of the two great Causes of Nature, which concur, one actively and the other passively, in the generation of all beings: which were symbolized by what we now term *Gemini*, the Twins, at that remote period when the Sun was in that Sign at the Vernal Equinox, and when they were Male and Female; and of which the Phallus was perhaps taken from the generative organ of the Bull, when about twenty-five hundred years before our era he opened that equinox, and became to the Ancient World the symbol of the creative and generative Power.

The Initiates at Eleusis commenced, Proclus says, by invoking the two great causes of nature, the Heavens and the Earth, on which in succession they fixed their eyes, addressing to each a prayer. And they deemed it their duty to do so, he adds, because they saw in them the Father and Mother of all generations. The concourse of these two agents of the Universe was termed in theological language a *marriage*. Tertullian, accusing the Valentinians of having borrowed these symbols from the Mysteries of Eleusis, yet admits that in those Mysteries they were explained in a manner consistent with decency, as representing the powers of nature. He was too little of a philosopher to comprehend the sublime esoteric meaning of these emblems, which will, if you advance, in other Degrees be unfolded to you.

The Christian Fathers contented themselves with reviling and ridiculing the use of these emblems. But as they in the earlier times created no indecent ideas, and were worn alike by the most innocent youths and virtuous women, it will be far wiser for us to seek to penetrate their meaning. Not only the Egyptians, says Diodorus Siculus, but every other people that consecrate this symbol (the Phallus), deem that they thereby do honor to the Active Force of the universal generation of all living things. For the same reason, as we learn from the geographer Ptolemy, it was revered among the Assyrians and Persians. Proclus remarks that in the distribution of the Zodiac among the twelve great Divinities, by ancient astrology, six signs were assigned to the male and six to the female principle.

There is another division of nature, which has in all ages struck all men, and which was not forgotten in the Mysteries; that of Light and Darkness, Day and Night, Good and Evil; which mingle with, and clash against, and pursue or are pursued by each other throughout the Universe. The Great Symbolic Egg distinctly reminded the Initiates of this great division of the world. Plutarch, treating of the dogma of a Providence, and of that of the two principles of Light and Darkness, which he regarded as the basis of the Ancient Theology, of the Orgies and the Myste-

of Chios and Tenedos, this death was represented by the sacrifice
of a man, actually immolated.

The mutilation and sufferings of the same Sun-God, honored
in Phrygia under the name of Atys, caused the tragic scenes that
were, as we learn from Diodorus Siculus, represented annually in
the Mysteries of Cybele, mother of the Gods. An image was
borne there, representing the corpse of a young man, over whose
tomb tears were shed, and to whom funeral honors were paid.

At Samothrace, in the Mysteries of the Cabiri or great Gods, a
representation was given of the death of one of them. This name
was given to the Sun, because the Ancient Astronomers gave the
name of Gods Cabiri and of Samothrace to the two Gods in the
Constellation Gemini; whom others term Apollo and Hercules,
two names of the Sun. Athenion says that the young Cabirus so
slain was the same as the Dionusos or Bakchos of the Greeks. The
Pelasgi, ancient inhabitants of Greece, and who settled Samothrace, celebrated these Mysteries, whose origin is unknown: and
they worshipped Castor and Pollux as patrons of navigation.

The tomb of Apollo was at Delphi, where his body was laid,
after Python, the Polar Serpent that annually heralds the coming
of autumn, cold, darkness, and winter, had slain him, and over
whom the God triumphs, on the 25th of March, on his return to
the lamb of the Vernal Equinox.

In Crete, Jupiter Ammon, or the Sun in Aries, painted with the
attributes of that equinoctial sign, the Ram or Lamb;—that Ammon who, Martianus Copella says, is the same as Osiris, Adoni,
Adonis, Atys, and the other Sun-Gods,—had also a tomb, and a
religious initiation; one of the principal ceremonies of which consisted in clothing the Initiate with the skin of a white lamb. And
in this we see the origin of the apron of white sheep-skin, used in
Masonry.

All these deaths and resurrections, these funeral emblems, these
anniversaries of mourning and joy, these cenotaphs raised in different places to the Sun-God, honored under different names, had
but a single object, the allegorical narration of the events which
happened here below to the Light of Nature, that sacred fire from
which our souls were deemed to emanate, warring with Matter and
the dark Principle resident therein, ever at variance with the Principle of Good and Light poured upon itself by the Supreme Divinity. All these Mysteries, says Clemens of Alexandria, displaying

PRINCE OF THE TABERNACLE.   411

and introduced the image of the sun into the body of the sanctuary, where he seemed to blaze as in the heights of Heaven, and to dissipate the darkness within that temple which was a representative symbol of the world. There the passion, death, and resurrection of Bakchos were represented.

So the Temple of Eleusis was lighted by a window in the roof. The sanctuary so lighted, Dion compares to the Universe, from which he says it differed in size alone; and in it the great lights of nature played a great part and were mystically represented. The images of the Sun, Moon, and Mercury were represented there, (the latter the same as Anubis who accompanied Isis); and they are still the three lights of a Masonic Lodge; except that for Mercury, the Master of the Lodge has been absurdly substituted.

Eusebius names as the principal Ministers in the Mysteries of Eleusis, first, the *Hierophant*, clothed with the attributes of the Grand Architect (Demiourgos) of the Universe. After him came the *Dadoukos*, or torch-bearer, representative of the Sun: then the altar-bearer, representing the Moon: and last, the *Hieroceryx*, bearing the caduceus, and representing Mercury. It was not permissible to reveal the different emblems and the mysterious pageantry of initiation to the Profane; and therefore we do not know the attributes, emblems, and ornaments of these and other officers; of which Apuleius and Pausanias dared not speak.

We know only that everything recounted there was marvellous; everything done there tended to astonish the Initiate: and that eyes and ears were equally astounded. The Hierophant, of lofty height, and noble features, with long hair, of a great age, grave and dignified, with a voice sweet and sonorous, sat upon a throne, clad in a long trailing robe; as the Motive-God of Nature was held to be enveloped in His work and hidden under a veil which no mortal can raise. Even His name was concealed, like that of the Demiourgos, whose name was ineffable.

The Dadoukos also wore a long robe, his hair long, and a bandeau on his forehead. Callias, when holding that office, fighting on the great day of Marathon, clothed with the insignia of his office, was taken by the Barbarians to be a King. The Dadoukos led the procession of the Initiates, and was charged with the purifications.

We do not know the functions of the *Epibomos* or assistant at the altar, who represented the moon. That planet was one of the

figure of the pyramid and that of the obelisk, resembling the shape of a flame, caused these monuments to be consecrated to the Sun and to Fire. And Timæus of Locria says: "The equilateral triangle enters into the composition of the pyramid, which has four equal faces and equal angles, and which in this is like fire, the most subtle and mobile of the elements." They and the obelisks were erected in honor of the Sun, termed in an inscription upon one of the latter, translated by the Egyptian Hermapion, and to be found in Ammianus Marcellinus, "Apollo the strong, Son of God, He who made the world, true Lord of the diadems, who possesses Egypt and fills it with His glory."

The two most famous divisions of the Heavens, by seven, which is that of the planets, and by twelve, which is that of the signs, are found on the religious monuments of all the people of the ancient world. The twelve Great Gods of Egypt are met with everywhere. They were adopted by the Greeks and Romans; and the latter assigned one of them to each sign of the Zodiac. Their images were seen at Athens, where an altar was erected to each; and they were painted on the porticos. The People of the North had their twelve *Azes,* or Senate of twelve great gods, of whom Odin was chief. The Japanese had the same number, and like the Egyptians divided them into classes, seven, who were the most ancient, and five, afterward added: both of which numbers are well known and consecrated in Masonry.

There is no more striking proof of the universal adoration paid the stars and constellations, than the arrangement of the Hebrew camp in the Desert, and the allegory in regard to the twelve Tribes of Israel, ascribed in the Hebrew legends to Jacob. The Hebrew camp was a quadrilateral, in sixteen divisions, of which the central four were occupied by images of the four elements. The four divisions at the four angles of the quadrilateral exhibited the four signs that the astrologers call *fixed,* and which they regard as subject to the influence of the four great Royal Stars, Regulus in Leo, Aldebaran in Taurus, Antares in Scorpio, and Fomalhaut in the mouth of Pisces, on which falls the water poured out by Aquarius; of which constellations the Scorpion was represented in the Hebrew blazonry by the Celestial Vulture or Eagle, that rises at the same time with it and is its paranatellon. The other signs were arranged on the four faces of the quadrilateral, and in the parallel and interior divisions.

Zodiac. The House of the Sun was in Leo, and that of the Moon in Cancer. Each other planet had two signs; Mercury had Gemini and Virgo; Venus, Taurus and Libra; Mars, Aries and Scorpio; Jupiter, Pisces and Sagittarius; and Saturn, Aquarius and Capricornus. From this distribution of the signs also came many mythological emblems and fables; as also many came from the places of exaltation of the planets. Diana of Ephesus, the Moon, wore the image of a crab on her bosom, because in that sign was the Moon's domicile; and lions bore up the throne of Horus, the Egyptian Apollo, the Sun personified, for a like reason: while the Egyptians consecrated the tauriform scarabæus to the Moon, because she had her place of exaltation in Taurus; and for the same reason Mercury is said to have presented Isis with a helmet like a bull's head.

A further division of the Zodiac was of each sign into three parts of 10° each, called Decans, or, in the whole Zodiac, 36 parts, among which the seven planets were apportioned anew, each planet having an equal number of Decans, except the first, which, opening and closing the series of planets five times repeated, necessarily had one Decan more than the others. This subdivision was not invented until after Aries opened the Vernal Equinox; and accordingly Mars, having his house in Aries, opens the series of decans and closes it; the planets following each other, five times in succession, in the following order, Mars, the Sun, Venus, Mercury, the Moon, Saturn, Jupiter, Mars, etc.; so that to each sign are assigned three planets, each occupying 10 degrees. To each Decan a God or Genius was assigned, making thirty-six in all, one of whom, the Chaldeans said, came down upon earth every ten days, remained so many days, and re-ascended to Heaven. This division is found on the Indian sphere, the Persian, and that Barbaric one which Aben Ezra describes. Each genius of the Decans had a name and special characteristics. They concur and aid in the effects produced by the Sun, Moon, and other planets charged with the administration of the world: and the doctrine in regard to them, secret and august as it was held, was considered of the gravest importance; and its principles, Firmicus says, were not entrusted by the ancients, inspired as they were by the Deity, to any but the Initiates, and to them only with great reserve, and a kind of fear, and when cautiously enveloped with an obscure veil, that they might not come to be known by the profane.

The creative action of Heaven was manifested, and all its de-
miurgic energy developed, most of all at the Vernal Equinox, to
which refer all the fables that typify the victory of Light over
Darkness, by the triumphs of Jupiter, Osiris, Ormuzd, and Apollo.
Always the triumphant god takes the form of the Bull, the Ram,
or the Lamb. Then Jupiter wrests from Typhon his thunderbolts,
of which that malignant Deity had possessed himself during the
Winter. Then the God of Light overwhelms his foe, pictured as a
huge Serpent. Then Winter ends; the Sun, seated on the Bull
and accompanied by Orion, blazes in the Heavens. All nature
rejoices at the victory; and Order and Harmony are everywhere
re-established, in place of the dire confusion that reigned while
gloomy Typhon domineered, and Ahriman prevailed against
Ormuzd.

The universal Soul of the World, motive power of Heaven and
of the Spheres, it was held, exercises its creative energy chiefly
through the medium of the Sun, during his revolution along the
signs of the Zodiac, with which signs unite the paranatellons that
modify their influence, and concur in furnishing the symbolic attributes of the Great Luminary that regulates Nature and is the
depository of her greatest powers. The action of this Universal
Soul of the World is displayed in the movements of the Spheres,
and above all in that of the Sun, in the successions of the risings
and settings of the Stars, and in their periodical returns. By these
are explainable all the metamorphoses of that Soul, personified as
Jupiter, as Bacchus, as Vishnu, or as Buddha, and all the various
attributes ascribed to it; and also the worship of those animals
that were consecrated in the ancient Temples, representatives on
earth of the Celestial Signs, and supposed to receive by transmis-
sion from them the rays and emanations which in them flow from
the Universal Soul.

All the old Adorers of Nature, the Theologians, Astrologers,
and Poets, as well as the most distinguished Philosophers, supposed that the Stars were so many animated and intelligent beings,
or eternal bodies, active causes of effect here below, animated by a
living principle, and directed by an intelligence that was itself but
an emanation from and a part of the life and universal intelligence of the world: and we find in the hierarchical order and
distribution of their eternal and divine Intelligences, known by
the names of Gods, Angels, and Genii, the same distributions and

the same divisions as those by which the ancients divided the visible Universe and distributed its parts. And the famous divisions by seven and by twelve, appertaining to the planets and the signs of the zodiac, is everywhere found in the hierarchical order of the Gods, and Angels, and the other Ministers that are the depositaries of that Divine Force which moves and rules the world.

These, and the other Intelligences assigned to the other Stars, have absolute dominion over all parts of Nature; over the elements, the animal and vegetable kingdoms, over man and all his actions, over his virtues and vices, and over good and evil, which divide between them his life. The passions of his soul and the maladies of his body,—these and the entire man are dependent on the heavens and the genii that there inhabit, who preside at his birth, control his fortunes during life, and receive his soul or active and intelligent part when it is to be re-united to the pure life of the lofty Stars. And all through the great body of the world are disseminated portions of the universal Soul, impressing movement on everything that seems to move of itself, giving life to the plants and trees, directing by a regular and settled plan the organization and development of their germs, imparting constant mobility to the running waters and maintaining their eternal motion, impelling the winds and changing their direction or stilling them, calming and arousing the ocean, unchaining the storms, pouring out the fires of volcanoes, or with earthquakes shaking the roots of huge mountains and the foundations of vast continents; by means of a force that, belonging to Nature, is a mystery to man.

And these invisible Intelligences, like the stars, are marshalled in two great divisions, under the banners of the two Principles of Good and Evil, Light and Darkness; under Ormuzd and Ahriman, Osiris and Typhon. The Evil Principle was the motive power of brute matter; and it, personified as Ahriman and Typhon, had its hosts and armies of Devs and Genii, Fallen Angels and Malevolent Spirits, who waged continual war with the Good Principle, the Principle of Empyreal Light and Splendor, Osiris, Ormuzd, Jupiter or Dionusos, with his bright hosts of Amshaspands, Izeds, Angels, and Archangels; a warfare that goes on from birth until death, in the soul of every man that lives.

We have heretofore, in the 24th Degree, recited the principal incidents in the legend of Osiris and Isis, and it remains but to point

organs of generation, which had been thrown into and devoured in the waters of the river that every year fertilized Egypt. The other portions were buried by Isis, and over them she erected a tomb. Thereafter she remained single, loading her subjects with blessings. She cured the sick, restored sight to the blind, made the paralytic whole, and even raised the dead. From her Horus or Apollo learned divination and the science of medicine.

Thus the Egyptians pictured the beneficent action of the two luminaries that, from the bosom of the elements, produced all animals and men, and all bodies that are born, grow, and die in the eternal circle of generation and destruction here below.

When the Celestial Bull opened the new year at the Vernal Equinox, Osiris, united with the Moon, communicated to her the seeds of fruitfulness which she poured upon the air, and therewith impregnated the generative principles which gave activity to universal vegetation. Apis, represented by a bull, was the living and sensible image of the Sun or Osiris, when in union with Isis or the Moon at the Vernal Equinox, concurring with her in provoking everything that lives to generation. This conjunction of the Sun with the Moon at the Vernal Equinox, in the constellation Taurus, required the Bull Apis to have on his shoulder a mark resembling the Crescent Moon. And the fecundating influence of these two luminaries was expressed by images that would now be deemed gross and indecent, but which then were not misunderstood.

Everything good in Nature comes from Osiris,—order, harmony, and the favorable temperature of the seasons and celestial periods. From Typhon come the stormy passions and irregular impulses that agitate the brute and material part of man; maladies of the body, and violent shocks that injure the health and derange the system; inclement weather, derangement of the seasons, and eclipses. Osiris and Typhon were the Ormuzd and Ahriman of the Persians; principles of good and evil, of light and darkness, ever at war in the administration of the Universe.

Osiris was the image of generative power. This was expressed by his symbolic statues, and by the sign into which he entered at the Vernal Equinox. He especially dispensed the humid principle of Nature, generative element of all things; and the Nile and all moisture were regarded as emanations from him, without which there could be no vegetation.

That Osiris and Isis were the Sun and Moon, is attested by many

At Dedan and Saba it was thirty-six days, from the beginning of the *aphanisin,* i. e. the *disappearances* of these stars, to the heliacal rising of Aldebaran. During these days, or forty at Medina, or a few more at Babylon and Byblos, the stars of the Husbandman successively sank out of sight, during the *crepusculum* or short-lived morning twilight of those Southern climes. They disappear during the glancings of the dawn, the special season of ancient sidereal observation.

Thus the forty days of mourning for Osiris were measured out by the period of the departure of his Stars. When the last had sunken out of sight, the vernal season was ushered in; and the Sun arose with the splendid Aldebaran, the Tauric leader of the Hosts of Heaven; and the whole East rejoiced and kept holiday.

With the exception of the Stars x, ϵ and ϑ, Boötes did not begin to reappear in the Eastern quarter of the Heavens till after the lapse of about four months. Then the Stars of Taurus had declined Westward, and Virgo was rising heliacally. In that latitude, also, the Stars of Ursa Major [termed anciently the Ark of Osiris] set; and Benetnasch, the last of them, returned to the Eastern horizon, with those in the head of Leo, a little before the Summer Solstice. In about a month, followed the Stars of the Husbandman; the chief of them, Ras, Mirach, and Arcturus, being very nearly simultaneous in their heliacal rising.

Thus the Stars of Boötes rose in the East immediately after Vindemiatrix, and as if under the genial influence of its rays; he had his annual career of prosperity; he revelled orientally for a quarter of a year, and attained his meridian altitude with Virgo; and then, as the Stars of the Water-Urn rose, and Aquarius began to pour forth his annual deluge, he declined Westward, preceded by the Ark of Osiris. In the East, he was the sign of that happiness in which Nature, the great Goddess of passive production, rejoiced. Now, in the West, as he declines toward the Northwestern horizon, his generative vigor gradually abates; the Solar year grows old; and as his Stars descend beneath the Western Wave, Osiris dies, and the world mourns.

The Ancient Astronomers saw all the great Symbols of Masonry in the Stars. Sirius still glitters in our Lodges as the Blazing Star, (*l'Etoile Flamboyante*). The Sun is still symbolized by the point within a Circle; and, with the Moon and Mercury or Anubis, in the three Great Lights of the Lodge. Not only to these, but to the figures and numbers exhibited by the Stars, were ascribed peculiar and divine powers. The veneration paid to numbers had its source there. The three Kings in Orion are in a straight line, and equidistant from each other, the two extreme Stars being 3° apart, and each of the three distant from the one nearest it 1° 30'. And as the number *three* is peculiar to apprentices, so the straight line is the first principle of Geometry, having length but no breadth, and being but the extension of a point, and an emblem of Unity, and thus of Good, as the divided or broken line is of Duality or Evil. Near these Stars are the Hyades, *five* in number, appropriate to the Fellow-Craft; and close to them the Pleiades, of the master's number, *seven;* and thus these three sacred numbers, consecrated in Masonry as they were in the Pythagorean philosophy, always appear together in the Heavens, when the Bull, emblem of fertility and production, glitters among the Stars, and Aldebaran leads the Hosts of Heaven (*Tsbauth*).

Algenib in Perseus and Almaach and Algol in Andromeda form a right-angled triangle, illustrate the 47th problem, and display the Grand Master's square upon the skies. Denebola in Leo, Arcturus in Boötes, and Spica in Virgo form an equilateral triangle, universal emblem of Perfection, and the Deity with His Trinity of Infinite Attributes, Wisdom, Power, and Harmony; and that other, the generative, preserving, and destroying Powers. The Three Kings form, with Rigel in Orion, two triangles included in one: and Capella and Menkalina in Auriga, with Bellatrix and Betelgueux in Orion, form two isosceles triangles with β Tauri, that is equidistant from each pair; while the first four make a right-angled parallelogram,—the oblong square so often mentioned in our Degrees.

Julius Firmicus, in his description of the Mysteries, says, "But in those funerals and lamentations which are annually celebrated in honor of Osiris, their defenders pretend a physical reason. They call the seeds of fruit, Osiris; the Earth, Isis; the natural heat, Typhon: and because the fruits are ripened by the natural heat, and collected for the life of man, and are separated from their marriage to the earth, and are sown again when Winter approaches. this they would have to be the death of Osiris: but when the fruits, by the genial fostering of the earth, begin again to be generated by a new procreation, this is the finding of Osiris."

No doubt the decay of vegetation and the falling of the leaves,

God, of a creative, productive, governing unity, resided in the earliest exertion of thought: and this monotheism of the primitive ages, makes every succeeding epoch, unless it be the present, appear only as a stage in the progress of degeneracy and aberration. Everywhere in the old faiths we find the idea of a supreme or presiding Deity. Amun or Osiris presides among the many gods of Egypt; Pan, with the music of his pipe, directs the chorus of the constellations, as Zeus leads the solemn procession of the celestial troops in the astronomical theology of the Pythagoreans. "Amidst an infinite diversity of opinions on all other subjects," says Maximus Tyrius, "the whole world is unanimous in the belief of one only almighty King and Father of all."

There is always a Sovereign Power, a Zeus or Deus, Mahadeva or Adideva, to whom belongs the maintenance of the order of the Universe. Among the thousand gods of India, the doctrine of Divine Unity is never lost sight of; and the ethereal Jove, worshipped by the Persian in an age long before Xenophanes or Anaxagoras, appears as supremely comprehensive and independent of planetary or elemental subdivisions, as the "Vast One" or "Great Soul" of the Vedas.

But the simplicity of belief of the patriarchs did not exclude the employment of symbolical representations. The mind never rests satisfied with a mere feeling. That feeling ever strives to assume precision and durability as an idea, by some *outward* delineation of its thought. Even the ideas that are above and beyond the senses, as all ideas of God are, require the aid of the senses for their expression and communication. Hence come the representative forms and symbols which constitute the external investiture of every religion; attempts to express a religious sentiment that is essentially *one,* and that vainly struggles for adequate external utterance, striving to tell to one man, to *paint* to him, an idea existing in the mind of another, and essentially incapable of utterance or description, in a language all the words of which have a sensuous meaning. Thus, the idea being perhaps the same in all, its expressions and utterances are infinitely various, and branch into an infinite diversity of creeds and sects.

All religious expression is symbolism; since we can describe only what we see; and the true objects of religion are unseen. The earliest instruments of education were symbols; and they and all other religious forms differed and still differ according to

XXVI.

PRINCE OF MERCY, OR SCOTTISH TRINITARIAN.

WHILE you were veiled in darkness, you heard repeated by the Voice of the Great Past its most ancient doctrines. None has the right to object, if the Christian Mason sees foreshadowed in Chrishna and Sosiosch, in Mithras and Osiris, the Divine WORD that, as he believes, became Man, and died upon the cross to redeem a fallen race. Nor can *he* object if others see reproduced, in the WORD of the beloved Disciple, that was in the beginning with God, and that was God, and by Whom everything was made, only the LOGOS of Plato, and the WORD or Uttered THOUGHT or first Emanation of LIGHT, or the Perfect REASON of the Great, Silent, Supreme, Uncreated Deity, believed in and adored by all.

We do not undervalue the importance of any Truth. We utter no word that can be deemed irreverent by any one of any faith. We do not tell the Moslem that it is only important for him to believe that there is but one God, and wholly unessential whether Mahomet was His prophet. We do not tell the Hebrew that the Messiah whom he expects was born in Bethlehem nearly two thousand years ago; and that he is a heretic because he will not so believe. And as little do we tell the sincere Christian that Jesus of Nazareth was but a man like us, or His history but the unreal revival of an older legend. To do either is beyond our jurisdiction. Masonry, of no one age, belongs to all time; of no one religion, it finds its great truths in all.

To every Mason, there is a GOD; ONE, Supreme, Infinite in Goodness, Wisdom, Foresight, Justice, and Benevolence; Creator, Disposer, and Preserver of all things. How, or by what intermediates He creates and acts, and in what way He unfolds and manifests Himself, Masonry leaves to creeds and Religions to inquire.

To every Mason, the soul of man is immortal. Whether it

emanates from and will return to God, and what its continued mode of existence hereafter, each judges for himself. Masonry was not made to settle that.

To every Mason, WISDOM or INTELLIGENCE, FORCE or STRENGTH, and HARMONY, or FITNESS and BEAUTY, are the Trinity of the attributes of God. With the subtleties of Philosophy concerning them Masonry does not meddle, nor decide as to the reality of the supposed Existences which are their Personifications : nor whether the Christian Trinity be such a personification. or a Reality of the gravest import and significance.

To every Mason, the Infinite Justice and Benevolence of God give ample assurance that Evil will ultimately be dethroned, and the Good, the True, and the Beautiful reign triumphant and eternal. It teaches, as it feels and knows, that Evil, and Pain, and Sorrow exist as part of a wise and beneficent plan, all the parts of which work together under God's eye to a result which shall be perfection. Whether the existence of evil is rightly explained in this creed or in that, by Typhon the Great Serpent, by Ahriman and his Armies of Wicked Spirits, by the Giants and Titans that war against Heaven, by the two co-existent Principles of Good and Evil, by Satan's temptation and the fall of Man, by Lok and the Serpent Fenris, it is beyond the domain of Masonry to decide, nor does it need to inquire. Nor is it within its Province to determine how the ultimate triumph of Light and Truth and Good, over Darkness and Error and Evil, is to be achieved ; nor whether the Redeemer, looked and longed for by all nations, hath appeared in Judea, or is yet to come.

It reverences all the great reformers. It sees in Moses, the Lawgiver of the Jews, in Confucius and Zoroaster, in Jesus of Nazareth, and in the Arabian Iconoclast, Great Teachers of Morality, and Eminent Reformers, if no more : and allows every brother of the Order to assign to each such higher and even Divine Character as his Creed and Truth require.

Thus Masonry disbelieves no truth, and teaches unbelief in no creed, except so far as such creed may lower its lofty estimate of the Deity, degrade Him to the level of the passions of humanity, deny the high destiny of man, impugn the goodness and benevolence of the Supreme God, strike at those great columns of Masonry, Faith, Hope, and Charity, or inculcate immorality, and disregard of the active duties of the Order.

return to God and be forever happy, in His good time; as our mortal bodies, dissolving, return to the elements from which they came, their particles coming and going ever in perpetual genesis. To our Jewish Brethren, this supper is symbolical of the Passover: to the Christian Mason, of that eaten by Christ and His Disciples, when, celebrating the Passover, He broke bread and gave it to them, saying, "Take! eat! this is My body:" and giving them the cup, He said, "Drink ye all of it! for this is My blood of the New Testament, which is shed for many for the remission of sins:" thus symbolizing the perfect harmony and union between Himself and the faithful; and His death upon the cross for the salvation of man.

The history of Masonry is the history of Philosophy. Masons do not pretend to set themselves up for instructors of the human race: but, though Asia produced and preserved the Mysteries, Masonry has, in Europe and America, given regularity to their doctrines, spirit, and action, and developed the moral advantages which mankind may reap from them. More consistent, and more simple in its mode of procedure, it has put an end to the vast allegorical pantheon of ancient mythologies, and itself become a science.

None can deny that Christ taught a lofty morality. "Love one another: forgive those that despitefully use you and persecute you: be pure of heart, meek, humble, contented: lay not up riches on earth, but in Heaven: submit to the powers lawfully over you: become like these little children, or ye cannot be saved, for of such is the Kingdom of Heaven: forgive the repentant; and cast no stone at the sinner, if you too have sinned: do unto others as ye would have others do unto you:" such, and not abstruse questions of theology, were His simple and sublime teachings.

The early Christians followed in His footsteps. The first preachers of the faith had no thought of domination. Entirely animated by His saying, that he among them should be first, who should serve with the greatest devotion, they were humble, modest, and charitable, and they knew how to communicate this spirit of the inner man to the churches under their direction. These churches were at first but spontaneous meetings of all Christians inhabiting the same locality. A pure and severe morality, mingled with religious enthusiasm, was the characteristic of each, and excited the admiration even of their persecutors. Everything was in common among them; their property, their joys, and their sorrows. In the silence of night they met for instruction and to pray together. Their love-feasts, or fraternal repasts, ended these reunions, in which all differences in social position and rank were effaced in the presence of a paternal Divinity. Their sole object was to make men better, by bringing them back to a simple worship, of which universal morality was the basis; and to end those numerous and cruel sacrifices which everywhere inundated with blood the altars of the gods. Thus did Christianity reform the world, and obey the teachings of its founder. It gave to woman her proper rank and influence; it regulated domestic life: and by admitting the slaves to the love-feasts, it by degrees raised them above that oppression under which half of mankind had groaned for ages.

This, in its purity, as taught by Christ Himself, was the true primitive religion, as communicated by God to the Patriarchs. It was no new religion, but the reproduction of the oldest of all; and its true and perfect morality is the morality of Masonry, as is the morality of every creed of antiquity.

In the early days of Christianity, there was an initiation like those of the Pagans. Persons were admitted on special conditions only. To arrive at a complete knowledge of the doctrine, they had to pass three degrees of instruction. The Initiates were consequently divided into three classes; the first, *Auditors*, the second, *Catechumens*, and the third, *the Faithful*. The Auditors were a sort of novices, who were prepared by certain ceremonies and certain instruction to receive the dogmas of Christianity. A portion of these dogmas was made known to the Catechumens; who, after particular purifications, received baptism, or the initiation of the *theogenesis* (*divine generation*); but in the grand mysteries of that religion, the incarnation, nativity, passion, and resurrection of Christ, none were initiated but *the Faithful*. These doctrines, and the celebration of the Holy Sacraments, particularly the Eucharist, were kept with profound secrecy. These Mysteries were divided into two parts; the first styled the Mass of the Catechumens; the second, the Mass of the Faithful. The celebration of the Mysteries of Mithras was also styled *a mass;* and the ceremonies used were the same. There were found all the sacraments of the Catholic Church, even the breath of confirmation. The Priest of Mithras promised the Initiates deliverance from sin, by means

the Faithful [Πιστοι], who possess the knowledge, may be still more informed, and those who are not acquainted with it, may suffer no disadvantage."

Cyril, Bishop of Jerusalem, was born in the year 315, and died in 386. In his *Catechesis* he says: "The Lord spake in parables to His hearers in general; but to His disciples He explained in private the parables and allegories which He spoke in public. 'The splendor of glory is for those who are early enlightened: obscurity and darkness are the portion of the unbelievers and ignorant. Just so the church discovers its Mysteries to those who have advanced beyond the class of Catechumens: we employ obscure terms with others."

St. Basil, the Great Bishop of Cæsarea born in the year 326, and dying in the year 376, says: "We receive the dogmas transmitted to us by writing, and those which have descended to us from the Apostles, beneath the mystery of oral tradition: for several things have been handed to us without writing, lest the vulgar, too familiar with our dogmas, should lose a due respect for them. . . .This is what the uninitiated are not permitted to contemplate; and how should it ever be proper to write and circulate among the people an account of them?"

St. Gregory Nazianzen, Bishop of Constantinople, A. D. 379, says: "You have heard as much of the Mystery as we are allowed to speak openly in the ears of all; the rest will be communicated to you in private; and that you must retain within yourself. . . . . Our Mysteries are not to be made known to strangers."

St. Ambrose, Archbishop of Milan, who was born in 340, and died in 393, says in his work *De Mysteriis:* "All the Mystery should be kept concealed, guarded by faithful silence, lest it should be inconsiderately divulged to the ears of the Profane. . . . . It is not given to all to contemplate the depths of our Mysteries. . . . that they may not be seen by those who ought not to behold them; nor received by those who cannot preserve them." And in another work: "He sins against God, who divulges to the unworthy the Mysteries confided to him. The danger is not merely in violating truth, but in telling truth, if he allow himself to give hints of them to those from whom they ought to be concealed.....Beware of casting pearls before swine!....Every Mystery ought to be kept secret; and, as it were, to be covered over by silence, lest it should rashly be

that are themselves *not* matter. We give them names, but *what* they really are, and what their essence, we are wholly ignorant.

But, fortunately, it does not follow that we may not *believe*, or even *know*, that which we cannot *explain* to ourselves, or that which is beyond the reach of our comprehension. If we believed only that which our intellect can grasp, measure, comprehend, and have distinct and clear ideas of, we should believe scarce anything. The senses are not the witnesses that bear testimony to us of the loftiest truths.

Our greatest difficulty is, that language is not adequate to express our ideas; because our words refer to *things*, and are images of what is substantial and material. If we use the word *"emanation,"* our mind involuntarily recurs to something material, *flowing out* of some other thing that is material; and if we *reject* this idea of materiality, nothing is left of the emanation but an unreality. The word "thing" itself suggests to us that which is material and within the cognizance and jurisdiction of the senses. If we cut away from it the idea of materiality, it presents itself to us as *no* thing, but an intangible unreality, which the mind vainly endeavors to grasp. *Existence* and *Being* are terms that have the same color of materiality; and when we speak of a *Power* or *Force*, the mind immediately images to itself one physical and material thing acting upon another. Eliminate that idea; and the Power or Force, devoid of physical characteristics, seems as unreal as the shadow that dances on a wall, itself a mere *absence* of light; as spirit is to us merely that which is *not* matter.

Infinite space and infinite time are the two primary ideas. We formulize them thus: add body to body and sphere to sphere, until the imagination wearies; and still there will remain beyond, a void, empty, unoccupied SPACE, limitless, because it *is* void. Add event to event in continuous succession, forever and forever, and there will still remain, before and after, a TIME in which there was and will be no event, and also endless because it too *is* void.

Thus these two ideas of the boundlessness of space and the endlessness of time seem to *involve* the ideas that matter and events are limited and finite. We cannot conceive of an *infinity* of worlds or of events; but only of an *indefinite* number of each; for, as we struggle to conceive of their *infinity*, the thought ever occurs in despite of all our efforts—there must be *space* in which

Infinite Being penetrated the brain, and became the Soul: and lo, MAN THE IMMORTAL! Thus, threefold, fruit of God's thought, is Man; that sees and hears and feels; that thinks and reasons; that loves and is in harmony with the Universe.

Before the world grew old, the primitive Truth faded out from men's Souls. Then man asked himself, *"What am I? and how and whence am I? and whither do I go?"* And the Soul, looking inward upon itself, strove to learn whether that "I" were mere matter; its thought and reason and its passions and affections mere results of material combination; or a material Being enveloping an immaterial Spirit: . . and further it strove, by self-examination, to learn whether that Spirit were an individual essence, with a separate immortal existence, or an infinitesimal portion of a Great First Principle, inter-penetrating the Universe and the infinitude of space, and undulating like light and heat: . . and so they wandered further amid the mazes of error; and imagined vain philosophies; wallowing in the sloughs of materialism and sensualism, of beating their wings vainly in the vacuum of abstractions and idealities.

While yet the first oaks still put forth their leaves, man lost the perfect knowledge of the One True God, the Ancient Absolute Existence, the Infinite Mind and Supreme Intelligence; and floated helplessly out upon the shoreless ocean of conjecture. Then the soul vexed itself with seeking to learn whether the material Universe was a mere chance combination of atoms, or the work of Infinite, Uncreated Wisdom: . . whether the Deity was a concentrated, and the Universe an extended immateriality; or whether He was a personal existence, an Omnipotent, Eternal, Supreme Essence, regulating matter at will; or subjecting it to unchangeable laws throughout eternity; and to Whom, Himself Infinite and Eternal, Space and Time are unknown. With their finite limited vision, they sought to learn the source and explain the existence of Evil, and Pain, and Sorrow; and so they wandered ever deeper into the darkness, and were lost; and there was for them no longer any God; but only a great, dumb, soulless Universe, full of mere emblems and symbols.

You have heretofore, in some of the Degrees through which you have passed, heard much of the ancient worship of the Sun, the Moon, and the other bright luminaries of Heaven, and of the Elements and Powers of Universal Nature. You have been made, to some extent, familiar with their personifications as Heroes suffering or triumphant, or as personal Gods or Goddesses, with human characteristics and passions, and with the multitude of legends and fables that do but allegorically represent their risings and settings, their courses, their conjunctions and oppositions, their domiciles and places of exaltation.

Perhaps you have supposed that we, like many who have written on these subjects, have intended to represent this worship to you as the most ancient and original worship of the first men that lived. To undeceive you, if such was your conclusion, we have caused the Personifications of the Great Luminary of Heaven, under the names by which he was known to the most ancient nations, to proclaim the old primitive truths that were known to the Fathers of our race, before men came to worship the visible manifestations of the Supreme Power and Magnificence and the Supposed Attributes of the Universal Deity in the Elements and in the glittering armies that Night regularly marshals and arrays upon the blue field of the firmament.

We ask now your attention to a still further development of these truths, after we shall have added something to what we have already said in regard to the Chief Luminary of Heaven, in explanation of the names and characteristics of the several imaginary Deities that represented him among the ancient races of men.

ATHOM or ATHOM-RE, was the Chief and Oldest Supreme God of Upper Egypt, worshipped at Thebes; the same as the OM or AUM of the Hindūs, whose name was unpronounceable, and who, like the BREHM of the latter People, was "The Being that was, and is, and is to come; the Great God, the Great Omnipotent, Omniscient, and Omnipresent One, the Greatest in the Universe, the Lord;" whose emblem was a perfect sphere, showing that He was first, last, midst, and without end; superior to all Nature-Gods, and all personifications of Powers, Elements, and Luminaries; symbolized by Light, the Principle of Life.

AMUN was the Nature-God, or Spirit of Nature, called by that name or AMUN-RE, and worshipped at Memphis in Lower Egypt, and in Libya, as well as in Upper Egypt. He was the Libyan Jupiter, and represented the intelligent and organizing force that develops itself in Nature, when the intellectual types or forms of bodies are revealed to the senses in the world's order, by their

Nature-God AL, and still beyond him, Abstract Existence, IHUH—He that IS, WAS, and SHALL BE. Above all the Persian Deities was the Unlimited Time, ZERUANE-AKHERENE; and over Odin and Thor was the Great Scandinavian Deity ALFADIR.

The worship of Universal Nature as a God was too near akin to the worship of a Universal Soul, to have been the instinctive creed of any savage people or rude race of men. To imagine all nature, with all its apparently independent parts, as forming one consistent whole, and as itself a unit, required an amount of experience and a faculty of generalization not possessed by the rude uncivilized mind, and is but a step below the idea of a universal Soul.

In the beginning man had the WORD; and that WORD was from God; and out of the living POWER communicated to man in and by that WORD, came THE LIGHT of His Existence.

God made man in His own likeness. When, by a long succession of geological changes, He had prepared the earth to be his habitation, He created him, and placed him in that part of Asia which all the old nations agreed in calling the cradle of the human race, and whence afterward the stream of human life flowed forth to India, China, Egypt, Persia, Arabia, and Phœnicia. HE communicated to him a knowledge of the nature of his Creator, and of the pure, primitive, undefiled religion. The peculiar and distinctive excellence and real essence of the primitive man, and his true nature and destiny, consisted in his likeness to God. HE stamped HIS own image upon man's soul. That image has been, in the breast of every individual man and of mankind in general, greatly altered, impaired, and defaced; but its old, half-obliterated characters are still to be found on all the pages of primitive history; and the impress, not entirely effaced, every reflecting mind may discover in its own interior.

Of the original revelation to mankind, of the primitive WORD of Divine TRUTH, we find clear indications and scattered traces in the sacred traditions of all the primitive Nations; traces which, when separately examined, appear like the broken remnants, the mysterious and hieroglyphic characters, of a mighty edifice that has been destroyed; and its fragments, like those of the old Temples and Palaces of Nimroud, wrought incongruously into edifices many centuries younger. And, although amid the ever-growing degeneracy of mankind, this primeval word of revelation was falsified by the admixture of various errors, and overlaid and obscured by numberless and manifold fictions, inextricably confused, and disfigured almost beyond the power of recognition, still a profound inquiry will discover in heathenism many luminous vestiges of primitive Truth.

For the old Heathenism had everywhere a foundation in Truth; and if we could separate that pure intuition into nature and into the simple symbols of nature, that constituted the basis of all Heathenism, from the alloy of error and the additions of fiction, those first hieroglyphic traits of the instinctive science of the first men, would be found to agree with truth and a true knowledge of nature, and to afford an image of a free, pure, comprehensive, and finished philosophy of life.

The struggle, thenceforward to be eternal, between the Divine will and the natural will in the souls of men, commenced immediately after the creation. Cain slew his brother Abel, and went forth to people parts of the earth with an impious race, forgetters and defiers of the true God. The other Descendants of the Common Father of the race intermarried with the daughters of Cain's Descendants: and all nations preserved the remembrance of that division of the human family into the righteous and impious, in their distorted legends of the wars between the Gods, and the Giants and Titans. When, afterward, another similar division occurred, the Descendants of Seth alone preserved the true primitive religion and science, and transmitted them to posterity in the ancient symbolical character, on monuments of stone: and many nations preserved in their legendary traditions the memory of the columns of Enoch and Seth.

Then the world declined from its original happy condition and fortunate estate, into idolatry and barbarism: but all nations retained the memory of that old estate; and the poets, in those early days the only historians, commemorated the succession of the ages of gold, silver, brass, and iron.

In the lapse of those ages, the sacred tradition followed various courses among each of the most ancient nations; and from its original source, as from a common centre, its various streams flowed downward; some diffusing through favored regions of the world fertility and life; but others soon losing themselves, and being dried up in the sterile sands of human error.

After the internal and Divine WORD originally communicated

by God to man, had become obscured; after man's connection
with his Creator had been broken, even outward language necessarily fell into disorder and confusion. The simple and Divine
Truth was overlaid with various and sensual fictions, buried under
illusive symbols, and at last perverted into horrible phantoms.

For in the progress of idolatry it needs came to pass, that what
was originally revered as the symbol of a higher principle, became
gradually confounded or identified with the object itself, and was
worshipped; until this error led to a more degraded form of idolatry. The early nations received much from the primeval source
of sacred tradition; but that haughty pride which seems an
inherent part of human nature led each to represent these
fragmentary relics of original truth as a possession peculiar to
themselves; thus exaggerating their value, and their own importance, as peculiar favorites of the Deity, who had chosen them as
the favored people to whom to commit these truths. To make
these fragments, as far as possible, their private property, they
reproduced them under peculiar forms, wrapped them up in
symbols, concealed them in allegories, and invented fables to
account for their own special possession of them. So that, instead
of preserving in their primitive simplicity and purity these blessings of original revelation, they overlaid them with poetical
ornament; and the whole wears a fabulous aspect, until by close
and severe examination we discover the truth which the apparent
fable contains.

These being the conflicting elements in the breast of man; the
old inheritance or original dowry of truth, imparted to him by
God in the primitive revelation; and error, or the foundation for
error, in his degraded sense and spirit now turned from God to
nature, false faiths easily sprung up and grew rank and luxuriant,
when the Divine Truth was no longer guarded with jealous care,
nor preserved in its pristine purity. This soon happened among
most Eastern nations, and especially the Indians, the Chaldeans,
the Arabians, the Persians, and the Egyptians; with whom imagination, and a very deep but still sensual feeling for nature, were
very predominant. The Northern firmament, visible to their eyes,
possesses by far the largest and most brilliant constellations; and
they were more alive to the impressions made by such objects, than
are the men of the present day.

With the Chinese, a patriarchal, simple, and secluded people, idolatry long made but little progress. They invented writing within three or four generations after the flood ; and they long preserved the memory of much of the primitive revelation : less overlaid with fiction than those fragments which other nations have remembered. They were among those who stood nearest to the source of sacred tradition ; and many passages in their old writings contain remarkable vestiges of eternal truth, and of the WORD of primitive revelation, the heritage of old thought, which attest to us their original eminence.

But among the other early nations, a wild enthusiasm and a sensual idolatry of nature soon superseded the simple worship of the Almighty God, and set aside or disfigured the pure belief in the Eternal Uncreated Spirit. The great powers and elements of nature, and the vital principle of production and procreation through all generations; then the celestial spirits or heavenly Host, the luminous armies of the Stars, and the great Sun, and mysterious, ever-changing Moon (all of which the whole ancient world regarded not as mere globes of light or bodies of fire, but as animated living substances, potent over man's fate and destinies) ; next the genii and tutelar spirits, and even the souls of the dead, received divine worship. The animals, representing the starry constellations, first reverenced as symbols merely, came to be worshipped as gods ; the heavens, earth, and the operations of nature were personified ; and fictitious personages invented to account for the introduction of science and arts, and the fragments of the old religious truths ; and the good and bad principles personified, became also objects of worship ; while, through all, still shone the silver threads of the old primitive revelation.

Increasing familiarity with early oriental records seems more and more to confirm the probability that they all originally emanated from one source. The eastern and southern slopes of the Paropismus, or Hindukusch, appear to have been inhabited by kindred Iranian races, similar in habits, language, and religion. The earliest Indian and Persian Deities are for the most part symbols of celestial light, their agency being regarded as an eternal warfare with the powers of Winter, storm, and darkness. The religion of both was originally a worship of outward nature, especially the manifestations of fire and light ; the coincidences being too marked to be merely accidental. Deva, God, is derived from the root *div*, to shine. Indra, like Ormuzd or Ahura-Mazda, is the bright firmative idea of the creation: "In the beginning, the Universe was but a Soul: nothing else, active or inactive, existed. Then HE had this thought, *I will create worlds;* and thus HE created these different worlds; air, the light, mortal beings, and the waters.

"HE had this thought: *Behold the worlds; I will create guardians for the worlds.* So HE took of the water and fashioned a being clothed with the human form. He looked upon him, and of that being so contemplated, the mouth opened like an egg, and speech came forth, and from the speech fire. The nostrils opened, and through them went the breath of respiration, and by it the air was propagated. The eyes opened; from them came a luminous ray, and from it was produced the sun. The ears dilated; from them came hearing, and from hearing space:" . . . and, after the body of man, with the senses, was formed;—"HE, the Universal Soul, thus reflected: *How can this body exist without Me?* He examined through what extremity He could penetrate it. He said to Himself: If, *without Me, the World is articulated, breath exhales, and sight sees; if hearing hears, the skin feels, and the mind reflects, deglutition swallows, and the generative organ fulfils its functions, what then am I?* And separating the suture of the cranium, He penetrated into man."

Behold the great fundamental primitive truths! God, an infinite Eternal Soul or Spirit. Matter, not eternal nor self-existent, but created—created by a thought of God. After matter, and worlds, then man, by a like thought: and finally, after endowing him with the senses and a thinking mind, a portion, a spark, of God Himself penetrates the man, and becomes a living spirit within him.

The Vedas thus detail the creation of the world:

"In the beginning there was a single God, existing of Himself; Who, after having passed an eternity absorbed in the contemplation of His own being, desired to manifest His perfections outwardly of Himself; and created the matter of the world. The four elements being thus produced, but still mingled in confusion, He breathed upon the waters, which swelled up into an immense ball in the shape of an egg, and, developing themselves, became the vault and orb of Heaven which encircles the earth. Having made the earth and the bodies of animal beings, this God, the essence of movement, gave to them, to animate them, a portion of His own being. Thus, the soul of everything that breathes being a fraction of the universal soul, none perishes; but each soul merely changes its mould and form, by passing successively into different bodies. Of all forms, that which most pleases the Divine Being is Man, as nearest approaching His own perfections. When a man, absolutely disengaging himself from his senses, absorbs himself in self-contemplation, he comes to discern the Divinity, and becomes part of Him."

The Ancient Persians in many respects resembled the Hindūs,—in their language, their poetry, and their poetic legends. Their conquests brought them in contact with China; and they subdued Egypt and Judea. Their views of God and religion more resembled those of the Hebrews than those of any other nation; and indeed the latter people borrowed from them some prominent doctrines, that we are in the habit of regarding as an essential part of the original Hebrew creed.

Of the King of Heaven and Father of Eternal Light, of the pure World of LIGHT, of the Eternal WORD by which all things were created, of the Seven Mighty Spirits that stand next to the Throne of Light and Omnipotence, and of the glory of those Heavenly Hosts that encompass that Throne, of the Origin of Evil, and the Prince of Darkness, Monarch of the rebellious spirits, enemies of all good, they entertained tenets very similar to those of the Hebrews. Toward Egyptian idolatry they felt the strongest abhorrence, and under Cambyses pursued a regular plan for its utter extirpation. Xerxes, when he invaded Greece, destroyed the Temples and erected fire-chapels along the whole course of his march. Their religion was eminently spiritual, and the earthly fire and earthly sacrifice were but the signs and emblems of another devotion and a higher power.

Thus the fundamental doctrine of the ancient religion of India and Persia was at first nothing more than a simple veneration of nature, its pure elements and its primary energies, the sacred fire, and above all, Light,—the air, not the lower atmospheric air, but the purer and brighter air of Heaven, the breath that animates and pervades the breath of mortal life. This pure and simple veneration of nature is perhaps the most ancient, and was by far the most generally prevalent in the primitive and patriarchal world. It was not originally a deification of nature, or a denial of the sovereignty of God. Those pure elements and primitive essences of created nature offered to the first men, still in a close communication with the Deity, not a likeness of resemblance, nor a mere fanciful image or a poetical figure, but a natural and true symbol of Divine power. Everywhere in the Hebrew writings the pure light or sacred fire is employed as an image of the all-pervading and all-consuming power and omnipresence of the Divinity. His breath was the first source of life; and the faint whisper of the breeze announced to the prophet His immediate presence.

"All things are the progeny of one fire. The Father perfected all things, and delivered them over to the Second Mind, whom all nations of men call the First. Natural works co-exist with the intellectual light of the Father; for it is the Soul which adorns the great Heaven, and which adorns it after the Father. The Soul, being a bright fire, by the power of the Father, remains immortal, and is mistress of life, and fills up the recesses of the world. For the fire which is first beyond, did not shut up his power in matter by works, but by mind, for the framer of the fiery world is the mind of mind, who first sprang from mind, clothing fire with fire. Father-begotten Light! for He alone, having from the Father's power received the essence of intellect, is enabled to understand the mind of the Father; and to instill into all sources and principles the capacity of understanding, and of ever continuing in ceaseless revolving motion." Such was the language of Zoroaster, embodying the old Persian ideas.

And the same ancient sage thus spoke of the Sun and Stars: "The Father made the whole Universe of fire and water and earth, and all-nourishing ether. He fixed a great multitude of moveless stars, that stand still forever, not by compulsion and unwillingly, but without desire to wander, fire acting upon fire. He congregated the seven firmaments of the world, and so surrounded the earth with the convexity of the Heavens; and therein set seven living existences, arranging their apparent disorder in regular orbits, six of them planets, and the Sun, placed in the centre, the seventh;—in that centre from which all lines, diverging which way soever, are equal; and the swift sun himself, revolving around a principal centre, and ever striving to reach the central and all-pervading light, bearing with him the bright Moon."

And yet Zoroaster added: "Measure not the journeyings of the Sun, nor attempt to reduce them to rule: for he is carried by the eternal will of the Father, not for your sake. Do not endeavor to understand the impetuous course of the Moon; for she runs

earth will then sink down into *Duzakh,* and become for three periods a place of punishment for the wicked. Then, by degrees, all will be pardoned, even *Ahriman* and the *Devs,* and admitted to the regions of bliss, and thus there will be a new Heaven and a new earth."

In the doctrines of Lamaism also, we find, obscured, and partly concealed in fiction, fragments of the primitive truth. For, according to that faith, "There is to be a final judgment before Eslik Khan : The good are to be admitted to Paradise, the bad to be banished to hell, where there are eight regions burning hot and eight freezing cold."

In the Mysteries, wherever they were practised, was taught that truth of the primitive revelation, the existence of One Great Being, Infinite and pervading the Universe, Who was there worshipped without superstition ; and His marvellous nature, essence, and attributes taught to the Initiates ; while the vulgar attributed His works to Secondary Gods, personified, and isolated from Him in fabulous independence.

These truths were covered from the common people as with a veil ; and the Mysteries were carried into every country, that, without disturbing the popular beliefs, truth, the arts, and the sciences might be known to those who were capable of understanding them, and maintaining the true doctrine incorrupt; which the people, prone to superstition and idolatry, have in no age been able to do; nor, as many strange aberrations and superstitions of the present day prove, any more now than heretofore. For we need but point to the doctrines of so many sects that degrade the Creator to the rank, and assign to Him the passions of humanity, to prove that now, as always, the old truths must be committed to a few, or they will be overlaid with fiction and error; and irretrievably lost.

Though Masonry is identical with the Ancient Mysteries, it is so in this qualified sense ; that it presents but an imperfect image of their brilliancy; the ruins only of their grandeur, and a system that has experienced progressive alterations, the fruits of social events and political circumstances. Upon leaving Egypt, the Mysteries were modified by the habits of the different nations among whom they were introduced. Though originally more moral and political than religious, they soon became the heritage, as it were, of the priests, and essentially religious, though in reality limiting the sacerdotal power, by teaching the intelligent laity the folly and absurdity of the creeds of the populace. They were therefore necessarily changed by the religious systems of the counries into which they were transplanted. In Greece, they were the Mysteries of Ceres; in Rome, of *Bona Dea,* the Good Goddess; in Gaul, the School of Mars; in Sicily, the Academy of the Sciences; among the Hebrews, they partook of the rites and ceremonies of a religion which placed all the powers of government, and all the knowledge, in the hands of the Priests and Levites. The pagodas of India, the retreats of the Magi of Persia and Chaldea, and the pyramids of Egypt, were no longer the sources at which men drank in knowledge. Each people, at all informed, had its Mysteries. After a time the Temples of Greece and the School of Pythagoras lost their reputation, and Freemasonry took their place.

Masonry, when properly expounded, is at once the interpretation of the great book of nature, the recital of physical and astronomical phenomena, the purest philosophy, and the place of deposit, where, as in a Treasury, are kept in safety all the great truths of the primitive revelation, that form the basis of all religions. In the modern Degrees three things are to be recognized: The image of primeval times, the tableau of the efficient causes of the Universe, and the book in which are written the morality of all peoples, and the code by which they must govern themselves if they would be prosperous.

The Kabalistic doctrine was long the religion of the Sage and the Savant; because, like Freemasonry, it incessantly tends toward spiritual perfection, and the fusion of the creeds and Nationalities of Mankind. In the eyes of the Kabalist, all men are his brothers; and their relative ignorance is, to him, but a reason for instructing them. There were illustrious Kabalists among the Egyptians and Greeks, whose doctrines the Orthodox Church has accepted; and among the Arabs were many, whose wisdom was not slighted by the Mediæval Church.

The Sages proudly wore the name of Kabalists. The Kabalah embodied a noble philosophy, pure, not mysterious, but symbolic. It taught the doctrine of the Unity of God, the art of knowing and explaining the essence and operations of the Supreme Being, of spiritual powers and natural forces, and of determining their action by symbolic figures; by the arrangement of the alphabet,

And so the cubes:

$27^2 = 729 \times 729 = 18 = 9$ $18^2 = 324 = 9$ $9^2 = 81$ $81^2 = ..6561 = 18 = 9$

729	324	6561

$6561 = 18 = 9$	$1296 = 18 = 9$	$6561 = 18 = 9$
$1458 = 18 = 9$	$648 = 18 = 9$	$39366 = 27 = 9$
$5103 = 9$	$972 = 18 = 9$	$32805 = 18 = 9$
		$39366 = 27 = 9$

$531441 = 18 = 9$	$104976 = 27 = 9$	$43,046,721 = 27 = 9.$

The number 10, or the Denary, is the measure of everything; and reduces multiplied numbers to unity. Containing all the numerical and harmonic relations, and all the properties of the numbers which precede it, it concludes the Abacus or Table of Pythagoras. To the Mysterious Societies, this number typified the assemblage of all the wonders of the Universe. They wrote it thus θ, that is to say, Unity in the middle of Zero, as the centre of a circle, or symbol of Deity. They saw in this figure everything that should lead to reflection: the centre, the ray, and the circumference, represented to them God, Man, and the Universe.

This number was, among the Sages, a sign of concord, love, and peace. To Masons it is a sign of union and good faith; because it is expressed by joining two hands, or the Master's grip, when the number of fingers gives 10: and it was represented by the Tetractys of Pythagoras.

The number 12, like the number 7, is celebrated in the worship of nature. The two most famous divisions of the heavens, that by 7, which is that of the planets, and that by 12, which is that of the Signs of the Zodiac, are found upon the religious monuments of all the peoples of the Ancient World, even to the remote extremes of the East. Although Pythagoras does not speak of the number 12, it is none the less a sacred number. It is the image of the Zodiac; and consequently that of the Sun, which rules over it.

Such are the ancient ideas in regard to those numbers which so often appear in Masonry; and rightly understood, as the old Sages understood them, they contain many a pregnant lesson.

Before we enter upon the final lesson of Masonic Philosophy, we will delay a few moments to repeat to you the Christian interpretations of the Blue Degrees.

In the First Degree, they said, there are three symbols to be applied.

1st. Man, after the fall, was left naked and defenceless against the just anger of the Deity. Prone to evil, the human race staggered blindly onward into the thick darkness of unbelief, bound fast by the strong cable-tow of the natural and sinful will. Moral corruption was followed by physical misery. Want and destitution invaded the earth. War and Famine and Pestilence filled up the measure of evil, and over the sharp flints of misfortune and wretchedness man toiled with naked and bleeding feet. This condition of blindness, destitution, misery, and bondage, from which to save the world the Redeemer came, is symbolized by the condition of the candidate, when he is brought up for the first time to the door of the Lodge.

2d. Notwithstanding the death of the Redeemer, man can be saved only by faith, repentance, and reformation. To repent, he must feel the sharp sting of conscience and remorse, like a sword piercing his bosom. His confidence in his guide, whom he is told to follow and fear no danger; his trust in God, which he is caused to profess; and the point of the sword that is pressed against his naked left breast over the heart, are symbolical of the faith, repentance and reformation necessary to bring him to the light of a life in Christ the Crucified.

3d. Having repented and reformed, and bound himself to the service of God by a firm promise and obligation, the light of Christian hope shines down into the darkness of the heart of the humble penitent, and blazes upon his pathway to Heaven. And this is symbolized by the candidate's being brought to light, after he is obligated, by the Worshipful Master, who in that is a symbol of the Redeemer, and so brings him to light, with the help of the brethren, as He taught the Word with the aid of the Apostles.

In the Second Degree there are two symbols:

4th. The Christian assumes new duties toward God and his fellows. Toward God, of love, gratitude, and veneration, and an anxious desire to serve and glorify Him; toward his fellows, of kindness, sympathy, and justice. And this assumption of duty, this entering upon good works, is symbolized by the Fellow-Craft's obligation; by which, bound as an apprentice to secrecy merely, and set in the Northeast corner of the Lodge, he descends as a Fellow-Craft into the body of the brethren, and assumes the active duties of a good Mason.

5th. The Christian, reconciled to God, sees the world in a new light. This great Universe is no longer a mere machine, wound up and set going six thousand or sixty million years ago, and left to run on afterward forever, by virtue of a law of mechanics created at the beginning, without further care or consideration on the part of the Deity; but it has now become to him a great emanation from God, the product of His thought, not a mere dead machine, but a thing of life, over which God watches continually, and every movement of which is immediately produced by His present action, the law of harmony being the essence of the Deity, re-enacted every instant. And this is symbolized by the imperfect instruction given in the Fellow-Craft's Degree, in the sciences, and particularly geometry, connected as the latter is with God Himself in the mind of a Mason, because the same letter, suspended in the East, represents both; and astronomy, or the knowledge of the laws of motion and harmony that govern the spheres, is but a portion of the wider science of geometry. It is so symbolized, because it is here, in the Second Degree, that the candidate first receives an other than moral instruction.

There are also two symbols in the Third Degree, which, with the 3 in the first, and 2 in the second, make the 7.

6th. The candidate, after passing through the first part of the ceremony, imagines himself a Master; and is surprised to be informed that as yet he is not, and that it is uncertain whether he ever will be. He is told of a difficult and dangerous path yet to be travelled, and is advised that upon that journey it depends whether he will become a Master. This is symbolical of that which our Saviour said to Nicodemus, that, notwithstanding his morals might be beyond reproach, he could not enter the Kingdom of Heaven unless he were born again; symbolically dying, and again entering the world regenerate, like a spotless infant.

7th. The murder of Hiram, his burial, and his being raised again by the Master, are symbols, both of the death, burial, and resurrection of the Redeemer; and of the death and burial in sins of the natural man, and his being raised again to a new life, or born again, by the direct action of the Redeemer; after Morality (symbolized by the Entered Apprentice's grip), and Philosophy (symbolized by the grip of the Fellow-Craft), had failed to raise him. That of the Lion of the House of Judah is the strong grip, never to be broken, with which Christ, of the royal line of that House, has clasped to Himself the whole human race, and embraces them in His wide arms as closely and affectionately as brethren embrace each other on the five points of fellowship.

As Entered Apprentices and Fellow-Crafts, Masons are taught to imitate the laudable example of those Masons who labored at the building of King Solomon's Temple; and to plant firmly and deep in their hearts those foundation-stones of principle, truth, justice, temperance, fortitude, prudence, and charity, on which to erect that Christian character which all the storms of misfortune and all the powers and temptations of Hell shall not prevail against; those feelings and noble affections which are the most proper homage that can be paid to the Grand Architect and Great Father of the Universe, and which make the heart a living temple builded to Him: when the unruly passions are made to submit to rule and measurement, and their excesses are struck off with the gavel of self-restraint; and when every action and every principle is accurately corrected and adjusted by the square of wisdom, the level of humility, and the plumb of justice.

The two columns, Jachin and Boaz, are the symbols of that profound faith and implicit trust in God and the Redeemer that are the Christian's *strength*; and of those good works by which alone that faith can be *established* and made operative and effectual to salvation.

The three pillars that support the Lodge are symbols of a Christian's HOPE in a future state of happiness; FAITH in the promises and the divine character and mission of the Redeemer; and CHARITABLE JUDGMENT of other men.

The three murderers of Khir-Om symbolize Pontius Pilate, Caiaphas the High-Priest, and Judas Iscariot: and the three blows given him are the betrayal by the last, the refusal of Roman protection by Pilate, and the condemnation by the High-Priest. They also symbolize the blow on the ear, the scourging, and the crown of thorns. The twelve fellow-crafts sent in search of the body are the twelve disciples, in doubt whether to believe that the Redeemer would rise from the dead.

The Master's word, supposed to be lost, symbolizes the Christian faith and religion, supposed to have been crushed and destroyed when the Saviour was crucified, after Iscariot had betrayed Him,

and Peter deserted Him, and when the other disciples doubted
whether He would arise from the dead; but which rose from His
tomb and flowed rapidly over the civilized world; and so that
which was supposed to be *lost* was *found*. It symbolizes also the
Saviour Himself; the WORD that was in the beginning—that was
with God, and that *was* God; the Word of life, that was made
flesh and dwelt among us, and was supposed to be lost, while He
lay in the tomb, for three days, and His disciples "as yet knew not
the scripture that He must rise again from the dead," and doubted when they heard of it, and were amazed and frightened and
still doubted when He appeared among them.

The bush of acacia placed at the head of the grave of Khir-Om
is an emblem of resurrection and immortality.

Such are the explanations of our Christian brethren; entitled,
like those of all other Masons, to a respectful consideration.

CLOSING INSTRUCTION.

There is no pretence to infallibility in Masonry. It is not for
us to dictate to any man what he shall believe. We have hitherto,
in the instruction of the several Degrees, confined ourselves to
laying before you the great thoughts that have found expression
in the different ages of the world, leaving you to decide for yourself as to the orthodoxy or heterodoxy of each, and what proportion of truth, if any, each contained. We shall pursue no other
course in this closing Philosophical instruction; in which we
propose to deal with the highest questions that have ever exercised
the human mind,—with the existence and the nature of a God,
with the existence and the nature of the human soul, and with the
relations of the divine and human spirit with the merely material
Universe. There can be no questions more important to an intelligent being, none that have for him a more direct and personal
interest; and to this last word of Scottish Masonry we invite your
serious and attentive consideration. And, as what we shall now
say will be but the completion and rounding-off of what we have
already said in several of the preceding Degrees, in regard to the
Old Thought and the Ancient Philosophies, we hope that you
have noted and not forgotten our previous lessons, without which
this would seem imperfect and fragmentary.

In its idea of rewarding a faithful and intelligent workman by
conferring upon him a knowledge of the True Word, Masonry

at once their existence and their intelligibility. It is by participating in the Divine reason that our own reason possesses something of the Absolute. Every judgment of reason envelopes a
necessary truth, and every necessary truth supposes the necessary
Existence.

Thus, from every direction,—from metaphysics, æsthetics, and
morality above all, we rise to the same Principle, the common
centre, and ultimate foundation of all truth, all beauty, all good.
The True, the Beautiful, the Good, are but diverse revelations of
one and the same Being. Thus we reach the threshold of religion ;
and are in communion with the great philosophies which all proclaim a God ; and at the same time with the religions which cover
the earth, and all repose on the sacred foundation of natural religion ; of that religion which reveals to us the natural light given
to all men, without the aid of a particular revelation. So long as
philosophy does not arrive at religion, it is below all worships,
even the most imperfect ; for they at least give man a Father, a
Witness, a Consoler, a Judge. By religion, philosophy connects
itself with humanity, which, from one end of the world to the
other, aspires to God, believes in God, hopes in God. Philosophy
contains in itself the common basis of all religious beliefs ; it, as
it were, borrows from them their principle, and returns it to them
surrounded with light, elevated above uncertainty, secure against
all attack.

From the necessity of His Nature, the Infinite Being must
create and preserve the Finite, and to the Finite must, in its
forms, give and communicate of His own kind. We cannot conceive of any finite thing existing without God, the Infinite basis
and ground thereof ; nor of God existing without something. God
is the necessary logical condition of a world, its necessitating
cause ; a world, the necessary logical condition of God, His neces-
sitated consequence. It is according to His Infinite Perfection to
create, and then to preserve and bless whatever He creates. That
is the conclusion of modern metaphysical science. The stream
of philosophy runs down from Aristotle to Hegel, and breaks off
with this conclusion : and then again recurs the ancient difficulty.
If it be of His nature to create,—if we cannot conceive of His
existing alone, without creating, without having created, then what
He created was co-existent with Himself. If He could exist an
instant without creating, He could as well do so for a myriad of

eternities. And so again comes round to us the old doctrine of a God, the Soul of the Universe, and co-existent with it. For what He created had a *beginning;* and however long since that creation occurred, an eternity had before elapsed. The difference between *a* beginning and *no* beginning is infinite.

But of some things we can be certain. We are conscious of our-selves—of ourselves if not as substances, at least as Powers to be, to do, to suffer. We are conscious of ourselves not as self-origin-ated at all or as self-sustained alone; but only as dependent, first for existence, ever since for support.

Among the primary ideas of consciousness, that are inseparable from it, the atoms of self-consciousness, we find the idea of God. Carefully examined by the scrutinizing intellect, it is the idea of God as infinite, perfectly powerful, wise, just, loving, holy: abso-lute being with no limitation. This made us, made all, sustains us, sustains all; made our body, not by a single act, but by a series of acts extending over a vast succession of years,—for man's body is the resultant of all created things,—made our spirit, our mind, conscience, affections, soul, will, appointed for each its natural mode of action, set each at its several aim. Thus self-con-sciousness leads us to consciousness of God, and at last to con-sciousness of an infinite God. That is the highest evidence of our own existence, and it is the highest evidence of His.

If there is a God at all, He must be omnipresent in space. Beyond the last Stars He must be, as He is here. There can be no mote that peoples the sunbeams, no little cell of life that the microscope discovers in the seed-sporule of a moss, but He is there.

He must also be omnipresent in time. There was no second of time before the Stars began to burn, but God was in that second. In the most distant nebulous spot in Orion's belt, and in every one of the millions that people a square inch of limestone. God is alike present. He is in the smallest imaginable or even unimagin-able portion of time, and in every second of its most vast and unimaginable volume; His Here conterminous with the All of Space, His Now coeval with the All of Time.

Through all this Space, in all this Time, His Being extends, spreads undivided, operates unspent: God in all His infinity, per-fectly powerful, wise, just, loving, and holy. His being is an infinite activity, a creating, and so a giving of Himself to the

46

World. The World's being is a *becoming*, a being created and continued. It is so now, and was so, incalculable and unimaginable millions of ages ago.

All this is philosophy, the unavoidable conclusion of the human mind. It is not the *opinion* of Coleridge and Kant, but their *science;* not what they *guess*, but what they *know*.

In virtue of this in-dwelling of God in matter, we say that the world is a revelation of Him, its existence a show of His. He is *in* His work. The manifold action of the Universe is only His mode of operation, and all material things are in communion with Him. All grow and move and live in Him, and by means of Him, and only so. Let Him withdraw from the space occupied by anything, and it ceases to be. Let Him withdraw any quality of His nature from anything, and it ceases to be. All must partake of Him, He dwelling in each, and yet transcending all.

The failure of fanciful religion to become philosophy, does not preclude philosophy from coinciding with true religion. Philosophy, or rather its object, the divine order of the Universe, is the intellectual guide which the religious sentiment needs; while exploring the real relations of the finite, it obtains a constantly improving and self-correcting measure of the perfect law of the Gospel of Love and Liberty, and a means of carrying into effect the spiritualism of revealed religion. It establishes law, by ascertaining its terms; it guides the spirit to see its way to the amelioration of life and the increase of happiness. While religion was stationary, science could not walk alone; when both are admitted to be progressive, their interests and aims become identified. Aristotle began to show how religion may be founded on an intellectual basis; but the basis he laid was too narrow. Bacon, by giving to philosophy a definite aim and method, gave it at the same time a safer and self-enlarging basis. Our position is that of intellectual beings surrounded by limitations; and the latter being constant, have to intelligence the practical value of laws, in whose investigation and application consists that seemingly endless career of intellectual and moral progress which the sentiment of religion inspires and ennobles. The title of Saint has commonly been claimed for those whose boast it has been to despise philosophy; yet faith will stumble and sentiment mislead, unless knowledge be present, in amount and quality sufficient to purify the one and to give beneficial direction to the other.

KNIGHT OF THE SUN, OR PRINCE ADEPT.   711

Science consists of those matured inferences from experience which all other experience confirms. It is no fixed system
superior to revision, but that progressive mediation between
ignorance and wisdom in part conceived by Plato, whose immediate object is happiness, and its impulse the highest kind of love.
Science realizes and unites all that was truly valuable in both the
old schemes of mediation; the heroic, or system of action and
effort; and the mystical theory of spiritual, contemplative communion. "Listen to me," says Galen, "as to the voice of the
Eleusinian Hierophant, and believe that the study of nature is a
mystery no less important than theirs, nor less adapted to display
the wisdom and power of the Great Creator. Their lessons and
demonstrations were obscure, but ours are clear and unmistak-
able."

To science we owe it that no man is any longer entitled to consider himself the central point around which the whole Universe
of life and motion revolves—the immensely important individual
for whose convenience and even luxurious ease and indulgence the
whole Universe was made. On one side it has shown us an infinite Universe of stars and suns and worlds at incalculable dis-
tances from each other, in whose majestic and awful presence we
sink and even our world sinks into insignificance; while, on the
other side, the microscope has placed us in communication with
new worlds of organized living beings, gifted with senses, nerves,
appetites, and instincts, in every tear and in every drop of putrid
water.

Thus science teaches us that we are but an infinitesimal portion
of a great whole, that stretches out on every side of us, and above
and below us, infinite in its complications, and which infinite wisdom alone can comprehend. Infinite wisdom has arranged the
infinite succession of beings, involving the necessity of birth,
decay, and death, and made the loftiest virtues possible by providing those conflicts, reverses, trials, and hardships, without which
even their names could never have been invented.

Knowledge is convertible into power, and axioms into rules of
utility and duty. Modern science is social and communicative.
It is moral as well as intellectual; powerful, yet pacific and disinterested; binding man to man as well as to the Universe; filling
up the details of obligation, and cherishing impulses of virtue,
and, by affording clear proof of the consistency and identity of all

interests, substituting co-operation for rivalry, liberality for jealousy, and tending far more powerfully than any other means to realize the spirit of religion, by healing those inveterate disorders which, traced to their real origin, will be found rooted in an ignorant assumption as to the penurious severity of Providence, and the consequent greed of selfish men to confine what seemed as if extorted from it to themselves, or to steal from each other rather than quietly to enjoy their own.

We shall probably never reach those higher forms containing the true differences of things, involving the full discovery and correct expression of their very self or essence. We shall ever fall short of the most general and most simple nature, the ultimate or most comprehensive law. Our widest axioms explain many phenomena, but so too in a degree did the principles or elements of the old philosophers, and the cycles and epicycles of ancient astronomy. We cannot in any case of causation assign the whole of the conditions, nor, though we may reproduce them in practice, can we mentally distinguish them all, without knowing the essences of the things including them; and we therefore must not unconsciously ascribe that absolute certainty to axioms, which the ancient religionists did to creeds, nor allow the mind, which ever strives to insulate itself and its acquisitions, to forget the nature of the process by which it substituted scientific for common notions, and so with one as with the other lay the basis of self-deception by a pedantic and superstitious employment of them.

Doubt, the essential preliminary of all improvement and discovery, must accompany all the stages of man's onward progress. His intellectual life is a perpetual beginning, a preparation for a birth. The faculty of doubting and questioning, without which those of comparison and judgment would be useless, is itself a divine prerogative of the reason. Knowledge is always imperfect, or complete only in a prospectively boundless career, in which discovery multiplies doubt, and doubt leads on to new discovery. The boast of science is not so much its manifested results, as its admitted imperfection and capacity of unlimited progress. The true religious philosophy of an imperfect being is not a system of creed, but, as Socrates thought, an infinite search or approximation. Finality is but another name for bewilderment or defeat. Science gratifies the religious feeling without arresting it, and opens out the unfathomable mystery of the One Supreme into more explicit and manageable Forms, which express not indeed His Essence, which is wholly beyond our reach and higher than our faculties can climb, but His Will, and so feeds an endless enthusiasm by accumulating forever new objects of pursuit. We have long experienced that knowledge is profitable, we are beginning to find out that it is moral, and we shall at last discover it to be religious.

God and truth are inseparable; a knowledge of God is possession of the saving oracles of truth. In proportion as the thought and purpose of the individual are trained to conformity with the rule of right prescribed by Supreme Intelligence, so far is his happiness promoted, and the purpose of his existence fulfilled. In this way a new life arises in him; he is no longer isolated, but is a part of the eternal harmonies around him. His erring will is directed by the influence of a higher will, informing and moulding it in the path of his true happiness.

Man's power of apprehending outward truth is a qualified privilege; the mental like the physical inspiration passing through a diluted medium; and yet, even when truth, imparted, as it were, by intuition, has been specious, or at least imperfect, the intoxication of sudden discovery has ever claimed it as full, infallible, and divine. And while human weakness needed ever to recur to the pure and perfect source, the revelations once popularly accepted and valued assumed an independent substantiality, perpetuating not themselves only, but the whole mass of derivitive forms accidentally connected with them, and legalized in their names. The mists of error thickened under the shadows of prescription, until the free light again broke in upon the night of ages, redeeming the genuine treasure from the superstition which obstinately doted on its accessories.

Even to the Barbarian, Nature reveals a mighty power and a wondrous wisdom, and continually points to God. It is no wonder that men worshipped the several things of the world. The world of matter is a revelation of fear to the savage in Northern climes; he trembles at his deity throned in ice and snow. The lightning, the storm, the earthquake startle the rude man, and he sees the divine in the extraordinary.

The grand objects of Nature perpetually constrain men to think of their Author. The Alps are the great altar of Europe; the nocturnal sky has been to mankind the dome of a temple, starred all over with admonitions to reverence, trust, and love. The Scriptures for the human race are writ in earth and Heaven. No organ or miserere touches the heart like the sonorous swell of the sea or the ocean-wave's immeasurable laugh. Every year the old world puts on new bridal beauty, and celebrates its Whit-Sunday, when in the sweet Spring each bush and tree dons reverently its new glories. Autumn is a long All-Saints' day; and the harvest is Hallowmass to Mankind. Before the human race marched down from the slopes of the Himalayas to take possession of Asia, Chaldea, and Egypt, men marked each annual crisis, the solstices and the equinoxes, and celebrated religious festivals therein; and even then, and ever since, the material was and has been the element of communion between man and God.

Nature is full of religious lessons to a thoughtful man. He dissolves the matter of the Universe, leaving only its forces; he dissolves away the phenomena of human history, leaving only immortal spirit; he studies the law, the mode of action of these forces and this spirit, which make up the material and the human world, and cannot fail to be filled with reverence, with trust, with boundless love of the Infinite God, who devised these laws of matter and of mind, and thereby bears·up this marvellous Universe óf things and men. Science has its New Testament; and the beatitudes of Philosophy are profoundly touching. An undevout astronomer is mad. Familiarity with the grass and the trees teaches us deeper lessons of love and trust than we can glean from the writings of Fénélon and Augustine. The great Bible of God is ever open before mankind. The eternal flowers of Heaven seem to shed sweet influence on the perishable blossoms of the earth. The great sermon of Jesus was preached on a mountain, which preached to Him as He did to the people, and His figures of speech were first natural figures of fact.

If to-morrow I am to perish utterly, then I shall only take counsel for to-day, and ask for qualities which last no longer. My fathers will be to me only as the ground out of which my bread-corn is grown; dead, they are but the rotten mould of earth, their memory of small concern to me. Posterity!—I shall care nothing for the future generations of mankind. I am one atom in the trunk of a tree, and care nothing for the roots below, or the branch above. I shall sow such seed only as will bear har vest to-day. Passion may enact my statutes to-day, and ambition repeal them to-morrow. I will know no other legislators. Morality will vanish, and expediency take its place. Heroism will be gone; and instead of it there will be the savage ferocity of the he-wolf, the brute cunning of the she-fox, the rapacity of the vulture, and the headlong daring of the wild bull; but no longer the cool, calm courage that, for truth's sake, and for love's sake, looks death firmly in the face, and then wheels into line ready to be slain. Affection, friendship, philanthrophy, will be but the wild fancies of the monomaniac, fit subjects for smiles or laughter or for pity.

But knowing that we shall live forever, and that the Infinite God loves all of us, we can look on all the evils of the world, and see that it is only the hour before sunrise, and that the light is coming; and so we also, even we, may light a little taper, to illuminate the darkness while it lasts, and help until the day-spring come. Eternal morning follows the night: a rainbow scarfs the shoulders of every cloud that weeps its rain away to be flowers on land and pearls at sea: Life rises out of the grave, the soul cannot be held by fettering flesh. No dawn is hopeless; and disaster is only the threshold of delight.

Beautifully, above the great wide chaos of human errors, shines the calm, clear light of natural human religion, revealing to us God as the Infinite Parent of all, perfectly powerful, wise, just, loving, and perfectly holy too. Beautiful around stretches off every way the Universe, the Great Bible of God. Material nature is its Old Testament, millions of years old, thick with eternal truths under our feet, glittering with everlasting glories over our heads; and Human Nature is the New Testament from the Infinite God, every day revealing a new page as Time turns over the leaves. Immortality stands waiting to give a recompense for every virtue not rewarded, for every tear not wiped away, for every sorrow undeserved, for every prayer, for every pure intention and emotion of the heart. And over the whole, over Nature, Material and Human, over this Mortal Life and over the eternal Past and Future, the infinite Loving-kindness of God the Father comes enfolding all and blessing everything that ever was, that is, that ever shall be.

Everything is a thought of the Infinite God. Nature is His prose, and man His Poetry. There is no Chance, no Fate; but God's Great Providence, enfolding the whole Universe in its bosom, and feeding it with everlasting life. In times past there has been evil which we cannot understand; now there are evils which we cannot solve, nor make square with God's perfect goodness by any theory our feeble intellect enables us to frame. There are sufferings, follies, and sins for all mankind, for every nation, for every man and every woman. They were all foreseen by the infinite wisdom of God, all provided for by His infinite power and justice, and all are consistent with His infinite love. To believe otherwise would be to believe that He made the world, to amuse His idle hours with the follies and agonies of mankind, as Domitian was wont to do with the wrigglings and contortions of insect agonies. Then indeed we might despairingly unite in that horrible utterance of Heine: "Alas, God's Satire weighs heavily on me! The Great Author of the Universe, the Aristophanes of Heaven, is bent on demonstrating, with crushing force, to me, the little, earthly, German Aristophanes, how my wittiest sarcasms are only pitiful attempts at jesting, in comparison with His, and how miserably I am beneath Him, in humor, in colossal mockery."

No, no! God is not thus amused with and prodigal of human suffering. The world is neither a Here without a Hereafter, a body without a soul, a chaos with no God; nor a body blasted by a soul, a Here with a worse Hereafter, a world with a God that hates more than half the creatures He has made. There is no Savage, Revengeful, and Evil God: but there is an Infinite God, seen everywhere as Perfect Cause, everywhere as Perfect Providence, transcending all, yet in-dwelling everywhere, with perfect power, wisdom, justice, holiness, and love, providing for the future welfare of each and all, foreseeing and forecaring for every bubble that breaks on the great stream of human life and human history.

The end of man and the object of existence in this world, being not only happiness, but happiness in virtue and through virtue, virtue in this world is the condition of happiness in another life, and the condition of virtue in this world is suffering, more or less frequent, briefer or longer continued, more or less intense. Take away suffering, and there is no longer any resignation or humanity, no more self-sacrifice, no more devotedness, no more heroic virtues, no more sublime morality. We are subjected to suffering, both because we are sensible, and because we ought to be virtuous. If there were no physical evil, there would be no possible virtue, and the world would be badly adapted to the destiny of man.

repulsion at the Sun or at the most distant Star could draw or drive these impalpable, weightless, infinitely minute particles, appreciable by the Sense of Sight alone, so far through space? What has become of the immense aggregate of particles that have reached the earth since the creation? Have they increased its bulk? Why cannot chemistry detect and analyze them? If matter, why can they travel only in right lines?

No characteristic of matter belongs to Light, or Heat, or flame, or to Galvanism, Electricity, and Magnetism. The electric spark is light, and so is that produced by the flint, when it cuts off particles of steel. Iron, melted or heated, radiates light; and insects, infusoria, and decayed wood emit it. Heat is produced by friction and by pressure; to explain which, Science tells us of *latent* Caloric, thus representing it to us as existing without its only known distinctive quality. What quality of matter enables lightning, blazing from the Heavens, to rend the oak? What quality of matter enables it to make the circuit of the earth in a score of seconds?

Profoundly ignorant of the nature of these mighty agents of Divine Power, we conceal our ignorance by words that have no meaning; and we might well be asked *why* Light may not be an effluence from the Deity, as has been agreed by all the religions of all the Ages of the World.

All truly dogmatic religions have issued from the Kabalah and return to it: everything scientific and grand in the religious dreams of all the illuminati, Jacob Bœhme, Swedenborg, Saint-Martin, and others, is borrowed from the Kabalah; all the Masonic associations owe to it their Secrets and their Symbols.

The Kabalah alone consecrates the alliance of the Universal Reason and the Divine Word; it establishes, by the counterpoises of two forces apparently opposite, the eternal balance of being; it alone reconciles Reason with Faith, Power with Liberty, Science with Mystery; it has the keys of the Present, the Past, and the Future.

The Bible, with all the allegories it contains, expresses, in an incomplete and veiled manner only, the religious science of the Hebrews. The doctrine of Moses and the Prophets, identical at bottom with that of the ancient Egyptians, also had its outward meaning and its veils. The Hebrew books were written only to recall to memory the traditions: and they were written in Symbols unintelligible to the Profane. The Pentateuch and the prophetic poems were merely elementary books of doctrine, morals, or liturgy; and the true secret and traditional philosophy was only written afterward, under veils still less transparent. Thus was a second Bible born, unknown to, or rather uncomprehended by, the Christians; a collection, *they* say, of monstrous absurdities; a monument, the adept says, wherein is everything that the genius of philosophy and that of religion have ever formed or imagined of the sublime; a treasure surrounded by thorns; a diamond concealed in a rough dark stone.

One is filled with admiration, on penetrating into the Sanctuary of the Kabalah, at seeing a doctrine so logical, so simple, and at the same time so absolute. The necessary union of ideas and signs, the consecration of the most fundamental realities by the primitive characters; the Trinity of Words, Letters, and Numbers; a philosophy simple as the alphabet, profound and infinite as the Word; theorems more complete and luminous than those of Pythagoras; a theology summed up by counting on one's fingers; an Infinite which can be held in the hollow of an infant's hand; ten ciphers and twenty-two letters, a triangle, a square, and a circle,—these are all the elements of the Kabalah. These are the elementary principles of the written Word, reflection of that spoken Word that created the world!

This is the doctrine of the Kabalah, with which you will no doubt seek to make yourself acquainted, as to the Creation.

The Absolute Deity, with the Kabalists, has no name. The terms applied to Him are אור פשוט, Aor Pasot, the Most Simple [or Pure] Light, "called אין סוף, Ayen Soph, or Infinite, before any Emanation. For then there was no space or vacant place, but all was infinite Light."

Before the Deity created any Ideal, any limited and intelligible Nature, or any form whatever, He was alone, and without form or similitude, and there could be no cognition or comprehension of Him in any wise. He was without Idea or Figure, and it is forbidden to form any Idea or Figure of Him, neither by the letter He [ה], nor by the letter Yōd [י], though these are contained in the Holy Name; nor by any other letter or point in the world.

But after He created this Idea [this limited and existing-in-intellection Nature, which the ten Numerations, Sephiroth or

XXX.

KNIGHT KADOSH.

WE often profit more by our enemies than by our friends. *"We support ourselves only on that which resists,"* and owe our success to opposition. The best friends of Masonry in America were the Anti-Masons of 1826, and at the same time they were its worst enemies. Men are but the automata of Providence, and it uses the demagogue, the fanatic, and the knave, a common trinity in Republics, as its tools and instruments to effect that of which they do not dream, and which they imagine themselves commissioned to prevent.

The Anti-Masons, traitors and perjurors some, and some mere political knaves, purified Masonry by persecution, and so proved to be its benefactors; for that which is persecuted, grows. To them its present popularity is. due, the cheapening of its Degrees, the invasion of its Lodges, that are no longer Sanctuaries, by the multitude; its pomp and pageantry and overdone display.

An hundred years ago it had become known that the קדש were the Templars under a veil, and therefore the Degree was proscribed, and, ceasing to be worked, became a mere brief and formal ceremony, under another name. Now, from the tomb in which after his murders he rotted, Clement the Fifth howls against the successors of his victims, in the Allocution of Pio Nono against the Free-Masons. The ghosts of the dead Templars haunt the Vati-

814

can and disturb the slumbers of the paralyzed Papacy, which,
dreading the dead, shrieks out its excommunications and impotent
anathemas against the living. It is a declaration of war, and was
needed to arouse apathy and inertness to action.

An enemy of the Templars shall tell us the secret of this Papal
hostility against an Order that has existed for centuries in despite
of its anathemas, and has its Sanctuaries and Asyla even in Rome.

It will be easy, as we read, to separate the false from the true,
the audacious conjectures from the simple facts.

"A power that ruled without antagonism and without concur-
rence, and consequently without control, proved fatal to the Sacerdotal Royalties; while the Republics, on the other hand, had perished by the conflict of liberties and franchises, which, in the
absence of all duty hierarchically sanctioned and enforced, had
soon become mere tyrannies, rivals one of the other. To find a
stable medium between these two abysses, the idea of the Christian Hierophants was to create a society devoted to abnegation by
solemn vows, protected by severe regulations; which should be re-
cruited by initiation, and which, sole depositary of the great religious and social secrets, should make Kings and Pontiffs, without
exposing it to the corruptions of Power. In that was the secret
of that kingdom of Jesus Christ, which, without being of this
world, would govern all its grandeurs.

"This idea presided at the foundation of the great religious
orders, so often at war with the secular authorities, ecclesiastical
or civil. Its realization was also the dream of the dissident sects
of Gnostics or Illuminati who pretended to connect their faith
with the primitive tradition of the Christianity of Saint John. It
at length became a menace for the Church and Society, when a
rich and dissolute Order, initiated in the mysterious doctrines of
the Kabalah, seemed disposed to turn against legitimate authority
the conservative principle of Hierarchy, and threatened the entire
world with an immense revolution.

"The Templars, whose history is so imperfectly known, were
those terrible conspirators. In 1118, nine Knights Crusaders in
the East, among whom were Geoffroi de Saint-Omer and Hugues
de Payens, consecrated themselves to religion, and took an oath
between the hands of the Patriarch of Constantinople, a See
always secretly or openly hostile to that of Rome from the time
of Photius. The avowed object of the Templars was to protect

the Christians who came to visit the Holy Places: their secret
object was the re-building of the Temple of Solomon on the model
prophesied by Ezekiel.

"This re-building, formally predicted by the Judaïzing Mystics
of the earlier ages, had become the secret dream of the Patriarchs
of the Orient. The Temple of Solomon, re-built and consecrated
to the Catholic worship would become, in effect, the Metropolis of
the Universe; the East would prevail over the West, and the Patriarchs of Constantinople would possess themselves of the Papal
power.

"The Templars, or *Poor Fellow-Soldiery of the Holy House of
the Temple* intended to be re-built, took as their models, in the
Bible, the Warrior-Masons of Zorobabel, who worked, holding the
sword in one hand and the trowel in the other. Therefore it was
that the Sword and the Trowel were the insignia of the Templars,
who subsequently, as will be seen, concealed themselves under the
name of *Brethren Masons.* [This name, *Frères Maçons* in the
French, adopted by way of secret reference to the Builders of the
Second Temple, was corrupted in English into *Free*-Masons, as
Pythagore de Crotone was into *Peter Gower* of *Groton* in England.
Khairûm or *Khûr-ûm*, (a name mis-rendered into *Hiram*) from
an artificer in brass and other metals, became the Chief Builder
of the *Haikal Kadosh*, the Holy House, of the Temple, the 'Ιερος
Δομος; and the words *Bonai* and *Banaim* yet appear in the Ma-
sonic Degrees, meaning Builder and Builders.]

"The trowel of the Templars is quadruple, and the triangular
plates of it are arranged in the form of a cross, making the Kabalistic pantacle known by the name of the Cross of the East. The
Knight of the East, and the Knight of the East and West, have
in their titles secret allusions to the Templars of whom they were
at first the successors.

"The secret thought of Hugues de Payens, in founding his
Order, was not exactly to serve the ambition of the Patriarchs of
Constantinople. There existed at that period in the East a Sect
of Johannite Christians, who claimed to be the only true Initiates
into the real mysteries of the religion of the Saviour. They pretended to know the real history of YESUS the ANOINTED, and,
adopting in part the Jewish traditions and the tales of the Tal-
mud, they held that the facts recounted in the Evangels are but
allegories, the key of which Saint John gives, in saying that the

world might be filled with the books that could be written upon the words and deeds of Jesus Christ; words which, they thought, would be only a ridiculous exaggeration, if he were not speaking of an allegory and a legend, that might be varied and prolonged to infinity.

"The Johannites ascribed to Saint John the foundation of their Secret Church, and the Grand Pontiffs of the Sect assumed the title of *Christos, Anointed,* or *Consecrated,* and claimed to have succeeded one another from Saint John by an uninterrupted succession of pontifical powers. He who, at the period of the foundation of the Order of the Temple, claimed these imaginary prerogatives, was named THEOCLET; he knew HUGUES DE PAYENS, he initiated him into the Mysteries and hopes of his pretended church, he seduced him by the notions of Sovereign Priesthood and Supreme royalty, and finally designated him as his successor.

"Thus the Order of Knights of the Temple was at its very origin devoted to the cause of opposition to the tiara of Rome and the crowns of Kings, and the Apostolate of Kabalistic Gnosticism was vested in its chiefs. For Saint John himself was the Father of the Gnostics, and the current translation of his polemic against the heretical of his Sect and the pagans who denied that Christ was the Word, is throughout a misrepresentation, or misunderstanding at least, of the whole Spirit of that Evangel.

"The tendencies and tenets of the Order were enveloped in profound mystery, and it externally professed the most perfect orthodoxy. The Chiefs alone knew the aim of the Order: the Subalterns followed them without distrust.

"To acquire influence and wealth, then to intrigue, and at need to fight, to establish the Johannite or Gnostic and Kabalistic dogma, were the object and means proposed to the initiated Brethren. The Papacy and the rival monarchies, they said to them, are sold and bought in these days, become corrupt, and to-morrow, perhaps, will destroy each other. All that will become the heritage of the Temple: the World will soon come to us for its Sovereigns and Pontiffs. We shall constitute the equilibrium of the Universe, and be rulers over the Masters of the World.

"The Templars, like all other Secret Orders and Associations, had two doctrines, one concealed and reserved for the Masters, which was Johannism: the other public, which was the *Roman Catholic.* Thus they deceived the adversaries whom they sought

to supplant. Hence Free-Masonry, vulgarly imagined to have begun with the Dionysian Architects or the German Stone-workers,
adopted Saint John the Evangelist as one of its patrons, associat-
ing with him, in order not to arouse the suspicions of Rome, Saint
John the Baptist, and thus covertly proclaiming itself the child
of the Kabalah and Essenism together."

[For the Johannism of the Adepts was the Kabalah of the
earlier Gnostics, degenerating afterward into those heretical forms
which Gnosticism developed, so that even Manes had his followers
among them. Many adopted his doctrines of the two Principles,
the recollection of which is perpetuated by the handle of the dagger and the tesselated pavement or floor of the Lodge, stupidly
called *"the Indented Tessel,"* and represented by great hanging
tassels, when it really means a *tesserated* floor (from the Latin
tesscra) of white and black lozenges, with a necessarily *denticulated* or *indented* border or edging. And wherever, in the higher
Degrees, the two colors white and black, are in juxtaposition, the
two Principles of Zoroaster and Manes are alluded to. With others the doctrine became a mystic Pantheism, descended from that
of the Brahmins, and even pushed to an idolatry of Nature and
hatred of every revealed dogma.

[To all this the absurd reading of the established Church, taking literally the figurative, allegorical, and mythical language of a
collection of Oriental books of different ages, directly and inevitably led. The same result long after followed the folly of regarding the Hebrew books as if they had been written by the unimagi-
native, hard, practical intellect of the England of James the First
and the bigoted stolidity of Scottish Presbyterianism.]

"The better to succeed and win partisans, the Templars sympa-
thized with regrets for dethroned creeds and encouraged the hopes
of new worships, promising to all liberty of conscience and a new
orthodoxy that should be the synthesis of all the persecuted creeds."

[It is absurd to suppose that men of intellect adored a monstrous
idol called Baphomet, or recognized Mahomet as an inspired
prophet. Their symbolism, invented ages before, to conceal what
it was dangerous to avow, was of course misunderstood by those
who were not adepts, and to their enemies seemed to be pantheistic. The calf of gold, made by Aaron for the Israelites, was but one of
the oxen under the laver of bronze, and the Karobim on the Pro-
pitiatory, misunderstood. The symbols of the wise always become

the idols of the ignorant multitude. What the Chiefs of the Order really believed and taught, is indicated to the Adepts by the hints contained in the high Degrees of Free-Masonry, and by the symbols which only the Adepts understand.

[The Blue Degrees are but the outer court or portico of the Temple. Part of the symbols are displayed there to the Initiate, but he is intentionally misled by false interpretations. It is not intended that he shall understand them; but it is intended that he shall imagine he understands them. Their true explication is reserved for the Adepts, the Princes of Masonry. The whole body of the Royal and Sacerdotal Art was hidden so carefully, centuries since, in the High Degrees, as that it is even yet impossible to solve many of the enigmas which they contain. It is well enough for the mass of those called Masons, to imagine that all is contained in the Blue Degrees; and whoso attempts to undeceive them will labor in vain, and without any true reward violate his obligations as an Adept. Masonry is the veritable Sphinx, buried to the head in the sands heaped round it by the ages.]

"The seeds of decay were sown in the Order of the Temple at its origin. Hypocrisy is a mortal disease. It had conceived a great work which it was incapable of executing, because it knew neither humility nor personal abnegation, because Rome was then invincible, and because the later Chiefs of the Order did not comprehend its mission. Moreover, the Templars were in general uneducated, and capable only of wielding the sword, with no qualifications for governing, and at need enchaining, that queen of the world called Opinion." [The doctrines of the Chiefs would, if expounded to the masses, have seemed to them the babblings of folly. The symbols of the wise are the idols of the vulgar, or else as meaningless as the hieroglyphics of Egypt to the nomadic Arabs. There must always be a common-place interpretation for the mass of Initiates, of the symbols that are eloquent to the Adepts.]

"Hugues de Payens himself had not that keen and far-sighted intellect nor that grandeur of purpose which afterward distinguished the military founder of another soldiery that became formidable to kings. The Templars were unintelligent and therefore unsuccessful Jesuits.

"Their watchword was, to become wealthy, in order to buy the world. They became so, and 'n 1312 they possessed in Europe

alone more than nine thousand seignories. Riches were the shoal
on which they were wrecked. They became insolent, and un-
wisely showed their contempt for the religious and social institutions which they aimed to overthrow. Their ambition was fatal
to them. Their projects were divined and prevented. [Rome,
more intolerant of heresy than of vice and crime, came to fear the
Order, and fear is always cruel. It has always deemed philosophical truth the most dangerous of heresies, and has never been at a
loss for a false accusation, by means of which to crush free
thought.] Pope Clement V. and King Philip le Bel gave the signal to Europe, and the Templars, taken as it were in an immense
net, were arrested, disarmed, and cast into prison. Never was a
Coup d' Etat accomplished with a more formidable concert of
action. The whole world was struck with stupor, and eagerly
waited for the strange revelations of a process that was to echo
through so many ages.

"It was impossible to unfold to the people the conspiracy of the
Templars against the Thrones and the Tiara. It was impossible
to expose to them the doctrines of the Chiefs of the Order. [This
would have been to initiate the multitude into the secrets of the
Masters, and to have uplifted the veil of Isis. Recourse was therefore had to the charge of magic, and denouncers and false witnesses were easily found. When the temporal and spiritual tyrannies unite to crush a victim they never want for serviceable instruments.] The Templars were gravely accused of spitting upon
Christ and denying God at their receptions, of gross obscenities,
conversations with female devils, and the worship of a monstrous
idol.

"The end of the drama is well known, and how Jacques de
Molai and his fellows perished in the flames. But before his execution, the Chief of the doomed Order organized and instituted
what afterward came to be called the Occult, Hermetic, or Scottish Masonry. In the gloom of his prison, the Grand Master created four Metropolitan Lodges, at Naples for the East, at Edinburg
for the West, at Stockholm for the North, and at Paris for the
South." [The initials of his name, J∴ B∴ M∴ found in the same
order in the first three Degrees, are but one of the many internal
and cogent proofs that such was the origin of modern Free-Masonry. The legend of Osiris was revived and adopted, to symbolize
the destruction of the Order, and the resurrection of Khûrûm,

slain in the body of the Temple, of KHŪRŪM ABAI, the Master, as the martyr of fidelity to obligation, of Truth and Conscience, prophesied the restoration to life of the buried association.]

"The Pope and the King soon after perished in a strange and sudden manner. Squin de Florian, the chief denouncer of the Order, died assassinated. In breaking the sword of the Templars, they made of it a poniard; and their proscribed trowels thenceforward built only tombs."

[The Order disappeared at once. Its estates and wealth were confiscated, and it seemed to have ceased to exist. Nevertheless it lived, under other names and governed by unknown Chiefs, revealing itself only to those who, in passing through a series of Degrees, had proven themselves worthy to be entrusted with the dangerous Secret. The modern Orders that style themselves Templars have assumed a name to which they have not the shadow of a title.]

"The Successors of the Ancient Adepts Rose-Croix, abandoning by degrees the austere and hierarchical Science of their Ancestors in initiation, became a Mystic Sect, united with many of the Templars, the dogmas of the two intermingling, and believed themselves to be the sole depositaries of the secrets of the Gospel of St. John, seeing in its recitals an allegorical series of rites proper to complete the initiation.

"The Initiates, in fact, thought in the eighteenth century that their time had arrived, some to found a new Hierarchy, others to overturn all authority, and to press down all the summits of the Social Order under the level of Equality."

The mystical meanings of the Rose as a Symbol are to be looked for in the Kabalistic Commentaries on the Canticles.

The Rose was for the Initiates the living and blooming symbol of the revelation of the harmonies of being. It was the emblem of beauty, life, love, and pleasure. Flamel, or the Book of the Jew Abraham, made it the hieroglyphical sign of the accomplishment of the great Work. Such is the key of the Roman de la Rose. The Conquest of the Rose was the problem propounded to Science by Initiation, while Religion was laboring to prepare and establish the universal triumph, exclusive and definitive, of the Cross.

To unite the Rose to the Cross, was the problem proposed by the High Initiation; and in fact the Occult philosophy being the

53

Universal Synthesis, ought to explain all the phenomena of Being. Religion, considered solely as a physiological fact, is the revelation and satisfaction of a necessity of souls. Its existence is a scientific fact; to deny it, would be to deny humanity itself.

The Rose-Croix Adepts respected the dominant, hierarchical, and revealed religion. Consequently they could no more be the enemies of the Papacy than of legitimate Monarchy; and if they conspired against the Popes and Kings, it was because they considered them personally as apostates from duty and supreme favorers of anarchy.

What, in fact, is a despot, spiritual or temporal, but a crowned anarchist?

One of the magnificent pantacles that express the esoteric and unutterable part of Science, is a Rose of Light, in the centre of which a human form extends its arms in the form of a cross.

Commentaries and studies have been multiplied upon the *Divine Comedy,* the work of DANTE, and yet no one, so far as we know, has pointed out its especial character. The work of the great Ghibellin is a declaration of war against the Papacy, by bold revelation of the Mysteries. The Epic of Dante is Johannite and Gnostic, an audacious application, like that of the Apocalypse, of the figures and numbers of the Kabalah to the Christian dogmas, and a secret negation of every thing absolute in these dogmas. His journey through the supernatural worlds is accomplished like the initiation into the Mysteries of Eleusis and Thebes. He escapes from that gulf of Hell over the gate of which the sentence of despair was written, *by reversing the positions of his head and feet,* that is to say, *by accepting the direct opposite of the Catholic dogma;* and then he reascends to the light, by using the Devil himself as a monstrous ladder. Faust ascends to Heaven, by stepping on the head of the vanquished Mephistopheles. Hell is impassable for those only who know not how to turn back from it. We free ourselves from its bondage by audacity.

His Hell is but a negative Purgatory. His Heaven is composed of a series of Kabalistic circles, divided by a cross, like the Pantacle of Ezekiel. In the centre of this cross blooms a rose, and we see the symbol of the Adepts of the Rose-Croix for the first time publicly expounded and almost categorically explained.

For the first time, because Guillaume de Lorris, who died in 1260, five years before the birth of Alighieri, had not completed his *Roman de la Rose*, which was continued by Chopinel, a half century afterward. One is astonished to discover that the Roman de la Rose and the Divina Commedia are two opposite forms of one and the same work, initiation into independence of spirit, a satire on all contemporary institutions, and the allegorical formula of the great Secrets of the Society of the Roses-Croix.

The important manifestations of Occultism coincide with the period of the fall of the Templars; since Jean de Meung or Chopinel, contemporary of the old age of Dante, flourished during the best years of his life at the Court of Philippe le Bel. The Roman de la Rose is the Epic of old France. It is a profound book, under the form of levity, a revelation as learned as that of Apuleius, of the Mysteries of Occultism. The Rose of Flamel, that of Jean de Meung, and that of Dante, grew on the same stem.

Swedenborg's system was nothing else than the Kabalah, minus the principle of the Hierarchy. It is the Temple, without the keystone and the foundation.

Cagliostro was the Agent of the Templars, and therefore wrote to the Free-Masons of London that the time had come to begin the work of re-building the Temple of the Eternal. He had introduced into Masonry a new Rite called the *Egyptian*, and endeavored to resuscitate the mysterious worship of Isis. The three letters L.∴ P.∴ D.∴ on his seal, were the initials of the words "*Lilia pedibus destruc;*" *tread under foot the Lilies* [of France], and a Masonic medal of the sixteenth or seventeenth century has upon it a sword cutting off the stalk of a lily, and the words "*talem dabit ultio messem,*" such harvest revenge will give.

A Lodge inaugurated under the auspices of Rousseau, the fanatic of Geneva, became the centre of the revolutionary movement in France, and a Prince of the blood-royal went thither to swear the destruction of the successors of Philippe le Bel on the tomb of Jacques de Molai. The registers of the Order of Templars attest that the Regent, the Duc d' Orleans, was Grand Master of that formidable Secret Society, and that his successors were the Duc de Maine, the Prince of Bourbon-Condé, and the Duc de Cossé-Brissac.

The Templars compromitted the King; they saved him from the rage of the People, to exasperate that rage and bring on the catastrophe prepared for centuries; it was a scaffold that the vengeance of the Templars demanded. The secret movers of the

French Revolution had sworn to overturn the Throne and the Altar upon the Tomb of Jacques de Molai. When Louis XVI. was executed, half the work was done; and thenceforward the Army of the Temple was to direct all its efforts against the Pope.

Jacques de Molai and his companions were perhaps martyrs, but their avengers dishonored their memory. Royalty was regenerated on the scaffold of Louis XVI., the Church triumphed in the captivity of Pius VI., carried a prisoner to Valence. and dying of fatigue and sorrow, but the successors of the Ancient Knights of the Temple perished, overwhelmed in their fatal victory.

Return now, with us, to the Degrees of the Blue Masonry, and for your last lesson, receive the explanation of one of their Symbols.

You see upon the altar of those Degrees the SQUARE and the COMPASS, and you remember how they lay upon the altar in each Degree.

The SQUARE is an instrument adapted for plane surfaces only, and therefore appropriate to Geometry, or measurement of the Earth, which appears to be, and was by the Ancients supposed to be, a plane. The COMPASS is an instrument that has relation to spheres and spherical surfaces, and is adapted to spherical trigonometry, or that branch of mathematics which deals with the Heavens and the orbits of the planetary bodies.

The SQUARE, therefore, is a natural and appropriate Symbol of this Earth and the things that belong to it, are of it, or concern it. The Compass is an equally natural and appropriate Symbol of the Heavens, and of all celestial things and celestial natures.

You see at the beginning of this reading, an old Hermetic Symbol, copied from the "MATERIA PRIMA" of Valentinus, printed at Franckfurt, in 1613, with a treatise entitled "AZOTH." Upon it you see a Triangle upon a Square, both of these contained in a circle; and above this, standing upon a dragon, a human body, with two arms only, but two heads, one male and the other female. By the side of the male head is the Sun, and by that of the female head, the Moon, the crescent within the circle of the full moon. And the hand on the *male* side holds a *Compass*, and that on the *female* side, a *Square*.

The Heavens and the Earth were personified as Deities, even among the Aryan Ancestors of the European nations of the Hindus, Zends, Bactrians, and Persians; and the Rig Veda Sanhita contains hymns addressed to them as gods. They were deified also among the Phœnicians; and among the Greeks OURANOS and GEA, Heaven and Earth, were sung as the most ancient of the Deities, by Hesiod.

It is the great, fertile, beautiful MOTHER, Earth, that produces, with limitless profusion of beneficence, everything that ministers to the needs, to the comfort, and to the luxury of man. From her teeming and inexhaustible bosom come the fruits, the grain, the flowers, in their season. From it comes all that feeds the animals which serve man as laborers and for food. She, in the fair

Springtime, is green with abundant grass, and the trees spring from her soil, and from her teeming vitality take their wealth of green leaves. In her womb are found the useful and valuable minerals; hers are the seas that swarm with life; hers the rivers that furnish food and irrigation, and the mountains that send down the streams which swell into these rivers; hers the forests that feed the sacred fires for the sacrifices, and blaze upon the domestic hearths. The EARTH, therefore, the great PRODUCER, was always represented as a *female,* as the MOTHER,—Great, Bounteous, Beneficent Mother Earth.

On the other hand, it is the light and heat of the Sun in the Heavens, and the rains that seem to come from them, that in the Springtime make fruitful this bountifully-producing Earth, that restore life and warmth to her veins, chilled by Winter, set running free her streams, and *beget,* as it were, that greenness and that abundance of which she is so prolific. As the procreative and generative agents, the Heavens and the Sun have always been regarded as *male;* as the generators that fructify the Earth and cause it to produce.

The Hermaphroditic figure is the Symbol of the double nature anciently assigned to the Deity, as Generator and Producer, as BRAHM and MAYA among the Aryans, Osiris and Isis among the Egyptians. As the Sun was male, so the Moon was female; and Isis was both the sister and the wife of Osiris. The Compass, therefore, is the Hermetic Symbol of the Creative Deity, and the Square of the productive Earth or Universe.

From the Heavens come the spiritual and immortal portion of man; from the Earth his material and mortal portion. The Hebrew Genesis says that YEHOUAH formed man of the dust of the Earth, and breathed into his nostrils the breath of life. Through the seven planetary spheres, represented by the Mystic Ladder of the Mithriac Initiations, and it by that which Jacob saw in his dream (not with *three,* but with *seven* steps), the Souls, emanating from the Deity, descended, to be united to their human bodies; and through those seven spheres they must re-ascend, to return to their origin and home in the bosom of the Deity.

The COMPASS, therefore, as the Symbol of the *Heavens,* represents the spiritual, intellectual, and moral portion of this double nature of Humanity; and the SQUARE, as the Symbol of the *Earth,* its material, sensual, and baser portion.

55